TRIATHLONING for ORDINARY MORTALS

Steven Jonas, M.D., M.P.H.

Foreword by Dr. Jack Ramsay
Coach, Portland Trail Blazers
National Basketball Association

Nutrition for Ordinary Mortals (Chapter 9)
by Virginia Aronson, R.D., M.S.

W · W · NORTON & COMPANY
New York · London

Printed in the United States of America

The text of this book is composed in 11/13 Sabon, with display type in Sabon. Composition and manufacturing by The Maple-Vail Book Manufacturing Group. Book design by Nancy Dale Muldoon.

Library of Congress Cataloging in Publication Data

Jonas, Steven.
    Triathloning for ordinary mortals.

    Bibliography: p. 247
    Includes index.
    1. Triathlon.   2. Aerobic exercises.   I. Title.
GV1060.7.J66   1986   796.4'07   85–5022

ISBN 0-393-02251-X

ISBN 0-393-30279-2   {PBK.}

W. W. Norton & Company, Inc., 500 Fifth Avenue, New York, NY 10110
W. W. Norton & Company Ltd, 10 Coptic Street, London WC1A 1PU

        6 7 8 9 0

This book is not intended to be a substitute for medical advice. If there are any doubts in your mind about the advisability of undertaking the exercise programs described in this book, you should consult with a physician.

Appendix III is excerpted from Stretching © by Bob and Jean Anderson. $9.95 Shelter Publications, Inc., Bolinas, California, 1980. Distributed in bookstores by Random House. Reprinted by permission.

Much of the material in Chapter 9 was excerpted from Thirty Days to Better Nutrition by Virginia Aronson. Copyright © 1982, 1984 by Virginia Aronson. Reprinted by permission of Doubleday & Company, Inc.

The drawing of the bicycle which appears on pages 83 and 158 is used with permission of Macmillan Publishing Company, from Serious Cycling for the Beginner by Ray Adams, Copyright © 1977 by Anderson World, Inc.

FOR . . . PROFESSOR EMERITUS HAROLD J. JONAS
Beloved father and friend

Contents . . .

Foreword

IF YOU, like me, are among the legions who are or would like to be involved in the sport of triathloning for the sheer enjoyment of participation and the health benefits you derive from the activity, you will thoroughly enjoy *Triathloning for Ordinary Mortals.*

Dr. Steven Jonas has put together a most readable and comprehensive work that will serve well the recreational triathloner. The time allotments indicated in the training schedules are reasonable to follow. Their adoption will guarantee the participant readiness on race day. The chapter on nutrition by Virginia Aronson removes uncertainty from the minds of fitness enthusiasts who may be groping for guidance in determining what to eat, how much to eat, and when to eat it. Technique for the major sports of the triathlon—swimming, biking, and running—is presented with a simplicity and clarity that make sense. Steve's treatment of "race day" is overflowing with helpful hints that participants are sure to recall during competition.

Steve also details the need for and the mechanics of well-thought-out programs in stretching and weight training. He makes the whole project seem within the reach of the average competitor—the Ordinary Mortal, as he puts it—not just the superstar.

Those readers who are interested in fitness but have not yet dared to think that triathloning is possible for them, will be encouraged to try the event. And well they should, because this sport is one in which the usual qualities for athletic success—speed, agility, and physical coordination—are not the prime requisites. One needs only to be physically fit and mentally disciplined, as Steve points out.

This is an excellent work. Both beginners and readers who are already involved in triathloning will benefit greatly from its contents. The number of first-time participants is certain to grow larger as a result of the confidence gained from reading *Triathloning for Ordinary Mortals*. Steve Jonas writes from a personal perspective that will jog flecks of recollection from one's own experiences in training and competition. That is what happened for me. I found this book to be both enjoyable and informative. My guess is that you will too.

Jack Ramsay
Coach, Portland Trail Blazers
4th-year triathloner

Acknowledgments . . .

I WISH to thank my friends in the Port Jefferson (New York) Road Runners' Club for helping this middle-aged, former nonathlete to become a recreational endurance athlete and triathlete. Deserving of special mention in this regard are: Paul Lennon, Joe Dessi, Ed Miller, Joe and Sara Grillo, Ed Berkowitz, Ed and Carol Melendez, and Sheila Breck.

In the sport itself, Ray and Donna Charron, Ambrose Salmini, Howard Bashant, Dan Honig, Stan Wunderlich, and a number of the elite triathletes have offered assistance and encouragement.

As usual with my books, my father, Professor Harold J. Jonas played a major role in editing the final draft. As well, thanks go to Karen McGullam, my copy editor at W. W. Norton, and to Kathy Longobardo and Paddy Plagge of Creative Word Systems, Hauppauge, New York, who did such a fine job of word processing on the manuscript.

My children, Jacob and Lillian, and my former wife Linda Friedman Jonas, have provided much support and encouragement for my development as a triathlete.

I wish to thank my department chairman, Professor Andre Varma, M.D. for his support during the writing of this book.

Finally, many thanks to Eric Swenson, senior editor at W. W. Norton, for his friendship and confidence.

Steven Jonas, M.D., M.P.H.

DR. STEVEN JONAS is professor of Community and Preventive Medicine, School of Medicine, State University of New York at Stony Brook. Born and educated in New York City, he received his B.A. from Columbia College in 1958, his M.D. from Harvard Medical School in 1962, and his M.P.H. from the Yale School of Medicine in 1967. He interned at the Lenox Hill Hospital and also studied at the London School of Economics. He took his residency in Preventive Medicine/Public Health in the New York City Department of Health. He is board certified in Preventive Medicine.

He is a fellow of the American College of Preventive Medicine, the American Public Health Association, and the New York Academy of Medicine. He is a member of the Academy's Committee on Medical Education, a past-president of the Association of Teachers of Preventive Medicine, and an associate editor of *Preventive Medicine*. He is a member of the New York State Board for Medicine. He is chairman of the Quality Assurance and Utilization Review Committee, University Hospital at Stony Brook. He is vice-chairman of the American Medical Triathlon Association.

Dr. Jonas has written two books, *Medical Mystery: The Training of Doctors in the United States* (New York: W. W. Norton, 1979), and *Quality Control of Ambulatory Care* (New York: Springer Publishing Co., 1977). He is editor and co-author of another book, *Health Care Delivery in the United States,* also published by Springer, which will appear in its third edition in 1986. Dr. Jonas has also published close to 100 articles and book reviews in professional journals and books and has delivered over 50 papers at conferences and seminars.

Dr. Jonas lives in Port Jefferson, New York. He has two children, Jacob Henry, 12, and Lillian Sara, 11. For recreation, in addition to running, biking, and swimming, Dr. Jonas sails, skis, and listens to classical music.

Preface . . .

THIS BOOK is written for the beginner and novice triathlete, the average recreational endurance athlete, the "Ordinary Mortal" who wants to complete a swim-bike-run triathlon that would take him or her about as long as it would to complete a marathon. It is not aimed at those whose objective it is to do an Ironman triathlon. Nor is it aimed at those who want to win in their age class. It is for those who would like to get fit and stay fit doing more than one endurance sport and to race occasionally just for the fun and indeed the thrill of it.

The central focus of the book is the Triathloning for Ordinary Mortals Training Program (TFOMTP) presented in Chapter 7. The program provides for 3900 minutes of workout time over 13 weeks (5 hours per week on the average). One prerequisite is the establishment of an "aerobic base" of 2.5–3 hours of aerobic exercise per week for 6 months before commencing the TFOMTP. The other prerequisite is knowing how to run, cycle, and swim. Completion of the TFOMTP will enable the athlete to finish a marathon-equivalent triathlon, happily and healthily. Chapter 5 of this book sets out the basic principles of training. The training programs contained in Chapter 6 will enable someone who is doing little or no aerobic exercise now to start from scratch and 9 months later be ready to commence the TFOMTP.

Leading up to the training program chapters are four pre-

paratory ones. Chapter 1 introduces the sport, its basic con-
cepts and the criteria you should consider when deciding if
triathloning is for you. In Chapter 2 I describe my own journey from nonathleticism at age 44 to the starting line of my
first triathlon, the 1983 Mighty Hamptons at Sag Harbor,
New York, at age 46. Chapter 3 presents criteria that you
can use to help you choose your first triathlon. It also briefly
describes some usual and unusual triathlons. In Chapter 4, I
discuss some basic aspects of technique in swimming, cycling,
and running.

Following the training program chapters, Chapter 8 exam-
ines equipment for swimming, cycling, and running. Chapter
9 is a fine treatise on nutrition by my friend and colleague
Virginia Aronson, R.D., M.S. Not only does this chapter tell
you everything you need to know about nutrition for triathloning, it also tells you just about everything you need to know
about nutrition, period. In Chapter 10 I take you with me
through my first triathlon and offer some general advice on
triathlon racing. Chapter 11 concludes the book with a consideration of the "morning after" your first race and the view
ahead from the vantage point of a new triathlon finisher.

If you read the book through, cover to cover, you will notice
that there is some repetition. I have done this on purpose.
People reading sports books often do not read them straight
through, but pick and choose among the chapters, selecting
those that will be particularly useful for themselves. Thus there
are certain important matters that I have chosen to repeat, to
make sure that you will see them even if you do not read the
whole book.

My central message is simple. If you are a recreational
endurance athlete, or would like to become one, and you set
for yourself as a clear goal the completion of a marathon-
equivalent triathlon happily and healthily, you can achieve
that goal with a relatively modest amount of time and effort.
You can do this if you follow the principles and practice of

the Triathloning for Ordinary Mortals Training Program, on a consistent, regular basis. I can assure you that when you cross the finish line of your first race, regardless of your time, you will experience feelings of accomplishment and self-satisfaction unlike any you have experienced previously. In spirit, I will be there to greet you. Good luck!

Steven Jonas, M.D., M.P.H.
Port Jefferson, New York
December 4, 1984

TRIATHLONING
for
ORDINARY MORTALS

> *I encourage all of you ... triathletes to reach for your goals, whether they be to win or just to try. The trying is everything.*
>
> Dave Scott,
> four-time Hawaii Ironman champion,
> in *Triathlon*, December/January 1985

1 . . . *Introduction*

The difference between a jogger and a runner is an entry blank.

George Sheehan, M.D.,
quoted in "The Voice of Reason" by Eric Olsen,
The Runner, February 1985, p. 27

"LIFE IS what you do till the moment you die." It is this wonderful, mind-expanding concept with which The Woman opens the musical-stage version of Nikos Kazantzakis' powerful story *Zorba*. What a challenge to us all. Life is in our hands. Life is what we do with our time, what we make of it. George Sheehan, runner, cardiologist, philosopher, inspirer of thousands of endurance athletes, talks about energy, clarity, and self-esteem. He says that they are the principal products of a program of regular running, indeed of a regular program in any aerobic sport or combination of them.[1] Aerobic exercise increases life expectancy, a long-term result.[2] But, as George Sheehan points out, perhaps more importantly it improves the *quality* of life, a here-and-now concept as well as a long-term concept, by adding: energy, clarity, self-esteem.

---

1. George Sheehan in a talk given at the Presidential Sports Fitness Festival, Dallas, Texas, December 3, 1983.
2. Ralph Paffenbarger, "A Natural History of Athletism and Cardiovascular Health," *Journal of the American Medical Association*, 252, 1984, p. 491.

The rules for enjoying life in the positive sense are really quite simple:

Eat less, exercise more.
Talk less, think more.
Ride less, walk more.
Worry less, work more.
Waste less, give more.
Preach less, practice more.
Frown less, laugh more.
Grumble less, thank more.
Scold less, praise more.
Regret less, aspire more.
Hate less, love more.[3]

And thus we come to the sport of triathloning, the reason you are reading this book. In describing triathloning, Jim Curl put the concept very well:

It's a personal growth sport. Your body will change and you'll feel great. It's about waking up in the morning and knowing that you've done something that you didn't know that you could do the day before. There aren't that many things around that will give you that sense of accomplishment that fast. And, nobody can take it away from you. It's just you.[4]

Jeff MacMillan, a medical student from Pennsylvania, expands on this notion in a Sheehanesque mode:

It's a celebration of life, a way of being grateful for a gift I was given—that gift being a strong healthy body. If you don't keep set-

3. Glenn Clark, "The 7 Baths of Purification for Athletes," Chapter 2, Book I, in Bob Johnson's and Patricia Bragg's *The Complete Triathlon Distance Training Manual*, Santa Barbara, California: Health Science, 1982, p. 37.
4. Jim Curl is quoted in "Triathlon: Sport of the 80s?" by Margaret O. Kirk, which appeared in *The Boston Phoenix* of February 28, 1984, p. 1. Jim Curl is the cofounder of the Bud Light United States Triathlon Series, a set of races for both elite and amateur triathletes held all across the country each season.

ting goals, you might as well die. If you don't achieve or if you don't progress, you stagnate. For some people that's fine. I just like to feel that as every day goes by, I'm better than I was the day before.[5]

I overheard it put even more succinctly at the rain-drenched starting line of the 1984 Brooklyn Biathlon, a short but challenging run-bike-run event. Two women who appeared to be in their fifties were chatting. One said to the other: "Are you going to do the whole thing?" "Yes I am," came the reply, "God willing." God was willing. She did it. And you can do it too.

WHO THIS BOOK IS FOR . . .

"Ruts long traveled," it has been said, "grow comfortable." If you are reading this book, I think that it is safe for me to assume that you are a person who wants a new challenge and is at least thinking about trying this marvelous, zany, captivating, made-in-America phenomenon, the sport of triathloning. This book is for you if you are an average recreational endurance athlete of modest ability who would like to do a triathlon of modest proportions. It is also for you if you are not yet an "average recreational endurance athlete of modest ability" but would like to become one, with the goal in mind of doing a triathlon of "modest proportions." (Readers in this category should turn to Chapter 6 before doing anything silly, like buying a $2,500.00 bicycle or building their own private Olympic-size swimming pool.) This book is not for you if your ambition is to do an "Ironman" triathlon (see below). In that case I refer you instead to Sally Edwards's book *Triathlon: A Triple Fitness Sport.* It is certainly the best book on the market in mid-1984 for aspiring Ironmen and

5. Jeff MacMillan is quoted in the article cited in note 4.

women. So, we have narrowed our focus, but hopefully broadened our audience: we are looking at triathlons of reasonable lengths and athletes of relatively modest abilities.

WHAT IS "TRIATHLONING"? . . .

"Triathlon" is a new word that sounds old because of its Greek roots. It refers to a race that combines three endurance sports, done consecutively. There is a variety of combinations of various sports that is offered under the rubric "triathlon," (discussed in more detail in Chapter 3). However, the most common combination is the swim-bike-run event, taken in that order. These events are offered in a wide range of lengths. In 1984, the "Mini-Tri/Fairmont Triathlon" scheduled for Mandato, Minnesota, on September 1, required the competitor to swim .38 miles, bike 9 miles, and run 3.1 miles.[6] A number of "Ironman" competitions that year required a 2.4-mile swim and a 112-mile bike ride, followed by a marathon (26.2 miles).

For those who find the latter too tame, there are various multiday events that can be done. The Minnesota Border-to-Border Triathlon lasts for four days.[7] On each of the first two days, the competitor cycles for 200 miles. On the third, he or she runs 50 miles, while on the last day, only a 50-mile canoe trip is required. Both individuals and relay teams may enter. For the Big Island Triathlon in Hawaii, competitors swim 6 miles, bike 225 miles, and run 50 miles over three consecutive days.[8] For those needing even more of a challenge there is the Baja 1000 Triathlon, a 16-day stage event covering 1000 miles of Baja, California, in the various sports. To enter this one you must not only be in shape, but you also must be able to

6. *Triathlon*, June / July 1984, pp. 87, 92.
7. Ibid.
8. *Triathlon*, Winter 1983, p. 70.

afford the $1,000.00 entry fee. However, entries are limited to 200.[9]

Coming back to reality, then, this book is written for the person who desires simply to finish a triathlon of modest proportions happily and healthily. By "modest" I mean one that will have you exercising aerobically for about the same amount of time that it would take you to run 20–26 miles. This usually means a 1.0–1.5-mile swim, followed by a 20–25-mile bike ride, concluding with a 10k–10-mile[10] run, what I call a "marathon-equivalent" event. For this achievement a training program of modest proportions can be designed. My version is presented in Chapter 7. Having developed this training program and having seen it work for me, I decided to do this book, based primarily on my own experience. (More about my own background appears in the next chapter.) There are also references to the work of others, including Joe Henderson, Ardy Friedberg, and Ferdy Massimino, on preparing for a "marathon-equivalent" triathlon.

TRIATHLON CATEGORIES AND A LITTLE HISTORY . . .

As anyone who has perused the race calendars in the national triathlon publications such as *Triathlon, Tri-Athlete,* and *The Beast* or any of the regional or local newsletters such as *The Tri-ing Times* (ouch!) of the Big Apple Triathlon Club can tell you, triathlons come in a bewildering variety of sizes and shapes. There is no standardization. In this rapidly expanding sport, there probably never will be, nor in my mind ought there to be. There are some common lengths which are used on the professional triathlon circuit and which are the accepted

9. *Tri-Athlete,* May 1984, p. 79.
10. One kilometer equals approximately 0.62 miles.

championship standards, both amateur and professional. However, many races, particularly those designed to attract a local or regional group of competitors, are set up to fit a certain available course and / or group of central facilities that form the physical focus of this logistically complicated sort of race. Thus the available course may dictate the length of the triathlon components rather than vice versa. Any attempt at standardization would serve only to reduce the number of available events. However, it is useful to roughly categorize triathlons.

The "Ironman" length itself was the product of an historical accident. In 1978, a United States Navy commander, John Collins, thought that it might be fun to take three of the Hawaiian Islands' premier endurance-race distances, string them together, and ask competitors to do them consecutively. The Waikiki Rough Water Swim happened to be for 2.4 miles, the Oahu Bike Race happened to be for 112 miles, and the Honolulu Marathon was, well, a marathon. Fifteen men entered the new, combination event. Twelve finished. The prize for the winner was a six-pack of beer. The race was repeated the next year with 100 entrants. However, the event which seemed to galvanize the growth of the sport was the women's finish of the February, 1982 Ironman Triathlon, starting on Kona Pier in Hawaii. It happened to be televised on ABC's "Wide World of Sports."

That finish was very dramatic. With about ¼ mile to go in the last event, the marathon, Julie Moss, who had been leading the female group by a wide margin, collapsed. Completely out of glycogen (the body's storage form for carbohydrates), her leg muscles turned to "rubber." She rested briefly, got up, ran for a bit, collapsed again, and repeated the cycle several times until she was within about 10 yards of the finish. She could not rise again. This gallant woman then proceeded to crawl towards the line. Before Julie got there, however, Kathleen McCartney, who had been second and far behind, passed her and won the race. Julie continued to crawl and took second place. She also indelibly etched herself into the memories of millions of Americans who watched that telecast and a subsequent repeat of it. Many times in talking to nonathletes about triathloning, I hear them tell me about that particular episode. They may know little else about the sport, but they do remember Julie.

Whether coincidentally or not, triathloning then took off. For the 1983 season, there were an estimated 1,000 triathlons being held all over the country, involving an estimated 250,000 competitors.[11] On the day that I did my first, September 10, 1983, there were at least 13 others being run at the same time. Thus, about 5,000 people, most of them amateurs, were triathloning that day. For 1984, the estimates were about 1,800 events involving 600,000 people. Some consideration is being given to attempting to have "it" (with some yet-to-be-determined combination of events and lengths) become an Olympic sport.[12]

In this "proliferative period," as I pointed out above, all kinds of lengths have appeared. The Triathlon Federation / USA, the sport's major governing body, has defined three event categories. The "Ultra-Course" consists of a 2.4-mile swim, a 112-mile bike ride, and a 26.2-mile run. These, of course, are the Ironman lengths. The "Long Course" includes a 1.2-mile swim, a 56-mile bike, and a 13.1-mile run, precisely half the Ironman lengths. Finally, the "Short Course," found in the United States Triathlon Series events, consists of a 1.5-kilometer (.93-mile) swim, a 40-kilometer (24.8-mile) bike ride, and a 10-kilometer (6.2-mile) run. The Tri Fed's "Short Course" is what I call the "marathon-equivalent" event. There is a fourth group of still shorter events, growing in popularity

11. *Big Apple Triathlon Club Newsletter*, "1983 Triathlon Facts" March / April 1984, p. 8.

12. Margy Rochlin, "Olympic Bound?" *Triathlon*, April / May 1984, p. 30.

but not defined by Tri Fed / USA. This group might be called
"Training Triathlons."

IS TRIATHLONING FOR YOU? . . .

If you have bought this book, you have probably already come
to the conclusion that yes, triathloning is for you. But let's go
over the basic criteria anyway. First of all, you must enjoy
doing one or more of the three principal endurance sports
that make up triathloning. If you are just beginning as an
endurance athlete (and after reading this introductory material, you are going to turn to Chapter 6 to help you get started),
you must believe that you *will* enjoy one or more of triathloning's sports. Now the word "enjoy" in the context of endurance sports has different meanings for different people.

Some endurance athletes enjoy their sports while they are
doing them, most of the time. They feel good while they are
running, for example. They get off into a private mind-world
and do not have, do not feel, or just ignore any aches or pains
that may crop up. Others actually enjoy doing the sport itself
only occasionally. They do feel the pain, they do get bored,
they do have trouble getting underway in the morning. However, there is virtually no endurance athlete that I have ever
met who does not "enjoy" what he or she is doing in the
larger context of his / her whole life, who does not derive
enjoyment from what performance of an endurance sport on
a regular basis does for him or her as a whole person.

In an article in the *New York Running News*, Sofia Shafquat
reported on a series of interviews with runners on the question "Is Running Fun?"[13] The answers were quite varied. A
24-year-old male said: "Running is what you make it. It could

13. Sofia Shafquat, "Is Running Fun?" *New York Running News*, June / July 1984,
p. 13.

be fun or it could be torturous." To me, this is a very important concept that certainly applies to triathloning and triathlon training. To make it a positive, enjoyable experience, *you* must remain in control of *your* training. You must run your training program. If you let it run you, enjoyment will be hard to find. The corollary of this thought is that you must set reasonable, realistic, attainable goals if the experience is to be enjoyable. If it is not going to be enjoyable in one sense or another, why do it? Thus I will stress over and over again the goal of *finishing* a marathon-equivalent triathlon happily and healthily, without worrying about your time and where you place. If winning is important to you, that can come later, with the help of other books and programs. This book and my program will introduce you to the sport as enjoyment for its own sake and show you that you can do it.

Another person interviewed by Ms. Shafquat said that while running itself was not fun, *not* running is unhappiness, misery. This person went on to say that being in the shower after a run is always fun. Some people report the "runner's high." I have felt a specific response perhaps half-a-dozen times a year, always towards the end of a long, hard run. I will suddenly get a buzzing sensation on the top of my head which will then cascade down my body. I will get a release of my normally very tight musculature so that every motion is free, easy, painless, and wonderful. I will feel like vocalising and sometimes do. I will speed up effortlessly. This state of grace lasts no more than 2 minutes and for me is a rare pleasure.

I almost always feel good in the shower after a workout, however. When I have to stop running (or, in the winter, doing other aerobic exercises indoors) for more than 4–5 days because of injury, I do begin to feel very unhappy. (*Scheduled* cessation of training for a week or two every few months is quite another matter, however. It is very important, does *not* create misery, and is very beneficial. See also Chapter 5.) In any case, enjoyment of endurance sports in one sense or another is the first prerequisite for successful triathloning.

The next criterion is that you must be physically able to do each of the three sports, even if you are not yet trained in any of them. (In my view, running is the basic sport of triathloning, a subject to which I will return in more detail later in this chapter.) This does not mean that you need to be an expert in any of the sports. Running, except as done by top competitors, is not a technically complicated sport. Harold Schwab, owner with his Dad of my local running-shoe store, 2nd Wind in Setauket, New York, was a world-class hurdler and is now a recreational marathoner. He was asked by a beginning runner who had just bought his first pair of shoes about running technique. Harold put it very simply: "Stand up straight, hold your arms comfortably, and then go right, left, right, left." There is a bit more to it than that (see Chapter 4) but not much.

On the other hand, cycling, when done well, is a highly technical sport which requires a great deal of mental concentration. However, for the beginner triathlete, the most important aspects of cycling are safety and comfort. You must be comfortable on your machine and you must ride safely. Once you get to know your bike, a process which takes some time, you can then start to learn about technique, build up your miles, and gradually increase your speed, if that is of interest to you.

The beginner triathlete must also know how to swim, safely. Like cycling, swimming when done well is a highly technical sport requiring a great deal of mental concentration. However, previous experience in distance swimming is not a prerequisite for triathloning. Nor is mastery of the stroke used by the top triathletes, the free style (crawl). Any stroke is permitted in the swim leg, and you may use any combination of strokes that you find works. I learned how to swim as a child. I was thought to have good swimming form (by my parents at least) but I never raced and never swam for distance. After my 12th year, I did little swimming of any kind. For my first triathlon, the 1983 Mighty Hamptons, I went in the water for training exactly 9 times, as I recount in more detail in Chapter 2. Swimming slowly, I had no trouble with the swim leg because I was in good shape aerobically.

The third criterion for deciding if triathloning is for you is whether you have or can make available the time to train. We will talk more about training time in Chapter 5, but the basic requirements are as follows. You must have done or plan to do your principal sports or sports at the aerobic level[14] for 2½–3 hours per week for at least 6 months before you start specific triathlon training. Two and a half to 3 hours of aerobic work weekly, according to the American College of Sports Medicine, establishes the "aerobic base." Once having done that, you should be prepared to spend an average of 5 hours per week training for 13 weeks leading up to the triathlon that you have entered. The "Triathloning for Ordinary Mortals Training Program" is spelled out in detail in Chapter 7. You should be prepared to do 6 workouts per week over 5 days, resting 2 days per week. You should be able to assign a regular time of day for your workouts. If your swim training is to be done in a pool, the hours that the one that is available for your use is open to you will hopefully be ones that fit comfortably into your existing life and work schedule. In sum, you must be prepared to commit time on a regular basis, but the time commitment necessary is not one that most people interested in endurance sports will find inordinate.

The fourth criterion, related very much to the third, is that you must be prepared to be consistent in your training. If you already are an endurance athlete you know that getting out there is usually not a problem. It is *not* getting out there that

14. The aerobic level of exercise is defined by your heart rate. The "aerobic-threshold" heart rate is 70% of 220 minus your age. Once your heart rate is over that rate, accompanied by an increase in the depth and frequency of breathing, you are doing aerobic work.

most often creates problems. But you also know that there are those times when it is not so easy to get out there. You must be prepared to push yourself when necessary. Dick Brown, coach of the top middle-distance runner Mary Decker, stresses consistency. "It is more important to do less [miles] more often than to do more less often. . . . You'll probably avoid the three reasons for breaks in training: illness, injury, and lack of motivation."[15] Rod Dixon, winner of the 1983 New York Marathon, has 10 Rules of Running, to which we shall return in some depth later. Rod's first rule is: "Emphasize consistency in your training program."[16] This is a theme to which I will return—consistently.

Finally, if you are to be comfortable with what I am recommending in this book, your objective, as I said before, must be simply to finish a marathon-length triathlon happily and healthily. You must want to do the race just for the sake of doing it. You must be happy being *you*, doing what *you* can do, not what someone else can do or still another person thinks you ought to be able to do. Peter Leeds is a recreational triathlete who wrote a nice piece entitled "Tin and Proud" for *Triathlon* magazine. In it he discussed setting limits for race length, race time, and training program.

Peter talked about people who regard doing a triathlon of less magnitude than the Ironman as an achievement not worth mentioning. He also talked about the possible negative outcomes of the extensive training and the tremendous commitment of mind, body, and time necessary to do an Ironman. Doing one, he said, is of course a great achievement. However, it is not good for everyone, nor is everyone capable of doing it. He recognizes that for himself doing a marathon-equivalent or training triathlon is indeed an important achievement. In the 1983 New Preston Connecticut Tin Man

15. Dick Brown, "Running Smart," *The Runner*, January 1984, p. 12.
16. Rod Dixon, "Reaching Your Peak: Consistency Is the Key to Better Performance," *The Runner*, March 1984, p. 22.

Triathlon (0.5-mile swim, 22-mile bike, 7.7-mile run) Peter "enjoyed a fun, if unspectacular race." He has since established a consistent, balanced, and doable year-round training program that is very similar to what I recommend in this book. As he says:

I recognize other priorities, other life goals, and other daily objectives [as well as triathlon training]. . . . I'm satisfied with my goals, [but] I don't deny the Ironman his. . . . I'm a Tin Man—and I am proud of it.[17]

"Enjoy" and "fun" are the key words here. Dave Horning is a professional triathlete and race director. He has won his share of big races and has trained hard for them. But in describing the 1984 Liberty to Liberty Triathlon (a 2-mile swim, 90-mile bike, 6-mile run from New York's Statue of Liberty to Philadelphia's Liberty Bell) before a meeting of the Big Apple Triathlon Club, Dave said, "If it's not fun, there is no point in doing it." I couldn't agree more.

RUNNING AS THE BASIC SPORT FOR THE TRIATHLETE . . .

Some people may look at triathloning as the refuge for the road-race runner who is tired of running and wants to do something else. It is certainly true, in my own experience and that of many other marathon-equivalent triathletes with whom I have spoken, that doing a marathon-equivalent triathlon is easier—and more fun—than doing a marathon. I am certainly not knocking marathoning. In fact, I think that it is a great experience (which I have had), one not to be missed. It is just that exercising aerobically in three different events for

17. Peter Leeds, "Tin and Proud," *Triathlon*, April / May 1984, p. 19.

a given period of time is easier than exercising aerobically for the same amount of time in one event. This is especially true if that one event is running.

There are several reasons why this is so. First of all, swimming and cycling, neither of which involves pounding, are just easier on the body than is running. Second of all, in cycling—usually the longest segment despite the efforts of race organizers to achieve "balance" among the three events—you can rest and keep moving forward at the same time. So in the bike segment, usually second, you have a chance to recover a bit without giving up too much time. Third of all, triathloning is a colorful and very busy event. In marathoning it's "right, left, right, left" for 26 miles. In triathloning there are two clothing changes, lots of hustle and bustle, usually some complications to the course, logistics, and equipment to worry about. Fourthly, triathloning offers variety. The boredom that can accompany the later stages of a marathon has little chance to set in while triathloning, at least in marathon-equivalent events. Finally, if you are concerned about where you are going to place, strength in one sport can make up for weakness in another.

Nevertheless, despite all of this, running must be considered the basic sport of triathloning. You can come to triathloning from any of the three sports, of course. Just as runners can learn to ride and swim, bikers and swimmers can learn the other two sports as well. But running, because of the constant pounding of the body it involves, is the most demanding physically. Although you can get overuse and wear-and-tear injuries in any sport, swimming is generally good to the body. There is no pounding, your weight is partially supported by the water, and there are no hard surfaces against which to twist your body. In biking, you have to worry about the knee injury that can come from riding in too high gear at too low a cadence and the traumatic injuries that can result from falling off your machine, but again, the pounding and twisting that result from running are not present. But to triathlon you must run. You cannot consider triathloning a refuge from running. And running is the toughest sport. The French-Canadian Puntous twins, Patricia and Sylviane, winners together of almost every triathlon they have entered, put it well: "[Running] is the hard event. When you bike you can have a fun time and see the country. But when you go for a run, it's never really a fun time."[18]

Although physically demanding, running does have its advantages as a training sport, and the triathlete would do well to look at it in this light. You do not need a special facility to do it in as you do with swimming. You do not need a machine that can break and needs careful maintenance, as you do with biking. Running is cheap and its equipment demands are simple. It requires the least *total* time to get a good workout. It is relatively safe. It is highly portable. (When traveling, nothing is more fun than going for an easy morning run in a new city.) If you like socializing while exercising, running offers you the best opportunity to do so. Swimming is by its nature a solo sport. Most highways do not lend themselves to safe side-by-side bicycle riding.

THE PROS AND CONS OF RUNNING . . .

Runners run for many reasons. Some runners are truly cerebral about it. Bob Anderson, editor and publisher of *Runners World* magazine, puts it this way:

Running can certainly increase the length of your life in two ways: by contributing to both a strong mind and body, and by minimizing the influence of negative factors in human life, such as pollution, stress and so on. But after all the studies have been completed and

18. Michele Kort, "Twins," *Triathlon,* June / July 1984.

all the research is piled high on the table, after all the critics have
been laid to rest, it comes back to getting out there on that run
because you want to do it, because you enjoy it—because you'd do
it if there weren't one [future] physical or psychological benefit to
be derived from it.

We run because running is special to us. Anything else that accrues
to us because of it is merely icing on the cake.[19]

The late Jim Fixx, one of the great popularizers of the sport,
put it succinctly in the first paragraph of his *magnum opus,
The Complete Book of Running.*

One gray November morning I [met] . . . an old man shuffling along
slowly, using a cane. As I ran by him I called out, "Good morning!"
[He responded:] "Say, what do you gain by running?" I hollered
back: "It makes you feel good!"[20]

Even one of the great leaders of people of the twentieth
century, a man not ordinarily thought of in the context of
endurance sports, considered them important. He gave them
a political as well as a physical and psychological meaning.
In 1918, Mao Tse-tung wrote: "In general, any form of exercise, if pursued continuously, will help to train us in perse-
verance. Long-distance running is particularly good."[21] And
that was written long before distance running shoes were
developed.

How important can running become? Jim Fixx tells this
nic story: "The wife of a running friend of mine, asked how
her husband reconciled his Methodist convictions with the

19. Bob Anderson, "Is Running Good for You?" *Runners World,* April 1984, p.
13.
20. James F. Fixx, *The Complete Book of Running,* Chapter 1, "Feeling Better
Physically," New York: Random House, 1977, p. 3.
21. Mao Tse-tung, quoted in Fixx, p. 24.

fact that nearly all races are held on Sundays, replied, 'Tom *used* to be a Methodist. Now he's a runner.' "[22]

Before the 1982 New York Marathon, a *New York Times* / CBS News poll was taken among a sample of entrants. Neil Amdur of the *Times* summarized the results as follows:

Most runners who will compete in the New York City Marathon on Sunday say running has significantly improved their professional and personal lives, even though two-thirds of them have suffered serious training injuries.

Three of every four entrants surveyed said that running had helped them perform better at work. A similar proportion said that running had exerted a positive influence on their personal lives, from losing weight to meeting people or achieving a better sex life. But the price of almost daily training for long distances also had its price for some: 16 percent reported negative effects on their personal life.[23]

Eric Olsen summed up the pros and cons of running well in an article in *The Runner*.[24] Running improves the cardio-vascular system and the blood itself. It raises the level of "good" cholesterol (high-density lipoprotein, HDL in the serum) while lowering the "bad" (low-density lipoprotein, LDL). It can lower blood pressure (although persons with *highly* elevated blood pressure should consult their physician and get their blood pressure under at least partial control with medication before starting to exercise). It certainly improves respiratory system performance and help reverse deterioration in the early stages of chronic lung disease, especially if a smoker stops smoking in order to run. Running may reverse bone softening (osteo-

22. Ibid., p. xix.
23. Neil Amdur, "Marathon Runners Tell Poll Benefits Outweigh Problems," *The New York Times,* October 21, 1982, p. 1.
24. Eric Olsen, "What's So Terrific It Feels Good Even When It Feels Bad? Running, Of Course," *The Runner,* March 1984, p. 39.

porosis), especially in older women. It certainly builds leg muscles.

Turning to the gastrointestinal system, I have yet to meet a constipated runner, although some would certainly like to be before and / or during races. All that bouncing does have *some* positive benefit. Running is certainly a major factor in weight control. Have you noticed how in recent years the fad diet books (high-protein and / or high-fat diets) which produce early water loss but no really sustained weight loss, have faded from the best-seller lists? Leading the way now are various programs combining balanced calorie control with balanced exercise. A leading proponent of this approach is Virginia Aronson, R.D., M.S., author of Chapter 9, "The Triathlon Training Table," in this book.[25]

Running seems to improve a person's ability to handle stress. That has certainly been my own experience and it has been reported by many runners. My friend Charles Arnold, M.D., former vice-president of the American Health Foundation and now a medical director at Metropolitan Life, a runner himself, thinks that there is a biochemical basis to that finding. Running in a sense "teaches" the body how to handle in a positive, productive way substances that are produced by both running and stressful situations which can have both positive and negative effects. Running may ameliorate depression. It has a very important social aspect, especially for those people who are members of running clubs and / or race frequently. The highlight of my running week is Sunday morning with the Port Jefferson (New York) Road Runners: a nice, fun run for an hour or so with friends, followed by breakfast together in a local deli. Finally, many runners report an improvement in their sex lives.

Running also has its negative aspects. For whatever rea-

25. An excellent example of the genre is Virginia's own book, *Thirty Days to Better Nutrition*. Garden City, New York: Doubleday & Co., 1984.

sons, running is addictive. For most people, this addiction is a positive one, providing one or more of the benefits discussed above. For some, however, it can become a negative addiction. Obsessive or compulsive running can be very harmful. With virtually anything in life, too little or too much can each be bad. If you do not run your training but rather let your training run you, things can go wrong very quickly. "Gotta run, gotta run, gotta run" itself becomes a stress factor. Thus running, instead of helping a person deal with stress better, adds stress. Family, work, and other endeavors can be ignored. Weight control can become an obsession leading to harmful thinness. Finally, addictive running can quickly lead to one or more of the physical injuries of overuse.

Overuse or overtraining injuries constitute the major physical risks of running. There are many, ranging from minor aches and pains to chondromalacia patellae ("runner's knee," softening of the kneecap cartilage), plantar fasciitis (inflammation of the covering of the foot muscles), Achilles tendinitis, pulled muscles, shin splints, blisters, stress fractures, and numerous others. Virtually all of these problems result from doing too much running. They can be healed by rest combined with other interventions as appropriate, such as physical therapy, ultrasound, ice application, special stretching exercises, weight lifting, massage, and drugs.

Amenorrhea, irregular menstruation or lack of it, is a complication of running experienced by some women, possibly related to a loss of body fat. It too can be relieved by cutting back on running. Divorce may be a complication of overtraining, although the data are unclear. Finally, the "bad" pain of constant pounding or incipient injury, as contrasted with the "good" pain of a top-flight, muscle-burn workout, is a negative outcome of running. "Good" pain can be maximized and "bad" pain minimized by a reasonable consistant training program.

The best *preventive* measure for all of these problems is

balance. A major Navajo precept is an excellent one to strive for:"[When there is] balance between the individual and his total physical and social environment . . . good health is the result; an upset in this equilibrium causes disease."[26]

INJURIES, BALANCE, AND CROSS-TRAINING . . .

The goal of the endurance athlete should obviously be to achieve as many of the positives and incur as few of the negatives as possible. Balance and limiting your running seem to be the keys to doing this. Dr. Stan Newell, an experienced sports podiatrist from Seattle, says that running 15–25 miles per week is very reasonable. More than that rapidly increases the risk of injury. "When you get in the 30-to-50 mile range a week, that's when you start showing up with a lot of injuries."[27] Norbert Sander, a New York-based sports internist concurs: "If you run at a comfortable level, maybe three to five miles a day, you risk no more injury than in any other sport."[28]

All of this leads to cross-training. Cross-training is simply the combination of two or more aerobic endurance sports in one training program. Many athletes in one sport add another simply to reduce musculoskeletal stress, strengthen additional muscle groups, and diminish boredom. Sally Edwards was originally a long-distance road racer. In 1984, returning to ultramarathoning, she took 10 minutes off the course record for the American River 50-miler—running no more than 50

26. Sidney Kark. *Epidemiology and Community Medicine.* New York: Appleton-Century-Crofts, 1974, p. 11.

27. Stan Newell, M.D., quoted in "Prodiatrist Warns of Jogging Dangers," New York Times, Dec. 4, 1983.

28. Frank Litsky, 'A Second Wind in the Running Room," *New York Times,* April 16, 1984.

miles per week. She was also swimming 3 miles per day and cycling 100 or more miles per week.[29] Sally tells us that Brooks Johnson, coach of the 1984 women's Olympic track and field team had his athletes swimming every day. The 1984 Olympic women's marathon gold-medalist, Joan Benoit, who won the American women's 1984 Olympic Trials marathon just 17 days after having knee surgery, and then went on 3 months later to win the Olympic marathon itself, says that specializing in one sport to the exclusion of all others is hazardous— and passé.[30]

Although hardly in a class with Sally Edwards and Joan Benoit, I myself started on the road to triathloning in the fall of 1981 when I bought my first 10-speed bike after I had been running for about a year. I had never even heard of triathloning at the time. I doubt that I was familiar with the term "cross-training" either. But, even at only 15–20 miles of running per week, I just wanted to get some relief from the constant pounding of the sport while maintaining my aerobic base. Although I was absolutely fascinated by Julie Moss's feat in February, 1982, it wasn't until the following September when I heard about the Mighty Hamptons, a triathlon of reasonable length, that the first faint flicker of "maybe I could try that someday" crossed my mind. Cross-training is thus both a benefit in itself and an entree into triathloning.

Sally Edwards has posed a series of questions for evaluating the possible benefits of cross-training:

Are you interested in total-body fitness and not merely running [or swimming or biking] fitness?
Are you prone to frequent injury and looking for a solution?
Are you interested in expanding your friendships to other fitness-conscious people?

29. Sally Edwards, "First-Rate Fitness Means Getting All Wet," *Running and Fitness,* May / June 1984, p. 19.
30. "Informer": "Cross-Training Kudos," *Triathlon,* April / May 1984.

Are you looking for a new athletic experience?
Are you tired or bored with dong nothing but running [or biking
   or swimming]?
And finally, Are you thinking about trying a triathlon?[31]

Obviously, your answer to the last question is yes, or you
wouldn't be reading this book. And your answer to the other
questions is probably yes as well. Thus we arrive at what may
be the principal benefit of marathon-equivalent triathloning
and triathlon training. It permits and at the same time requires
the athlete to do the aerobic work required for a marathon
without subjecting him or her to the muscloskeletal stresses
and strains that running alone for all that time does. In preparing for a triathlon, cross-training in effect becomes insti-
tutionalized. Virtually all of the "pros" of running related to
extended aerobic exercise per se. Virtually all of its "cons"
relate to extended running itself. Thus triathloning gives you
the benefits and diminishes your risk of incurring the negatives. What could be better? In exercise, there is nothing else
that I can think of.

   31. Sally Edwards, "Bicycling and Synergistic Fitness," *Running and Fitness*, July /
August 1984, p. 24.

2 . . . The Road to Sag Harbor

> *Running gives you the chance to take charge of your*
> *own actions and thoughts. You alone choose the dis-*
> *tance and the pace. You leave behind the crowd and its*
> *conventions . . . you make friends with yourself and pre-*
> *pare to go back into the crowd on more peaceful terms.*
> Joe Henderson, "Thoughts on the Run,"
> *Runners World*, November 1984, p. 21

PRELUDE . . .

On September 10, 1983, I did my first triathlon, the Mighty
Hamptons, at Sag Harbor, New York. It was a little less than
4 years earlier, in December, 1979, that I had started down
the road that lead to the starting line of that event. A letter
arrived from a Texas physician named Charles ("Charlie")
Ogilvie, D.O. I didn't know it at the time, but that letter would
change my life in more ways than one. Charlie was then
chairman of the Department of Medical Humanities at the
Texas College of Osteopathic Medicine (TCOM) in Fort Worth.
With I. M. "Kim" Korr, PH.D., a neurophysiologist and medical educator, he was leading a movement for major change
at TCOM.

Virtually all medical schools in this country, whether

osteopathic (D.O.) or allopathic (M.D.) are disease oriented.[1]
They generally teach their students a great deal about what
to do for people after they become ill. However, they teach
very little if anything about what to do to help people stay
healthy and keep from getting sick in the first place. Kim and
Charlie, following the precepts of the original osteopathic
tradition, were in the process of designing a program to convert TCOM from the disease-oriented mode to a health-oriented one. About a year before, without knowing anything
about the developments at TCOM, I had published a book recommending that all medical education in the United States be
changed from what I described as the Disease-Oriented Physician Education approach (DOPE) to the Health-Oriented
Physician Education approach (HOPE).[2]

Charlie's letter inquired if I might be interested in discuss-
ing developments at TCOM with an eye towards possibly
assisting them in their endeavors. I leapt at the chance. When
I had written my book I had thought that I would not see a
HOPE-system medical school for 25 years. Now here was one
that was going to come into existence before my very eyes,
and I was being offered a chance to become a part of it. In
March 1980 I made a visit to the college and gave a talk.
Shortly thereafter, I was asked to become a consultant to the
college. I began work there in June 1980.

TCOM has a number of features which set it apart from
most medical schools. Among them is the existence of an
Institute of Human Fitness as an integral part of the school.
The Institute offers a wide variety of programs in fitness and
exercise to faculty, staff, and students, as well as to the gen-

1. Both M.D.s and D.O.s are physicians fully licensed in all 50 states to prescribe
drugs and practice surgery. The basic theory of allopathy focuses on single causes
and single cures of disease. The basic theory of osteopathy focuses on the unity of
the body and the central role of the musculoskeletal system in the maintenance of
health.
2. Steven Jonas, *Medical Mystery: The Training of Doctors in the United States*,
New York: W. W. Norton, 1978.

eral public. It turned out that there were a significant number of faculty members who took this health business quite seriously. First among them was Charlie Ogilvie himself.

Charlie was then 62 years old. He has been a track athlete in college but had gotten progressively more out of shape during his professional life, until he began running again at age 59. By the time I met him he was lean and hard, running 70–80 miles a week. He has been the North American record holder in his age class for the 10k- and the 15-mile run. He almost always wins his age class in the marathons he enters and often is faster than the winners of several of the younger age classes. In 1983, at age 65, he was invited to participate in the London Marathon. That year he ran in ten marathons, about one month apart from each other. His marathon Personal Record[3] is 3:03. Truly incredible. In addition to being a marvelous athlete, he is also a marvelous physician, and a marvelous person, as Hollis Walker attests, in the TCOM *Quarterly* article, "Country Doctor." He certainly influenced me, though always by example, never by direction.

At that time I was 43 years old. My risk factors[4] for cardiovascular disease, cancer, and the other major killers were in pretty good shape. I had never smoked cigarettes. My blood pressure was actually on the low side. I rarely drank alcoholic beverages, I was overweight but not significantly so (having recently lost about 10 pounds). My ability to handle stress was improving, and I always wore my automobile seat belt. However, I ate a diet fairly high in fat and cholesterol and I did not have an exercise program. For me in the TCOM context the latter was the biggest problem.

Exercise is the most visible health and fitness activity. Here I was, a consultant on health and prevention in medical edu-

3. A Personal Record or Personal Best is an athlete's own best time for a race on a particular distance or a particular course.
4. A risk factor is an element in the environment or personal behavior that increases a person's chance of contracting a particular disease.

cation, surrounded by a fit faculty, and I had no exercise program. I started thinking about developing one. I was sure that
I would hate it, but it would be very important politically to
be able to say that I was exercising regularly. And after all, I
said to myself, I had heard that 20 minutes 3 times a week
were the magic numbers, and that didn't seem too bad.

Over that summer and into that fall I thought about it. No
one put any pressure on me. It wasn't ever mentioned, and
while many of the faculty were in good shape, several of the
top leadership were not. Thus it was unlikely that I ever would
come under any overt pressure to begin exercising. But I continued to think about it. Somewhere alone the line, Bob Glover's and Jack Shepherd's *The Runner's Handbook* had found
its way into my library. I glanced at it briefly but still did not
actually get started. Then I had my moment of awakening.

In October of 1980 I was in Detroit for the annual meetings of the American Public Health Association, the Association of Teachers of Preventive Medicine, and the American
College of Preventive Medicine. Many of the sessions took
place in Cobo Hall, a large area whose floors are connected
to one another by ramps. One morning I walked up one flight
on one of those ramps. When I got to the top I was huffing
and puffing. "This is it," I said to myself. "When I get home
I am going to begin running."

I BECOME A RUNNER . . .

The high school outdoor track in my community, Port Jefferson, New York, is about three blocks from my house. The
Saturday morning after I returned from those meetings I laced
on a pair of old low-top basketball shoes. I had not bought
running shoes. I knew that it was not good to run in sneakers,
but I was not at all convinced that I was going to continue
this running business. I had several pieces of almost-new sports

equipment around the house, including a pair of soccer cleats. They had all been bought in bursts of enthusiasm for various new sports my participation in which proved to be short lived. I walked over to the track. I had a digital stopwatch that I used for timing sail-boat race starts. I began to run, slowly, just about three weeks before my 44th birthday.

I followed Bob Glover's "Run Easy" walk-run-walk approach. I think that I lasted about 12 minutes. That first day was *very* difficult. By the end of the first month, however, even as the weather got colder, I was "hooked." I had gotten over the hurdle that was supposed to be the most difficult one, the 1-month mark, and I was actually enjoying myself. I bought my first pair of running shoes. My workouts started getting longer: 25 minutes—30 minutes—35 minutes. The frequency increased from 3 to 4 times per week.

Snow fell. The track, which was starting to bore me anyway, became difficult to run on. I left it and started running around a "superblock" near my home which measured about 0.6 of a mile in length. It took 5–6 minutes for me to cover one lap. The weather got colder. I put on more clothing. I felt like a Michelin tire man. I sweated profusely. I thoroughly enjoyed myself. I was learning to run—in the winter. If this is fun, I thought, wait until you get to run in short pants. I took my first run out on the road. I ran about 2 miles after a 2-mile warm-up on "superblock". Was this really me?

At the end of March, 1981, my wife and I went out to Los Angeles for my brother-in-law's wedding. I took my running stuff. The temperature was hovering around 70°F. I went running in shorts for the first time. I was like a kid with a new toy. This was really *it!* I was now doing 35–45 minutes per workout, 4–5 workouts per week. Springtime arrived at home. One beautiful Sunday morning I went out and ran a total of 8 miles on the track and road. I didn't do them consecutively, and there was a lot of chit-chatting going on as I hooked up with various other runners jogging around the track.

But I had done 8 miles and had a really hard time tearing myself away from the physical activity.

I passed the 6-month mark, considered the second major time hurdle in running. I did notice a change around that time. The frequency of shin splints and minor muscle pulls in my legs dropped off sharply. My aerobic capacity was improving markedly. Although my enjoyment of the running itself was highly variable, I was enjoying the "afterward" more and more. I was really "into it." Considering my previous sports background this was rather amazing to me.

As a child, I had been a virtual nonathlete. I was small and slow. I had no aptitude for the hand-eye coordination sports (and still do not). Although my father had been a fine athlete the genes for that quality did not seem to have been passed through to me. I medical school I took up downhill skiing and became fairly proficient at it. I certainly loved doing it (and still do) because it was the first sport that I had tried that I was at all good at. But I had never been able to spend enough time skiing to become really good at it.

In the mid-70s, I took up sailing and became fairly good at that too. Because they both involve the balance sense, skiing and sailing actually have a great deal in common. And to my benefit, neither involves the hand-eye coordination sense. But sailing involves intense physical activity only on rare occasions (usually associated with panic) and skiing is aerobic only in very short spurts. Thus as 1980 rolled around I was entering middle age as a nonathlete with a spreading middle-age spread. Then along came Charlie Ogilvie, the Texas College of Osteopathic Medicine, and running.

NEXT STEPS . . .

By the summer of 1981, people would occasionally ask me about racing. "No, not for me," I would respond. "I'm doing this for my health and because it makes me feel good." That fall I bought my first 10-speed bike and began a bit of the cross-training that I spoke about in the first chapter. I watched the New York Marathon on television that year with the exciting record-setting performances of Allison Roe and Alberto Salazar. I watched the shots of the "back-of-the-packers" too, and there was a slight flicker of personal interest. "Impossible," I said to myself, and that was the end of that. As winter rolled around I decided to try something new. I joined a local "body shop" and took up lifting free weights (barbells and dumbells). I was really getting into my body.

I continued to run during the winter, 12–15 miles per week, I was also lifting weights for 3–4 hours per week. I noticed an improvement in my running almost immediately. On February 10, 1982, however, I suffered my first major injury. I broke my left ankle running on a cold, crisp, clear, but icy day. I took my eyes off the road for an instant, stepped on an icy patch, stumbled, twisted to my left over my shoe which had somehow snugged itself down into the ice surface, and broke my left ankle. Despite the fact that I had heard a loud "crack" as I fell, I engaged in massive denial. "Couldn't be broken," I thought, "just a bad sprain." But it was indeed broken, as I found out in X-ray a couple of hours later. My lower leg was placed in a fiber-glass cast.

As soon as the pain subsided, within 2 weeks of the accident, I was lifting weights, upper body (arms, shoulders, chest, and upper back). The cast came off at 5 weeks. I was riding my bike at 6 weeks, and was skiing (in boots that gave me more support than the cast had) at 9 weeks. Confident that I had retained my aerobic conditioning fairly well, I began running again at 10 weeks. What a letdown. It was like starting all over again. That first day I managed to run 1¼ miles and walk 1¼ miles. I felt awful. Over the next few weeks, I slowly worked my way up to 4 miles per day.

In the end, it took me about 8 months of running and cycling to get back to the shape that I had been in when I fell. There is a formula that says that 3 weeks of retraining are required for each week of aerobic exercise missed. I did not hear of that formula until the end of my recovery period. But it was indeed about 8 months before I felt "right" again following a 10-week injury-induced layoff: just about 3 for 1.

STARTING TO RACE . . .

For reasons which are still unclear to me, it was early during my recovery period that I decided to enter my first race. It was a 5-miler held in a neighboring community on Memorial Day, 1982. My friend, Charles Arnold, M.D., was to run it with me. My objective was to break 50 minutes. In the event I did 42:21. I had a glorious time. I hit the runner's high at the end. The feeling of satisfaction was wonderful. Surely I had the best time of all those persons in the race who had broken their ankles on February 10.

I would have tried a 10k the following week except that it rained and I didn't want to risk slipping and falling again. But I definitely liked this racing business. Through that summer I continued running and cycling doing a total equivalent to 20–25 miles of running per week.

In October, 1982 I ran my first 10k. I set a goal of 56 minutes. It was a great day and the course was almost flat. By the halfway mark I was really getting pumped up. I flew through the last 2 miles and finished in 50:10. I broke down and wept. I couldn't believe that I had finished my first 10k— at a minute per mile under the pace I thought I would be running. The Sunday before Thanksgiving, I did a local "Turkey Trot." I managed 7:40s for 5 miles. After 2 years of running and 3 whole races, I was a racer. I could barely wait for the next season to begin.

MARATHON THOUGHTS ...

With a strong assist from our local running-shoe store, Schwab's 2nd Wind, a local resident, Paul Lennon, had organized the 1982 Port Jefferson Turkey Trot. With the success of that race, Paul then proceeded to organize the Port Jefferson Road Runners Club. It was to become a major influence in my life. The club held group runs on Sunday mornings. Early in 1983 I began taking part in them. Among other things, a number of members were already training for the *Newsday* Long Island Marathon, held in May. I was asked about marathoning. "No way," I said. "Too far, too much training, too much pain. I will be happy to do some 10k's next season." Little did I know how quickly my mind would be changed on that question. And triathloning was a word that wasn't even in my vocabulary yet.

As one is wont to do when running with a club, I fell in with someone who ran at about the same speed I did (9:30–10-minute miles) for a distance that I was comfortable with for my "long" run, 6–8 miles. Ed Miller is an architect who lives in Port Jefferson. He had started running the previous September. He was planning to run the *Newsday* Long Island Marathon in May. He was planning to run the *Newsday* Long Island Marathon in May?!? How the devil was he going to do that?

He told me about a very interesting book by Ardy Friedberg called *How to Run Your First Marathon*. It provides a 22-week program that can be started by someone who is running no more than 20 minutes 3 times a week. Completion of it will enable almost anyone to finish a marathon, provided they do not attempt to run it at too fast a pace. I didn't know it at the time, but Ed Miller was telling me about the program which I would eventually use as the basis for my own triathlon training program. That program would enable me to complete the 1983 Mighty Hamptons Triathlon and would

then evolve into the Triathloning for Ordinary Mortals
Training Program. At any rate, Ed was talking about marathons and I was listening. "Why don't you try it?" the little
voice inside of me said. "No," came the reply, "too much
time, too much training, too much pain." A week or two later
my curiosity got the better of me, and I asked Ed if he could
bring the book along one Sunday.

A week or two after that I was pursuing what looked like
a reasonable, doable program. It was based on minutes, not
miles, which makes training much easier. When you feel good
you run fast. When you feel not-so-good, you run more slowly.
And you don't have to measure courses. You just go out for
half the required time, turn around and come back. Overall,
the program required an average of just over 4 hours per week
for 15 weeks, with a graded pattern of increasing and
decreasing weekly times leading to a peak 2 weeks before the
race.

Now I had taken up Nautilus that winter in place of free
weights. Between Nautilus and running I was already working out 3–4 hours per week. If I wanted to try a marathon, I
could hop in at Week 8 of the program, which required 220
minutes over 5 days, and then go on to finish a program which
did not take that much time and only had one run of more
than 2 hours in it.

Sensible me said "no." "But," said competitive me, "if *he*
could do it, *I* can do it, I *can* do it." After all, *he* had been
running only since the previous September. I had been at it
for 2½ years. I crossed the line from "I will never do a marathon" to "Yes, I'm training for my first marathon." I thought,
"There, that wasn't so hard, was it?"

Actually, I did not choose a marathon for my first long-
distance race. It was already too late to prepare for the *Newsday* Long Island Marathon, held in early May. Anyway, I
thought that it would be a good idea to get into this long-
distance racing business in stages, not easy ones, but stages
nevertheless. I would shoot for the Cross-Island Marathon

run between Port Jefferson and Patchogue, New York, in mid-June. This race is not actually a marathon, but at that time a 20-miler, (now under the sponsorship of Port Jefferson Road Runners, a 30k race). It would be a good test, I felt. If I managed to go 20 miles, I could probably run a marathon even though conventional wisdom says that at 20 miles you are only halfway to the finish of a marathon.

TRIATHLON THOUGHTS . . .

As my running time increased, I tapered off the Nautilus training. Overall, my program was going well. I had gotten on Ardy's program and was sticking with it consistently. Then in mid-May, I had a really wild idea. I saw an announcement for the 1983 Mighty Hamptons Triathlon, to be held the Saturday after Labor Day. I remembered Julie Moss in Hawaii. I remembered hearing about the 1982 Mighty Hamptons and Allison Roe's participation in it. "I can cycle," I thought. "My running is getting better, I can handle the increased training time, and I can swim." Looking at the distances involved, (1.5-mile swim, 25-mile bike, 10-mile run) and projecting completion times for each segment, I figured that it should take me just about as long to finish the Mighty Hamptons as it would take me to do a marathon 4:20 or so. (In the end I was just about right—for the actual racing time. I did a 4:46 including 23 minutes (!) changing my clothes. More on that in Chapter X.) And here I was already doing marathon-distance training.

The little voice spoke up again. "You can swim?!? What do you mean you can swim? You mean you know *how* to swim. What makes you think that you can go a mile and a half in the water and *then* cycle 25 and *then* run 10? You haven't swum in years and you have *never* swum for distance!" "I know, I know," I said to the little voice, "but this triathlon thing sounds like fun. I'll make a deal with you. I'll send in my entry to Mighty Hamptons. *If* I get in and *if* I finish the 20-miler, *then* I'll try the swimming. Maybe, just maybe, my aerobic conditioning will carry me through. I promise that if I can't do the swimming, I will pull out of the race. After all, I don't want to drown either me or you." "All right, all right," the little voice said, and retreated once again. After all, it knew that it had lost every debate about distance racing since the subject had first come up.

On June 18, 1983, I did the Cross-Island Marathon in 3:13, slightly under a 10-minute pace. I was okay until mile 17, but the last three were a real struggle. However, I didn't walk, and I passed a few people near the end. I was thrilled to have done it but I did hurt a lot—all over. I went into a postrace depression that lasted 2 weeks. In the meantime, I received my acceptance to the Mighty Hamptons Triathlon. Now I had to try swimming.

My first swim workout was in a pool on July 7. I did half a mile in half an hour. I alternated strokes by lap, doing crawl, side stroke, and elementary backstroke. I found that since I was in aerobic shape, if I didn't try to go too fast, I could do the distance without getting worn out. Paradoxical as it may seem, going slowly I progressed rapidly. I got up to a mile by the third workout. I dropped the side stroke by the sixth, splitting time evenly between crawl and elementary back-stroke. I was taking over 50 minutes to cover a mile, but I was doing the mile and I was comfortable at the end. I felt that I could do the race. I then set up a balanced swim-bike-run training program based on Ardy Friedberg's major con-cepts of hard / easy,[5] scheduled rest, and build up / cut back / build up further.

I did 3 open-water swims in preparation for that first

5. Hard / easy refers to a regular alternation of workouts that are difficult and challenging in length and / or intensity with ones that are relatively pleasant and relaxed.

triathlon. In the first I swam for an hour in fresh water, turning over on my back when I needed a blow and resting at halfway mark. In the second I swam for about 70 minutes without stopping in tidal salt water, returning to my starting point against an outgoing tide, again not worn out. I went slowly, still alternating strokes. I felt good.

I followed my program closely. I had a good August. About 2½ weeks before the race I went out to the racecourse and swam 1.2 miles of its 1.5-mile length. I knew then that I would be able to do the swim. And if I finished the swim without becoming a physical wreck doing so, I would be able to complete the bike and the run. Things were looking very good.

Two weeks before the race I had biked 25 miles and run 10 on a very hot Sunday morning. I was ready. I tapered my training over the next 2 weeks. I had my bike, all 30-odd pounds of it, "race prepared" at my bike shop. I pulled all the necessary bits and pieces of equipment and clothing together. I packed very carefully, trying hard not to fall into my usual pattern of forgetfulness. On the morning before the race, I loaded my bike into my car and took off for Sag Harbor. Upon arrival I checked into the guesthouse I was staying at and then checked myself and my bike into the race. I sorted out all of the paraphernalia. I took my bike over to the staging area and put it into its assigned stall. I was really going to do this thing.

The next morning I was up bright and early. I felt good and only slightly nervous. I laid out my equipment carefully at my assigned changing space. I pumped up my bike tires. Along with most of the other competitors I decided to walk the mile or so to the start of the swim rather than using one of the buses provided for transport. The walk gave us a chance to stretch out, to chit-chat, to relax. I got to the starting line and prepared for the swim. Almost 4 years before, Charlie Ogilvie's letter had set me off down the road to it. Until 6 months before the race date, neither I nor anyone I knew could have imagined that I would be at that place. But there I was. I did enter the water and I did finish the race. I describe the experience in detail in Chapter 10. It was a great one.

NEXT STEPS . . .

Contrasting with my experience in the Cross-Island Marathon, following the Mighty Hamptons I was on an emotional high for 2 weeks. I cast around for another event that I could do before the season ended. Three weeks later, I did the Ricoh East Coast Championship at Barnegat Light, New Jersey, an event similar in length to the Mighty Hamptons. In the interim between the two I did a metric century (100k) on my bike at near race pace[6] in an American Heart Association cyclethon. I was flying. I started thinking about doing this book, designed not for putative Ironmen but for people like me, and you, that is ordinary mortals who just happen to want to triathlon.

Immediately after the Barnegat Light race I began training for my first marathon, the White Rock in Dallas, Texas, held on December 4, 1983, again using Ardy Friedberg's program. I completed the marathon in a slow, comfortable 4:31, running most of the way. For the first time in my life, I thought of myself as an athlete. I was slow but steady. Winning was not my thing and it was unlikely that it ever would, or indeed could be. Doing it was my thing, just like it is for the overwhelming majority of competitors in these open endurance events. Doing it has rewards all its own.

For me, the single most important message of this book is this: if I, formerly a complete nonathlete can do it, you can do it too. And now on to the how-to.

6. Race pace is the speed at which one does an event when racing.

3 ... Choosing a Triathlon

The world is moving so fast now-a-days that a man who says it can't be done is generally interrupted by someone doing it.

Elbert Hubbard
in *The Complete Triathlon*, p. 219

INTRODUCTION . . .

Triathlons, as I pointed out in Chapter 1, come in many sizes and in a variety of different combinations of events. The standard combination is swim-bike-run, in that order. However, the order is occasionally changed. The alternative combinations usually include canoeing and often exclude swimming. Later in this chapter I will describe a few of the more exotic events. You might feel tempted, as I certainly have been, to try one. But it is likely that for your first event you will choose a swim-bike-run race.

There is a logic to the swim-bike-run order of events. Swimming is the sport in which the potential for serious accident is the highest. Therefore, it is a good idea to do it first when the athletes are physically fresh and mentally alert. Certainly it is preferable not to start a triathlon with the bike race. A mass start with bikes can easily produce a serious and potentially dangerous traffic jam. Furthermore, in most triathlons drafting (riding close behind another cyclist to take advantage of the wind-breaking effect) is prohibited. But drafting, even of the unintentional variety, is hard to avoid with a mass bike start.

The bike leg is usually the longest and physically the easiest. In biking, as contrasted with swimming and running, when you get tired you can always rest while continuing to move forward, by coasting while going downhill or even on the flat. It is obviously better to have the bike leg in the middle. Running, then, is left for last.

TRIATHLON LENGTHS . . .

I discussed the different lengths of triathlons in the first chapter. The Triathloning for Ordinary Mortals Training Program is designed to enable you to do a marathon-equivalent triathlon ("Short Course" in the Triathlon Federation/USA terminology) happily and healthily. As I pointed out in Chapter 1, marathon-equivalent is defined in functional terms: it takes the athlete of any ability about as long to do one as it would take him or her to run a marathon. As you can see, we are talking about some combination of a 1–1½-mile swim, a 20–25-mile bike ride, and a 10k–10-mile run. It is not likely that the TFOM Training Program will get you through an event any longer than this, but of course having done the program you will easily be able to handle a shorter, "training-length" race. There may be excellent reasons for doing just that for your first race.

The marathon-equivalent triathlon can be psychologically daunting before you have completed your first one. If you do a training-length event the first time around, you will convince yourself that you actually can do three sports consecutively under race conditions. You will be able to test yourself, your equipment, and your transition technique without getting too tired or strung out. You almost certainly will have a good time in your first shorter event. Finally, it might turn out to be logistically more convenient to do a shorter event for the first one if you can find one geographically close to home. But the TFOMTP will equip you, as it did me, to do a marathon-equivalent event even on the first time out.

THE BALANCE ISSUE . . .

In some quarters there is a great deal of concern with the issue of balance among the lengths of each of the three legs.[1] The concern focuses on the issue of racing advantage to those athletes most proficient in one of the events. If the cycling leg is functionally the longest, so the reasoning goes, cyclists will have an advantage in that race over people who are primarily swimmers or runners. However, this is a concern only for people who are in the race with an expectation of winning or placing, either overall or in their age-sex group. This group accounts for a relatively small percentage of all triathletes and, I expect, an even smaller percentage of the readers of this particular book. In any case, as Murphy Reinschreiber pointed out in his *Triathlon* article, since there are so many variations in athlete's abilities, the weather, temperature (air and water), course terrain, and topography, it is probably impossible to design a completely balanced triathlon. For your purposes, the best thing to do is to pick a race that has distances that you are mentally comfortable with.

WHERE TO FIND TRIATHLONS . . .

The best place to look is in the calendar of one of the growing number of triathlon publications (see Appendix 1). There is

1. Murphy Reinschreiber, "A Delicate Balance," *Triathlon,* Fall 1983, p. 15.

usually a calendar in every issue. The biggest ones appear in later winter/early spring, in time to plan your season. Since race dates and locations are sometimes changed, it is a good idea to check now and then if you have entered a race but have not yet heard about your acceptance. For example, in setting out my own schedule in the spring of 1984, I entered the Bud Light United States Triathlon Series (BLUSTS) event scheduled for Boston on August 4. I received a computer-printed confirmation of my entry but no details about the race. Then the changes began. First the race date was changed to August 12. I saw that in a USTS magazine ad. Then I heard through the grapevine that the location had been changed from Boston to Cape Cod. Finally, checking the race calendar in the July issue of *The Beast*, I discovered that the race had been moved back to Boston—for September 9. Since I was already planning to do the Mighty Hamptons on September 8, I had to withdraw. I did eventually receive notice from BLUSTS and a refund of my entry fee.

CHOOSING YOUR FIRST TRIATHLON . . .

There are a variety of factors to be taken into account when choosing which triathlon to do for your first one. Obviously, you must weigh all the variables for yourself and make the choice that suits you best and that you are most mentally and physically comfortable with. In this section, I will take you through the various criteria more or less in the order that I look at them. However, I do not propose this order as a rigid guide. You may well want to do your own evaluation differently. But I think that you will find these criteria helpful in making your choice.

DATE. This is obviously a major consideration. You must have enough time to train properly. The Triathloning for Ordinary

Mortals Training Program (TFOMTP) described in Chapter 7 requires 13 weeks. It assumes that before you start it you have been doing aerobic exercise consistently and regularly 2½–3 hours per week for about 6 months. (If you are starting from scratch, see Chapter 6. You will need about 3 additional months to get up to the 2½–3-hour-per-week level.) It also assumes that before you start the TFOMTP you know how to safely ride a bicycle (preferably one with derailleur shifters, commonly called a "10-speed") and swim using one or more of the strokes that can be employed effectively over long distances (crawl, side stroke, breast stroke, elementary backstroke, or back crawl). Thus the date that you pick for your first race will be anywhere from 3 months to 1 year from the time that you decide to become a triathlete. If you are going to need 9–12 months to prepare, choose an established race or two in the current season and write to them, enclosing a stamped, self-addressed envelope, asking to be placed on the mailing list for the following year. If you can attend a triathlon before doing one, all the better.

DISTANCE FROM HOME. This will also be a major consideration. You obviously must transport your bicycle to the race. People do fly around the country for races but that means packing your bike in an expensive, large, cumbersome container that most air lines charge extra to transport for you. For your first race you are well advised to pick one that you can drive to.

Unlike running road races, few triathlons provide for morning-of-the-race registration. Because all of the race places are usually taken in advance, virtually all require preregistration. It is normally held the day before the race. A bicycle safety inspection is *de rigueur*. Some races will then provide a secure, guarded area where you can safely leave your bike overnight. But in any case, unless the race is really close to home, you will have to stay overnight in the area. This requirement can lead to some considerable expense, especially if the race is held at a resort area during the season. In this case most motels and hotels require a minimum 2-night stay on the weekends.

Most race directors will send out a list of available accomodations with your notice of acceptance. Some are able to negotiate special triathloner rates with local hostelries. If a list is not provided, you can get one by writing to the local chamber of commerce or contacting an automobile club. In any case, if you need to stay overnight, be sure to make your reservations early. Accommodations convenient to the race tend to fill early, and many races are held in locations that do not have too many such facilities.

RACE LENGTH. As I said before, beginners may want to consider starting their triathlon career with a training-length event. While the TFOMTP is designed for the marathon-equilvalent event, it will obviously also prepare you for a shorter event and could even be cut down a bit (in minutes per week, not total weeks of training) if your choice is to be a race that is much shorter.

One way to figure out the maximum length that your first race should be is to calculate how long it will probably take you to do it. You will obviously need to know the rate at which you do each event. If your experience is like mine and that of many of my friends, in the race you will probably do the swim at a rate 2–4 minutes per mile more quickly than your training pace, the bike at or slightly above your training pace, and the run at 1–2 minutes per mile more slowly than your training pace. The TFOMTP will prepare you to engage in up to 4.5 hours of consecutive aerobic exercise. In addition, you will spend a total of 10–20 minutes in transition between events.

You *can* do that much your first time out. But if the prospect is daunting, why not try a "Tiny Tri" of 0.5k swim, 20k bike, 5k run as staged especially for beginners by the Southern California Triathlete's Club (Box 10033, Venice, California 90291) or the short Lancaster (Pennsylvania) Triathlon of .25-mile swim, 5-mile run, 15-mile bike (YMCA, 572 North Queen, Lancaster, Pennsylvania 17693) or the WAAY-TV Huntsville, Alabama) 3-in-1 Triathlon, 3-mile run, 6-mile bike, and 400-meter swim. There are in increasing number of training-length events appearing in the calendars. One of them may be just the ticket for you.

RACING ABILITY. Another criterion to use in deciding both when you are ready and what length to try is to apply to yourself a very nice race-pace test developed by Dr. E. C. Frederick and Stephen Kiesling.[2] To happily and healthily finish a U.S. Triathlon Series event (1.5k swim, 40k bike, 10k run) you should be able to do the following over a maximum 5-day span: swim 1k (0.6 miles) in no more than 31 minutes (a 52-minutes-per-mile pace), cycle 12k (7.5 miles) in no more than 34 minutes (a 13-mph pace), and run 5k (3 miles) in no more than 35 minutes (an 11.7-minutes-per-mile pace). Take this test before you start the TFOMTP, but after you have established your 6-month aerobic base (see Chapters 5 and 6). If you pass and then do the TFOMTP, you should be able to finish a marathon-equivalent tirathlon very comfortably. If you fail by a good deal, set your sights on a training-length event for your first race. If you fail only by a little, say in one event, try the test again during the sixth week of the TFOMTP.

If you pass on the second try, you will probably do just fine in a marathon-equivalent triathlon. If not, pick a training event, finish the TFOMTP, and do the race. Then in your subsequent training, work on improving your speed as well as your endurance. Of course if you have previous racing or time-trial

2. E. C. Frederick and Stephen Kiesling, "The Semi-Tough Triathlon," *American Health*, June 1984, p. 56.

experience in one or more of the sports, you don't have to formally take the full test, but rather can just plug in previous performances.

BALANCE. As I pointed out above, there is no completely "balanced" triathlon. As I did, however, you will want to consider the lengths of the legs and be certain that you have the capability of finishing each one. The balance of distances that you are looking for as an Ordinary-Mortal triathlete is one that is good for you.

RACECOURSE. As well as length, you will want to consider the characteristics of the course itself. There are many characteristics to be taken into account. For the swim, will it be in salt or fresh water? Most triathlon swims are held in natural bodies of water, but occasionally they are done in pools. Salt water means ocean, bay, or tidal river. It also means extra buoyancy, which I find very helpful. If the race is in open ocean, you must be prepared to deal with the possibility of breakers, tides, and an undertow. If the swim is in a bay, it is unlikely that you will have to worry about breakers, but there are still tides, currents, and waves to deal with.

In the 1983 Mighty Hamptons we were swimming into an incoming tide and wind-blown waves coming from the same direction. Luckily, I happen to breath to that side. I was able to time my swim stroke so that I was breathing at the top of each wave. In the 1983 East Coast Championships at Ships Bottom, New Jersey, for almost half of the swim we were beneficiaries of a 2-mile-per-hour current in our favor. Everybody had a really good swim time that day! The Northport (New York) Triathlon features relatively short bike and run legs but a 2.5-mile swim that because of tricky currents in Northport Harbor can turn into a 4-mile swim for the unwary. In the 1984 Virginia Beach (Virginia) Neptune Sandman Triathlon, which had an open-ocean, out-and-back swim, a

1.5-mph lateral current put me 200 yards up the beach at the end of the leg, even though I was aware of the current and tried to counter it.

Fresh water is in and of itself more pleasant than salt water, especially if you happen to take in a mouthful every now and then. But it doesn't have the buoyancy of salt water. And the lack of pleasantness of some lake bottoms can negatively balance out the pleasantness of the water. For the 1984 Empire State Triathlon held in Bear Mountain State Park (New York), a couple of practice sessions on my lawn really would have helped in dealing with the grasses of Lake Sebago!

Water temperature is also an important consideration. Below 70°F water starts to feel distinctly cold even after you have been swimming for a while. If you have a choice, pick a race in which the water temperature is at 70°F or above. If the temperature will be below 65°F you may well want to consider using a wet suit, ascertaining beforehand that they are permitted. Of course, different people react to the same water temperature in different ways. Even after 4 years of training I still have a layer of subskin body fat that I cannot get rid of. But it does help in cool-water swimming. In the 1984 Mighty Hamptons Triathlon I was happy as a clam in water that produced hypothermia in several very thin competitors. Only in those conditions is my fat layer an advantage.

For the bike and the run the course criteria to take into account are similar. Is the course a single loop or laps? The former is more interesting but the latter may make the race more comfortable and seem to go faster as you begin to deal with familiar terrain. If the course is hilly, just how hilly is it? My personal preference is for mildly to moderately hilly courses. I train for both the bike and run on hills, and I'm used to them. After you have worked your way up a hill on your bike you can always get an exhilarating ride down on the other side. On the other hand, on flat terrain, as at the East Coast Championships (all flat) and the Virginia Beach

Neptune Sandman (almost all flat) you have to keep going at a constant pace. This can get to be a real bother, especially on the bike.

What is the road surface like? Do you have to be extra-prepared for flat tires on the bike leg? Is there going to be any running done on uneven surfaces? What about shade? When the sun is brightly shining, the temperature is 85°F, and the humidity is 80%, running on a tree-lined road will be a lot more comfortable than running through a wide-open stretch of farmland. The time of day of the start is an important consideration too. Generally in my experience, the earlier the start the better.

CONCURRENT EVENTS. Some triathlons have concurrent events and this may be a factor to take into consideration. Is there a nice postrace awards ceremony with food and drink, possibly free? Is there a "carbo-loading" dinner[3] provided the night before? In the higher-cost events (also a consideration), this meal is usually included. If not included in the fee, perhaps it is offered at a nominal charge. Is there a raffle or a race-number drawing for prizes? Several triathlons have trade shows associated with them. Others have prerace programs with speakers, open to the general public (Mighty Hamptons), or conferences aimed at health professionals (Virginia Beach Neptune Sandman, Hawaii Ironman). Some races feature significant participation from local triathlon clubs while others may have special races-within-the-race for members of a particular group.

TRAINING SEASON. Finally, coming around full circle, you will have to consider the training season in making your choice of event. Some people run, ride, and swim all year round. I am not one of them, partly because winter in the Northeast-

---

3. Carbo-loading refers to eating foods high in complex carbohydrates like pasta, salad, and bread, but not simple sugars like candy and ice cream. See Chapter 9.

ern United States means consistently cold weather for 3 months, and partly because I believe in resting the body and in cyclical training. I generally go indoors for the winter. (For more detail on my winter training program, see Chapter 5). Further, I cannot stand bike riding in the cold weather even when the roads are dry. I find cold headwinds frustrating and hurtful. Even with booties on, my feet tend to turn into blocks of ice. Thus, if you are like me and you pay attention to the temperature in deciding upon your training regimen, you will want to allow at least 13 weeks of predictably decent weather before your first triathlon. Water temperature for the swim is also a factor here. Thus I never do my first triathlon of the season before mid-June. I do like to do a half-marathon and / or a short run-bike biathlon in the spring as a tune-up.

You now have some criteria to use in making your choice of your first triathlon. Following are some descriptions of actual races, conventional, and not-so-conventional.

SOME "ORDINARY" TRIATHLONS[4] ...

The Chicago race of the Bud Light United States Triathlon Series is held along the lakefront, a beautiful urban setting. The BLUSTS is a set of approximately 10 races run during the summer each year in cities all across the country. Elite triathletes compete for prizes in all the races, but the races are also open to all entrants so there is a nice mix of competitors. The 1.5k swim, 40k bike, 10k run distances (a "Short Course" race precisely) make them marathon-equivalent races and ideal choices for your first go. The use of Lake Michigan, with the magnificent Chicago skyline overlooking it, to swim in, and

4. This material is based in part on "8 Great Races," *Triathlon*, April/May 1984, p. 44.

the lakefront to bike and run along, make this event particularly appealing visually.

The Mighty Hamptons Triathlon (MHT) in Sag Harbor, New York, which began in 1982, quickly became one of the premier events in the East. A comparison of marathon times reported by competitors with their times in the MHT showed that its 1.5-mile swim, 25-mile bike, and 10-mile run very closely match the marathon for time needed for completion, making this race a true marathon-equivalent event. It is slightly longer than the Tri Fed/USA "Short Course" event. The swim is held in Noyac Bay near Sag Harbor, which on the weekend after Labor Day has a salt-water temperature above 70°F. The bike is over rolling hills and through pleasant farmland. The run is on well-shaded streets in and around the village of Sag Harbor. (For a detailed description of my first experience in this race, see Chapter 10.) If you want to try this one yourself, get your entry in early. It is very popular.

The Great Race Triathlon is held in Callaway Gardens Park, a resort and botanical gardens a bit over an hour outside of Atlanta, Georgia. It is a picturesque, relatively traffic-free 2k swim, 40k bike, 15k run. The swim is held in a small lake and the bike race consists of 3 laps over the same course.

The Los Angeles Championship Triathlon Series of three races are held in Bonelli Park over a 1k-swim, 38k-bike, 8k-run course. This is getting somewhat under marathon-equivalency, but they are excellent races. Early in the spring when the series starts, the lake water temperature can be quite cold, however. The bike race is over 3 laps of the same course.

The Empire State Triathlon is held in Bear Mountain State Park, a beautiful setting. The 1-mile swim is in Sebago Lake while the 25-mile bike and 10k run are held on smooth, generally traffic-free, picturesque parkways. The bike portion consists of 3 different out-and-back loops, while the run features 1 out-and-back loop. Each loop in both the bike and the run is uphill out and downhill back.

The Neptune Sandman Triathlon held in Virginia Beach, Virginia, is a 1.25-mile-swim, 18-mile-bike, 10k-run event which includes an open salt-water swim that starts in Atlantic Ocean surf. The swim, as I noted before, is tricky because of surf and current. The bike and the run are both flat. There is plenty of shade on the bike but not too much on the run.

SOME "NOT-SO-ORDINARY" TRIATHLONS . . .

The Kaaterskill Spring Rush is a downhill ski, run, bike, canoe-portage, canoe-paddle event starting at the Hunter Mountain (New York) ski area and finishing in Catskill, New York. It can be done by individuals or 2-person teams. It includes an 18-mile run and 47-mile bike ride over busy, narrow roads in the Catskill Mountains, followed by a 8-mile canoe paddle. There are no water stops or aid stations; you must supply your own support team. This race will test anyone's mettle.

Another New York State event held not too far from the site of the Kaaterskill Spring Rush is also a bit on the wild side. The Survival of the Shawangunks takes you consecutively and point-to-point on a 30-mile bike, 4-mile run, 1.25-mile swim, 6-mile run, .625-mile swim, 8.5-mile run, .625-mile swim, 1-mile run. You must carry your running shoes with you as you swim across each of the three lakes on the course. The runs are partly on wilderness trails. This event, in gorgeous country, is not for the faint of heart. For entry, there are required maximum qualifying times.

Also in New York State is a run-bike-canoe event with lengths (5.2-miles, 17.4-miles, and 5-miles respectively) that might well appeal to the first-time triathlete who would rather do something else than swim. This race is called the Incredible Journey Triathlon. It is held on and around Onondaga Lake in a county park. Again, a lovely setting and this time an event that is doable by Ordinary Mortals, either singly or in 2-person teams. Some canoe practice combined with the TFOMTP (actually reduced a bit) would set you up for this event very well.

The Greater Laurel Transfer held in and around Winsted, Connecticut, is another very doable bike-canoe-run event (27-7-9 miles) for singles and 5-person (1 cyclist, 2 runners, 2 canoeists) relay teams. The canoe portion is on a lake, which makes it especially appealing. The topographical maps supplied in the race instructions for this event are the best that I have seen anywhere.

Another New England bike-canoe-run event is the Great Josh Billings Run Aground held in the Great Bartington-Tanglewood area of the Berkshires. As of 1984 both this event and the Greater Laurel Transfer began with the bike race, always a dangerous way to go because of the increased possibility of collisions amongst racers inexperienced at riding in packs. But as in the Great Laurel Transfer, the canoe portion is held on a nice, small lake. This race is primarily for 4-person relay teams: 1 biker, 1 runner, 2 canoeists.

A nice bike-run-canoe event (12 miles-5 miles-3 miles) is held each spring in the Brandywine Creek State Park near Wilmington, Delaware. The Brandywine Classic/Gore-Tex Triathlon can be done by 1 person, 2 people, or 4 people. The course is a quite beautiful one, and proceeds from the race benefit the American Heart Association.

For those who might like to do a nonswimming triathlon but who are also put off by the thought of spending any time at all in a vessel as tippy as a canoe, there is Everybody's Triathlon held in Southwest Harbor, Maine. This is a 2.6-mile-run, 1-mile-*row*, 5.2-mile-bike event. This one, really of the "Tiny Tri" variety, is open to individuals and teams. As with so many of the others, the setting for this event, the rugged coast of Maine, is certainly a beautiful one.

You say that biking and running are okay, swimming is not, you cannot canoe, but you can sail? You should try the

Surf, Pedal, and Trot Triathlon held in Duxbury, Massachusetts. In this one you boardsail for 5 miles, cycle for 15, and
then run a 10k. Because it includes sailing, it is the only
triathlon I know of that schedules a rain date. This event is
open to individuals and relay teams. Forty-six individuals and
6 relay teams entered it when it was first run in 1984.

Finally, if biking is the event you would like to avoid and
paddling a boat is your thing, there is at least one race designed
just for you. The "Old Ironsiders" Kayathlon, held in Boston
Harbor, consists of a 2-mile ocean swim, a 2-mile run and a
30-mile paddle alone in a kayak. I wouldn't know what to
recommend as training for this one, but it certainly is a challenge. If *you* do it, please let me know how you trained and
how you made out.

CONCLUSION ...

Making a choice of which triathlon to do for your first one
becomes easier each year as more triathlons are developed in
all parts of the country. The majority of them are in the marathon-equivalent and training-length categories. You should
have an ample number from which to choose, regardless of
the region in which you live. In summary, the major factors
to consider are: length, combination of events, distance-from-
home / convenience, cost (of the event itself and of
travel / accomodations), time of year / time for training, course
characteristics, fresh water / salt water and water temperature, and of course your own ability. The choice you make
will obviously be the result of the balancing and weighing of
these factors and some others not on my list which may well
occur to you.

Once you have made your choice, send in for the application as early as you can. Be sure to enclose a stamped, self-
addressed envelope. Again, return your completed applica-

tion as soon as you can. Triathlons are complex events to stage and often accept relatively few competitors. The better-known ones often fill several months before they are held. Do not wait to receive a written acceptance to start your training. Sometimes acceptances are not mailed out until 1–2 weeks before the race.

Appearance of your canceled check for the registration fee is an excellent indication of acceptance. However, if you have heard nothing, after a decent interval you can telephone the race director for confirmation. But I would suggest not lobbying for acceptance if the decision has not yet been made. Most race directors do not take too kindly to that kind of special pleading. If you are worried about getting in, it may well pay to apply to two events being held around the same time in order to be sure of doing at least one. Who knows, if your training goes well and the events are separated in time by at least two weeks, you might well end up doing both! In my first triathlon season, I did my second race 3 weeks after I did my first, and between the two I did a metric century (100 k) at just below race pace on my bike. In my second season, I did 3 marathon-equivalent races in a 4-week period, felt fine at the end, and went on to run a marathon 6 weeks later. I am no Superman. I just followed the TFOMTP and did the races at a comfortable pace. At any rate, when you do get that first race acceptance you are well on your way to having one of the great experiences of your life—completing a triathlon.

4 ... *Run, Bike, and Swim: Technique*

I have two good doctors—my right leg and my left.
Anonymous

INTRODUCTION ...

Let me say right off the bat that I consider myself an expert on technique in none of the three principal sports of triathloning: running, cycling, and swimming. I do each sport well enough to finish happily and healthily at the back of the middle of the pack in the marathon-equivalent events that I do. Nevertheless, I do like to improve my performance each season, for the sake of improvement itself and to give myself something to shoot for. Better technique and better aerobic conditioning both contribute to better performance. Thus, while I work on conditioning in training by going at a faster pace but not by increasing training time, I also work on technique. I do this by going to some of the same sources that I recommend to you for this purpose: coaches, classes, books, and magazines.

At the beginning of this chapter I will review some of the principal sources of professional help that are available. Then I will describe the basic concepts of good technique in each of the three sports as I understand them from my own reading and conversations with experts. I will also share some of my training and racing experience as it bears on technique. But please understand that I am not setting myself up as a technical expert in any of the three sports. For technical expertise, you will have to seek additional guidance.

WRITTEN SOURCES OF ADVICE AND COUNSEL . . .

MAGAZINES. The principal triathlon magazines are listed in Appendix I. You will often find technical articles in these publications. I have frequently found such articles to be very helpful. There are also several single-sport magazines which publish useful technical articles on a regular basis. *Runner's World* and *The Runner* are the two main running magazines. I find the technical articles in RW to be particularly useful. Bicycle magazine publishing seems to be a growth industry these days, especially after the U.S. successes in bicycling at the 1984 Olympics. But *Bicycling* magazine is still the leader. It often has helpful technical articles. *Swim, Swim* offers useful advice in that sport. The better pieces from it are sometimes reprinted in *Triathlon* magazine.

BOOKS. The publishing world is replete with running books. There is an almost constant flow of them, and it is really difficult to keep up. My own favorites are listed in Appendix II, along with some of the leading books in cycling and swimming. Especially in running, there are certainly a number of fine ones available. Go to a bookstore with a good sports-book section. Browse. Take your time. Pick an author or two with whom you are comfortable. You can easily build up a nice little reference library for yourself.

I used *The Runner's Handbook* by Bob Glover and Jack

Shepherd to introduce me to running. I like that book and still consult it from time to time. The section on technique in Bob's newest book, *The Competitive Runner's Handbook* (written with Peter Schuder), I find to be particularly useful. I think that the late Jimmy Fixx's *The Complete Book of Running* will always be a classic, and who can be a runner and not read George Sheehan? Joe Henderson's *Jog, Run, Race* is a fine book on both technique and training for the beginner and novice runner. There are several running books written especially for women. I can recommend Dr. Joan Ullyot's *Running Free* (New York: G. P. Putnam's Sons), which also contains much useful nongender-specific information.

A very useful introductory cycling book is Thom Lieb's *Everybody's Book of Bicycle Riding*. The chapter on technique in Thom's book is excellent for the beginner. A good book *about* bicycles is Rosa and Kolin's *The Ten-Speed Bicycle*. A useful book on bike racing is Fred Matheny's *Beginning Bicycle-Racing*.

The standard text for the beginning and intermediate swimmer is Jane Katz's *Swimming for Total Fitness*. It is well written, well thought out and covers both technique and exercise programming very well.

Dan Honig, founder of New York's Big Apple Triathlon Club, has written three excellent, concise books on the three principal triathlon sports: *How to Run Better, How to Bike Better,* and *How to Swim Better.* Together, they provide a fine introduction for the prospective triathlete.

VERBAL SOURCES . . .

The best way to learn technique is with private coaching. This can be difficult to find and expensive, however. Classes in one or more of the sports may be offered in the Adult Education program of a local high school, college, or university, a "Y," a sports club, or a running-shoe, bicycle, or sporting-goods store. Adult summer camps for triathloning are appearing in various parts of the country. Those with 1-week programs seem to work better than the weekend variety. A particularly good one in the East is Triathlon World (Box 683, Dennis, Massachusetts). Finally, there are friends. Experienced friends can be very helpful but you must screen their advice with care. If a friend who offers technical help is often injured, I would smile, nod politely, and seek advice elsewhere.

SOME GENERAL THOUGHTS ON TECHNIQUE . . .

In endurance sports, as in medicine and sailing, there is often more than one way to do it right, although frequently someone who offers guidance will insist that his or hers is the *only* way to do it. There are also many different ways to do it wrong. Regardless of what the correct way (or ways) to do it is, you should learn all of the bad ways and make sure that you are doing none of them. How then do you judge?

Good technique in the endurance sports will first of all produce efficiency. You will cover maximum distance at good speed for any given expenditure of energy. Good technique will enable you to do this with the most comfort. For long races of the type you are planning to do, this should be translated as least pain. Endurance sports hurt. At the paces we are talking about the pain level is not that high, very far from unendurable or incapacitating. But there will be some pain, and good technique will keep the hurting at the lowest possible level. If speed is a concern to you, good technique will enable you to go as fast as your overall conditioning has equipped you to go, in terms of your cardiovascular functioning. Finally, good technique is one of the keys to injury prevention. (The others are appropriate goal setting, consistency, regularity, hard/easy, and avoidance of overtraining.) For example, running with your feet splayed out can lead to knee injury, while cycling in too high a gear and too low cadence can lead to the same thing.

Bad technique has effects generally opposite to those of good technique. One of the problems is, however, that the athlete is not necessarily aware that he or she is doing anything wrong. If bad technique leads to immediate discomfort, as it does for example when you cycle with the seat so low that your quads (front thigh muscles) never get stretched out, you will of course recognize it right away: "it hurts!" Even if you don't know the source of the discomfort, you will know that you are uncomfortable and hopefully will seek advice from a book, a friend, or a coach. However, unless you have an experienced person watch you, you may make a technical error that decreases your efficiency but does not produce pain and never know that you are doing anything wrong. Technical errors in swimming are often of this variety.

Recreational triathletes are not likely to swim fast enough to get into the pain or out-of-breath zone, because of the well-placed fear of getting into trouble and not being able to easily stop for a rest out on the water. Thus one tends to take it relatively easy while swimming. On the bike and the run you can stop at any point if you have to. Thus if you are swimming with poor technique, the usual outcome is not pain but loss of efficiency, wastage of energy, and decline in speed. This state of affairs could continue for a very long time without you knowing it. "I'm a slow swimmer and I will just have to live with that fact," you might say. Or in an effort to speed-up you might put in a lot of extra training time that could have been saved if only you were using correct technique.

Bad technique can also slow you down for simple mechanical reasons. Cycling in too upright a position increases wind resistance. If you run with too short a stride you will obviously cover less distance with each step. Since there is a limit to

how fast we can make our legs go, a shorter stride can mean
a slower rate of speed.

Finally, if good technique protects against injury, bad technique (as well as overtraining) increases your risk of being
injured. Injury is the most frequent cause of activity cessation
for the regular endurance athlete. Thus both bad technique
and overtraining are to be avoided as much as possible.

ON RUNNING . . .

I said in the first chapter, quoting my friend Harold Schwab,
running is mainly a matter of "right, left, right, left." But
when you sit down to talk with Harold, or any other expert,
you will find that there is a bit more to it than that. I have
found Part IV, "Technique" of *The Competitive Runner's
Handbook* by Bob Glover and Peter Schuder to be very helpful in this regard. In this section, I will just summarize some
of the basics.

Footstrike is the most important single component of running technique. There are several different "good" approaches,
but for most recreational endurance athletes the best one seems
to be "heel-ball." You land on the outside edge of your heel
first, but quickly roll along the outside edge of your foot,
rotating inward as the ball of your foot comes in contact with
the ground, then driving off the ball and big toe into the next
stride. Keep your toes pointed straight ahead. You do not
want to run solely on the balls of your feet, nor do you want
to land hard on your heels and then slap the rest of your foot
down on the ground. There is enough pounding and jarring
in running when it is done well; you do not want to do anything to accentuate it. Run lightly and in balance.

Your arms should be bent at the elbows. Arm swing should
be straight ahead, not across your chest. As in walking, the
arm going forward is the one opposite to the leg going for-

ward at the same time. According to Bob Glover, the bulk of the arm swing should be at the elbow, not the shoulder. If you are at all like me, you will find it unnatural to run with *no* shoulder swing at all, but the shoulders should come into play in a significant way only when you are driving up a hill. Keep your hands partially open and cupped. Neither clench your fists nor let your hands and fingers flop around aimlessly; both waste energy.

Stand up straight, but don't lock yourself into an erect posture. Bending at the waist inhibits movement of the diaphragm, the major muscle that you want to use for breathing. Making yourself rigidly upright, especially at the shoulders, produces only spasm and pain. I have a particular problem with shoulder cramping. When I get into the right gait and do not develop shoulder pain, the run is much more fun. As in everything else, the keys are balance, balance, and balance.

Hold your head erect. The books will all tell you to keep your gaze level, off in the distance. That is very good for posture. But if you are at all like me you will also be concerned about road conditions immediately in front of you: cracks, bumps, broken glass, holes, discarded mattresses, dead animals, animal droppings, and the like. Compromise. Keep your head up, cast your eyes down from time to time, but don't bend your neck.

Going up *and* coming down hills is a problem. Bob Glover and Peter Schuder have an excellent detailed section on this aspect of running. I will share with you my own experience. Since I live in a hilly area and train on hills, I actually like them. In a race, often when others are slowing down on a hill I am speeding up or at least maintaining my rate of speed. (If you don't like dirty looks however, *don't* pass fellow recreational racers on the hills.) I shorten my stride, bend slightly forward at the waist, pick up my pace, maintain heel-ball footstrike, and drive forward with my arms at the shoulders. My breathing rate increases, my quads begin to burn, but boy not by reaching our further in front. On really steep hills you will actually have to shorten your stride to stay in control. The most important thing about running downhill is in fact to stay in control. Your prime objectives should be to stay on your feet, stay in balance, and avoid injury, even if it means losing a few seconds here and there.

On breathing, you should do it through your mouth and primarily with your diaphragm. You will occasionally want to fully expand your lungs by consciously expanding your upper rib cage and raising your shoulders, but diaphramatic breathing is the key. If you are running fast enough to raise your respiratory rate a significant degree, most of the time you will want to fall into a rhythmic pattern. When I'm moving right along, I will be breathing in for 2 steps, out for 2 steps. In for 1 step, out for 1 step means that I am working hard and cannot hold that pace for too long. In for 3 steps, and out for 3 steps is a pretty leisurely pace for me. If I am breathing less hard than that on a training run (and on the easy days I am breathing less hard than that), I don't bother maintaining a rhythm.

When I am pushing hard and getting tired in running, biking, and swimming, I find that a pattern of quick, full inspiration / long, slow expiration for a few breaths is very helpful for recovery. Exactly why it works, I don't know. But it does. Develop your own pattern and try it. It should work for you too.

ON CYCLING . . .

The best written material that I have found on cycling technique for the beginner and the novice is in Chapters 6 and 7 of Thom Lieb's *Everybody's Book of Bicycle Riding*. Again, I will just share with you some of my own thoughts and experience.

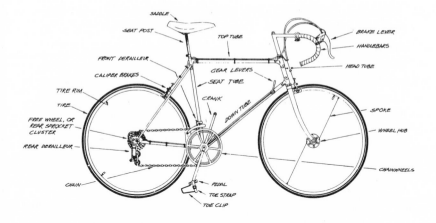

10-SPEED BICYCLE

to reach the brakes quickly if necessary. You let your hand rest on the hood, thumb to the inside, fingers to the outside. For more security, you can grasp the underside of the hood with your index and middle fingers. Your back is moderately bent, reducing wind resistance, but not so bent over as to be uncomfortable over the long haul.

With hands on the drops, you have maximum braking control and power. You also have good turning control. I always use that position when going downhill and coming into an intersection. It is the most aerodynamic position, but it is also the most uncomfortable one. You must bend your neck up so that you can look forward. Your diaphragm is compressed so that your breathing becomes less efficient. With your hips bent, you get less driving power from your legs because it is harder to bring the back muscles into play. Yet hands on the drops is certainly the position of choice for going into a headwind and for picking up speed when you need to. But until you become an experienced cyclist, you will not able to hold that position for too long.

Hands on the tops is fun-and-games and foolish and dangerous unless you have auxiliary brake handles which you shouldn't have anyway (see Chapter 8). It is comfortable because your back is straight, you are relatively upright and, believe it or not, the pressure on your bottom is the least. These are the reasons why leisurely bike riding in the 7–10 mph range is usually done in this position. BUT, as speed goes up, so does wind resistance. Upright is a no-no at 15–20 mph. Furthermore, with your hands close together on the tops you have the least turning control and your hands are the furthest away from the brakes. In June 1984, I learned this lesson the hard way.

Out on a training ride, I was going through a busy intersection very slowly, making a left-hand turn. I had my hands on the tops instead of on the hoods or, better yet, on the drops. Since I have a racing bike, there are no auxiliary brake handles. As I made my way through traffic at slow speed, the front wheel began to wobble. With my hands on the tops, I could neither stop the bike with the brakes nor effectively control the wobble (because my hands were too close together). I tipped over to the right, instinctively stuck out my right arm in a vain attempt to break the fall, and sustained a shoulder dislocation and a fracture of one of the bumps at the upper end of my upper arm bone. The injury was the result of a low-speed accident that was entirely my own fault. It would not have happened if my hands had been either on the hoods or the drops.

The third point of attachment between you and the bike is at the pedals. The considerations here mainly those of equipment rather than technique. I will deal with them in Chapter 8. I will say one thing about a pedaling technique called "ankling" which calls for active ankle flexion through the downstrike. Although used by many top bike racers, many expert-cyclist triathletes whom I know advise against it for triathloning. For one thing, it stresses the Achilles tendon, something that you do not want to do if you are a runner. Generally, it is recommended that the sole of your foot be kept more or less parallel with the ground throughout the whole pedaling cycle, except on the upstroke, in which the heel is elevated slightly as you pull up.

The most important element in the mechanics of cycling is the rate at which you turn the pedals. It is directly related to the gear which you select. The key to successful cycling is low gear, high revolutions per minute (rpm). This is called "spinning." For the triathlete, the rpm range to aim for is 80–100. This technique will take some practice to learn. Leisure-time cyclists are not used to pedaling that fast. But pedaling that fast does mean less legwork, less fatigue, more cardiovascular efficiency. The stroke should be smooth, not jerky, and you should be pulling with your leg in the upstroke as well as pushing on the downstroke. Pedaling at 70 rpm or less simply means more fatigue, more pain, and more risk of knee injury. There is no magic to gear selection. You have to learn what works for you.

Once you get comfortable with an rpm over 80, you should learn to shift gears constantly as the terrain changes so that you can stay at or near your target spinning rate, regardless of incline or decline of any particular hill. As you get even better and more conditioned, you will be able to reduce your gear shifting and stay in your target rpm range by adding muscle power as needed. For monitoring rpm, or "cadence" as it is called in the cycling jargon, I find an electronic cadence counter fitted to the bike to be very useful.

Shifting gears takes a bit of practice. You must be pedaling to shift gears on a 10-speed bike. The key to success is shifting with the pressure off the pedals, while at the same time turning them. It sounds contradictory, but a bit of practice will demonstrate to you how it works. The key to successful gear shifting on the hills is advance planning. Downshift early so that you don't get caught cranking at 20 rpm with searing

quads and knees about to pop. Think ahead. If you get into
a reasonable gear and are spinning at a reasonable cadence
before you start up a hill, should you have to downshift again
the bike will have enough forward momentum to enable you
to release the pressure on the pedals for an instant while continuing to crank, and then you can shift. Above all, remember
that bike pedaling is not a *macho* thing. Suffering up a hill in
too high a gear impresses no one except your knees and quads
and they are likely to hate you for it. Likewise, believe it or
not, on the flat if you are spinning at 90 in a middle gear you
will pass many a cyclist grinding away at 60 in top. And you
will be expending significantly less energy than he or she is.

Gear selection itself is a complicated, sometimes arcane
matter. Bike gears are quantified in "gear inches." The number of gear inches for any combination of chain ring (the big
sprockets to which the pedals are attached) and free-wheel
cogs (the little sprockets on the rear-wheel hub) connected by
the chain is determined as follows. Divide the number of teeth
on the chain ring by the number of teeth on the free-wheel
cog. Then multiply the result by the diameter of the bicycle's
wheels in inches, usually 27. This figure is the number of gear
inches you will be pedaling in for that combination of sprockets. Once you know the number of teeth on the respective
sprockets, however, you do not have to go through the arith-
metic yourself. Gear-inch tables covering any conceivable
combination are available in cycling books, bike-shop catalogs and at your friendly dealer. Once you know the gear
inches for your 10 or 12 or 18 chain-ring / free-wheel combinations, you know which ones are duplicative and you know
in which order to go as you shift up and down through the
range. Obviously, the larger the gear-inch number, the higher
the gear, and vice versa.

Braking is fairly simple. Rear wheel (usually the right brake
handle) first, then the front wheel. Front wheel first can lead
to very painful outcomes if you happen to somersault over

the handlebars. Try to anticipate situations. Bikes are inherently unstable. Slow down going into turns, especially sharp ones. Lose a few seconds rather than risk injury. You get the most leverage on the brake handles with your hands on the drops, but you can reach them with your hands on the hoods. By the way, long treatises have been written on turning and cornering. Suffice it to say here that the key to success is *not* to have the inside pedal in the 6 o'clock position.

On hill climbing. I have already talked about the importance of thinking ahead, shifting early, and maintaining your cadence. Equip your bike with a large enough free-wheel cog so that in combination with your small chain ring you will have a gear low enough to get you up any hill that you are likely to encounter, without grinding away at low rpm. Keep your hands on the brake hoods. This practice will give you maximum steering control and maximum diaphragmatic expansion capability. Also, you will add power if you grip the hoods, looping index and third fingers under them, pulling up with the arm on the same side as that of the leg going through the downstroke.

Standing up in the saddle can add tremendously to the power of any downstroke. Done correctly, your hands will be gripping the brake hoods, while your torso will be up over the handlebars. I must admit that I have trouble with balance on the bike and do not like to get up out of the saddle that far. Thus I will get up part way but still keep some intermittent contact between the insides of my thighs and the horn (forward protruberance) of the saddle. You can also get more power without standing by shifting back on the saddle and moving your hands to the tops for the greatest leverage. Obviously, if you take my advice you will do the latter only if you are sure that you will not have to brake or turn while your hands are up there.

As for going downhill, be careful! In training rides on busy, public roads with sometimes bumpy, obstacle-strewn shoulders, I rarely let 'er rip. Even in a race I will do so only on roads with smooth surfaces closed to vehicular traffic. Again, I would rather lose a bit of time than risk injury.

ON SWIMMING . . .

Swimming is the technically most complex of the three main triathlon sports. It is the one in which I am technically the weakest. Strangely enough, it is the one in which my relative performance is the best. This is not because I am a good swimmer but only because so many recreational triathletes swim even more poorly than I do. Why is this so?

First of all, swimming well is a skill which takes time to learn. Much practice of form is needed, aside from conditioning. Second, the immediate benefit to overall race performance from swimming faster is not great. In many marathon-length triathlons, the swim portion is a mile, taking the average recreational triathlete 35–45 minutes. Suppose you improve by 15%, a large amount. You may pick up 6 minutes. With much less practice and a little planning you can save that amount of time in the change from one event to another. A similar percentage improvement in the bike portion of the race could net you 12 minutes or more. A third factor in relatively poor swim performance by recreational triathletes is that boredom is a major problem in swim training.

However, swimming well will help your performance in the other two segments of the race by conserving both muscular and cardiovascular energy expenditure. Thus it is worthwhile to learn how to swim properly, although achieving that objective may not be at the top of your priority list, as it has not been at the top of mine. For example, in the swim, compared to my fellow recreational triathletes, I should use my upper body more and my leg less than I do. But the swim is my best event in terms of relative time of finish. I decided to work on other areas of weakness first.

When starting out in swim training, I strongly recommend using different strokes during each workout. Don't try to do the whole workout crawl (free style) right off the bat. That will come. When I started swimming for triathlons, I was doing one lap crawl, one lap side stroke, one lap elementary backstroke. After a few workouts, I dropped the side stroke and went to crawl for half the time, elementary backstroke for the balance. Now I do most of my workouts in the crawl but I still occasionally throw in a few laps of elementary backstroke. I still like to use it for a breather now and then in the races. Whatever stroke you are doing, try to concentrate on using the upper body. Doing that will certainly help your performance in the other two segments of the race, dependent as they are on leg power.

Swimming the crawl places you in a private world which you must get used to if you are going to be a successful swimmer. It is quiet and noisy at the same time. It is quiet in the sense that the outside world is almost totally excluded. The noises that you do hear are those of your own breathing and your passage through the water. Your vision is limited too, even if you are wearing goggles (and you certainly should be). When swimming you see only a small segment of the world, on the side on which you breathe, for the brief intervals that your head is out of the water. (In fact you should learn one stroke, breast or lifesaving crawl, that will enable to hold your head up out of the water and look straight ahead, for navigational purposes.) Compounding the problem is the fact that you can breathe only in a rhythmic fashion, when your head is out of the water. Unlike the experience in biking and running, your breathing is confined and feelings of claustrophobia can develop. (If they do, just turn over on your back and take a blow.) Of course millions of people swim correctly, happily, and successfully. You can, too. It will just take time and practice.

Most triathletes do most of their swim training in a pool. This is fine. Pool swimming can be done for endurance and for speed. It can be done in consecutive laps and it also be done in "sets." The latter can help relieve boredom. Sets done as "interval training,"[1] with increased speed, will also help you to lower your time if that is an objective. For a 25-yard pool, here are some lap patterns which you can use for variety and good training.[2]

1. "Pyramid 6" for 900 yards, a bit over half a mile.
   1 - 2 - 3 - 4 - 5 - 6 - 5 - 4 - 3 - 2 - 1
   (That is, you do one lap, then two laps, then three laps, and so on.) Rest 10–15 seconds between segments.
2. "Pyramid 8" for 1600 yards, a bit short of a mile. Rest 10–15 seconds between segments.
   1 - 2 - 3 - 4 - 5 - 6 - 7 - 8 - 7 - 6 - 5 - 4 - 3 - 2 - 1
3. "Ladder 16" for 1600 yards.
   4 - 8 - 12 - 16 - 12 - 8 - 4
   (That is, you do four laps, then eight laps, and so on.) Rest 20–30 seconds between sets.
4. "Countdown 12" for 1950 yards (1.1 miles).
   12 - 11 - 10 - 9 - 8 - 7 - 6 - 5 - 4 - 3 - 2 - 1
   Rest 5–10 seconds between sets. It is like swimming a mile non-stop. [This one is my own favorite pattern. It is always nice to know that the next set will have fewer laps than the one you are presently doing.]

As much pool swimming as you do, however, you will have to do some open-water swimming too, assuming that the swim portion of your triathlon is in open water. The type of open water that you choose to swim in should be the same as you

---

1. A set is a specified distance or number of laps. Interval training is doing sets repetitively with short rest periods in between.
2. Bob Krotee, "Swim Tricks," *Triathlon*, Winter 1983, p. 17.

will be swimming in for your race: fresh-water lake, salt-water bay, or ocean. There are several reasons for doing some open-water training. First, you will need practice in swimming continuously, uninterrupted by making turns and doing push-offs. Second, if you will be racing in salt water, you need to get used to it. I like it because of the buoyancy. Some people don't like salt water because of the unpleasant sensation you get when you swallow some. There is also the matter of tides, currents, and waves. Third, you need to get used to the racing-water temperature, usually colder than that encountered in a pool. Lastly, you will benefit from practice in open-water navigating. Thus open-water swimming in triathlon training is not just for conditioning but also for technical reasons.

CONCLUSION...

Technique is important in all three triathlon sports for efficiency and saving of energy, speed, and injury prevention. Good technique should be learned and practiced. But it should not be forgotten that the most important aspect of training, for the beginning triathlete, is aerobic conditioning. Being in the shape that following the Triathloning for Ordinary Mortals Training Program will get you into will enable you to finish a marathon-equivalent triathlon comfortably. Be concerned with technique, but don't get hung up on it. Be concerned first and foremost with consistency, regularity, and your overall aerobic fitness.

5 ... The Basic Principles of Triathlon Training for Ordinary Mortals

Consistency is the hobgoblin of small minds—except in training.

Anonymous (modified by author)

INTRODUCTION ...

You have decided to do a triathlon. You have picked out an event to enter. Depending upon your present state of personal fitness, the big day is anywhere from a few months to a year of more off. You either already can do each of the sports or you have allowed enough time in your preparation for the race to learn what you will need to learn. Thus you are ready to begin training.

In this chapter I will go over some principles of training which I recommend as the basis for your program regardless of what level of fitness you are at now. In the next chapter I will describe a "Basic Aerobic Fitness Program" which will "get you to the starting line" for triathlon training if you are presently doing little or nothing in the way of aerobic training. In Chapter 7, I will present the Triathloning for Ordinary

Mortals Training Program (TFOMTP). As I have said before, assuming that for at least 6 months you have been doing 15–20 miles per week of running or its equivalent, the 13-week TFOMTP will enable you to comfortably complete a marathon-equivalent triathlon.

EQUIVALENCY AMONG EVENTS . . .

In endurance spots, equivalency is an important concept. Much has been written about it. A variety of formulas for comparing the fitness effectiveness of the various forms of exercise have been worked out. According to Dr. Kenneth Cooper—the man who virtually "invented" aerobics—running, swimming, and bicycling are about the equivalent of each other in fitness effectiveness, *when they are done aerobically.*[1] Table 5.1 presents data gathered by the President's Council on Physical Fitness and Sports to rank the popular forms of endurance sports according to their health-and-fitness effects. Experts were asked to assign "benefit points" to each sport for each of the elements of physical fitness and general well-being. Although the top three vary somewhat in specific benefits, *in toto* they are all very beneficial for the body and very close to each other in overall ranking.[2]

The key elements, then, in developing *fitness* and *endurance* (as opposed to technical skill and athletic proficiency), are aerobic work and time. Your basic goal is completing a triathlon. The basic requirement is a level of aerobic fitness which will enable you to exercise for the amount of time necessary to complete the race at the speeds you can handle for that amount of time. Speed per se is not a factor since win-

1. Ken Cooper, *The Aerobics Program for Total Well-Being,* New York: M. Evans and Co., 1982.
2. James Fixx, *The Complete Book of Running,* New York: Random House, 1977, p. 39.

Table 5.1. COMPARATIVE FITNESS RATINGS OF SEVERAL SPORTS

	Running	Bicycling	Swimming	Handball/Squash	Tennis	Walking	Golf	Bowling
PHYSICAL FITNESS								
Cardiorespiratory endurance	21	19	21	19	16	13	8	5
Muscular endurance	20	18	20	18	16	14	8	5
Muscular strength	17	16	14	15	14	11	9	5
Flexibility	9	9	15	16	14	7	8	7
Balance	17	18	12	17	16	8	8	6
GENERAL WELL-BEING								
Weight Control	21	20	15	19	16	13	6	5
Muscle Definition	14	15	14	11	13	11	6	5
Digestion	13	12	13	13	12	11	7	7
Sleep	16	15	16	12	11	14	6	6
Total	148	142	140	140	128	102	66	51

ning is not a concern. The key variable in this approach to triathlon training is the time devoted to aerobic work. Thus the programs that I recommend are always set out in minutes of aerobic exercise not distance covered.

I first discovered this approach in Ardy Friedberg's book *How to Run Your First Marathon*. I have found it to be psychologically comfortable and logistically simple. In biking and running, you will generally do out-and-back courses at least until you find loops that take about the amount of time required for a particular day's workout. With the minutes approach, you no longer have to measure a variety of courses with your (often inaccurate) automobile odometer. In swimming, you don't have to count laps in the pool if you don't want to and you don't have to worry about hard-to-measure open-water distances. Most importantly, on each day of training, you go at the pace that is comfortable for you for that day. I have fast days and I have slow days. Many variables of weather, temperature, mood, and body state produce these differences. But without having mileage to worry about, as long as I have raised my heart rate into the aerobic range, I can feel that I have had a good, or least a useful workout.

Obviously, the time spent working out should be distributed among the three sports so that the sport-specific muscle groups each get a significant amount of exercise work and strengthening. But the specific balance among the sports is not critical. For example, suppose you have a bike ride on the program for a particular day and it happens to be raining. You don't like riding in the rain because of the safety factor. You certainly can go for a swim or a run (assuming that you don't mind running in the rain) as long as you do the number of minutes scheduled. The critical element is that those minutes be done at an aerobic pace.

The formula for determining that, you will recall, is as follows. Seventy percent of 220 minus your age is your aerobic-threshold heart rate. For a 45-year-old that number is 123

(70% of 175). Your theoretical maximum heart rate is 220 minus your age. The safe range for aerobic work is between the threshold level and 85% of the maximum.[3] Once again, the major factor in both the TFOMTP and the preparation to begin it is the amount of time spent exercising with a degree of exertion that will boost your heart rate into this range.[4]

Now I must admit that despite all my talk about the importance of minutes of training, when speaking with other people about my training more often than not I use the same language of comparison that almost everyone else does: miles. But this can be done easily without falling into the mileage trap for measuring training courses and setting up your program. You just determine your own average training rates in each of the three sports by doing measured courses a few times. Dividing that number into 60 gives you miles per hour for each sport. You can then determine mileage equivalencies for yourself. This is what counts. No one else's equivalency table means anything for you, unless they happen to train in each sport at the same rates you do.

I train at a rather slow pace in each sport: 9–10 minutes per mile running (6–6.7 mph), 3.5–4 minutes per mile biking (15–17 mph), and about 40 minutes per mile (1.5 mph) swimming. Thus for me the rates are (approximately) 2.5 miles biking = 1 mile running = 0.25 miles swimming. So if someone asks me, "Well, how many miles did you run today?" and it happens that I went biking for an hour, I can comfort-

3. Fixx, pp. 67, 68.
4. Quite obviously you will need a stopwatch and you will have to know how to take your own pulse. The latter can be found either by placing the tips of the index and middle fingers of one hand in the slight depression that you will find on the outer aspect (thumb side) of the opposite wrist (palm up) just about where your watch strap comes across, or in your neck about halfway up, between your windpipe and the front edge of the major group of neck muscles. The latter is easier to do for most people (including me), but you must not take it on both sides at the same time. If you do, you could cause yourself to pass out. Once having found your pulse, count it for 6 seconds and multiply by 10, or 12 seconds and multiply by 5. That will give you your heart rate in beats per minute.

ably say, "Oh, the equivalent of about six, six and a half miles of running." Another common medium of conversational exchange amongst endurance athletes is miles per week. When I am in training for a triathlon, I average 300 minutes fo aerobic exercise per week in all three sports for 13 weeks. Thus, at my usual pace I am doing the equivalent of 30–33 miles of running per week. When someone asks you how much you do, it is much easier to say, "Thirty miles per week," than to go into a long involved explanation of minutes, aerobic work, and equivalencies such as the one that you have just finished reading.

SOME BASIC GUIDELINES FOR TRAINING . . .

CONSISTENCY. Rod Dixon, winner in a very dramatic finish of the 1983 New York Marathon, has Ten Rules of Running which I think apply equally well to triathlon training.

1. Emphasize consistency in your training program.
2. Train in an environment that promotes a concentrated effort.
3. Maintain a strong commitment to being fit.
4. Realize that good, successful training is the best source of self-confidence.
5. Rest sufficiently after a race to restore energy levels.
6. Don't run when you don't feel up to it.
7. Enhance performance by going into a race with peace of mind.
8. Identify your nutritional needs as an athlete and nourish yourself properly.
9. Avoid injury by discarding shoes that are worn-out beyond 75 per cent of their "life."
10. Do not consider any one aspect of training more important than another. Each is integral to the total running program.[5]

5. Rod Dixon, "Reaching Your Peak: Consistency Is the Key to Better Performance," *The Runner*, March 1984, p. 22.

Some of these rules are at the philosophical level while some are practical. But the main message is consistency, regularity, wholeness. Rod can have a rule that says "Don't run when you don't feel up to it" because he knows that skipping a day now and then doesn't mean that he is giving up training. Training is a major part of his life. It will become, or already is, an important part of your life. Obviously, you won't train the way Rod Dixon does, but then your goals are not the same as his are. Training, if you follow my suggestions, will become important to you. At the same time, it will not, certainly it need not, take over your life, pushing everything else out. As long as you follow the consistency rule, you can maintain a balanced approach to training, placing limits on it, making it additive, not dominant in your life.

Dick Brown, coach of Mary Decker, talks about consistency in these terms:

It is more important to do less more often than to do more less often. When in doubt about a run, . . . the choice that will improve consistency is to be conservative. . . . Along with consistency should be a progression that taxes the system enough to improve it, but not enough to cause it to break down.[6]

THE TRAINING BASE. Consistency will be well developed if you are at or follow my recommendations for getting to the "aerobic base" as described by the American College of Sports Medicine[7] and the President's Council on Physical Fitness and Sports.[8] This base is not defined by a single point, however. It is now thought that as little as 20–30 minutes of aerobic

6. Dick Brown, "Running Smart," *The Runner,* January 1984, p. 12.

7. American College of Sports Medicine, "Position Statement on: The Recommended Quantity and Quality of Exercise for Developing and Maintaining Fitness in Healthy Adults," Indianapolis, Indiana, 1978.

8. H. Ebel, et al, eds., *Presidential Sports Award Fitness Manual,* Chapter I, Fitness 3 Council, "Your Way to Better Health," p. 11, and Chapter IV, "Starting an Exercise Program," p. 3, Havertown, Pennsylvania: Fit Com Corporation.

exercise 3–4 times per week will significantly reduce a person's chance of developing coronary artery disease later in life. Increasing exercise time up to 2.5–3 hours per week apparently increases the level of protection. Anything over that does not seem to add more protection. As Ken Cooper says, anyone who is running more than 15–20 miles per week (2.5–3 hours for the average 10-minute-per-mile jogger, the "aerobic base") is doing it for some reason *other* than cardiovascular protection. The equivalents are 35–45 miles per week for biking, 4–5 miles for swimming.

MAKING TRAINING FIT YOUR LIFESTYLE. In my own experience and in that of many recreational endurance athletes with whom I have spoken, one of the keys to achieving consistency is to adopt a training program that fits your lifestyle and your pattern of daily living. The time commitment for the TFOMTP is not overwhelming. Most of the long workouts are scheduled for weekends. However, as you will already know if you have done or are doing any exercise at all, the total time required is certainly more than the actual exercise time itself. You have to dress and stretch beforehand, cool down and shower afterwards. Unless it is in your backyard, you will have to travel to get to a pool. Thus, although the time requirement is not overwhelming, it is significant. You must be prepared to make that commitment. Carefully choosing when during your day and your week you will work out will make it easier to do so.

I like to get up early and exercise before going to work. Among other things, morning exercise usually sets me up for the day. Others like to work out after they get home from work. But if you have a family, that will usually mean delaying dinner for everyone or eating on your own. Either of these practices could create family-life problems. For swimming, I am fortunate enough to have a pool that is readily accessible from my office. I can usually get my swims in on a slightly extended lunch hour. For others, swims may have to be done early in the morning, in the evening, or on the weekend. However, the TFOM approach to training does not call for a great deal of swimming, just enough to get you through that segment of the race. Overall, with travel time, for most people a swim workout is the most time-consuming of the three. Thus I try to minimize daily-living-pattern disruption by not scheduling too many of them.

I find that laying out my workout schedule several months in advance is very useful. Within the general guidelines of time of day, and place to work out you can then plan around known events in your work and family life that might otherwise interfere with your training. I usually like to follow a Tuesday-Wednesday, Friday-Saturday-Sunday pattern. But planning my training schedule well in advance permits me to juggle workouts around other commitments and still get in the required number of minutes per week. I might not be able to do so if I waited until the last minute each week to set up my schedule.

I find that this approach is especially useful in dealing with travel. I travel a moderate amount in the course of my work. I find little more enjoyable in an exercise program than going out for an early morning run in different city now and then, even if I have been there before. In Fort Worth, I just love to run along the Trinity Trail on the banks of the Trinity River. This path is for runners and bikers only, quiet, smooth for the most part, no traffic, with measured miles. Even though I am an advocate of training by time not distance, and seldom run measured courses at home, it is fun and useful to check my training pace on the Trinity Trail once in a while.

In Philadelphia, I love to run over to the Fine Arts Museum and bound up the steps with the "Rocky" theme playing in my head. I then head out along the Schuylkill River on a beautiful path, usually in the company of a flock of local runners. Speaking of flocks of runners, Central Park in my birthplace, New York City, must be Mecca for the recreational endurance athlete. The running is delightful, and very picturesque. And you can find someone to run with most hours of the day or evening. Running along the East River is also pleasant and popular. Chicago's lakefront is a magnificent place to run. For me, however, it is Washington, D.C. which is the best city for runner-visitors (and runner-residents too, I should imagine). Rock Creek Park, either bank of the Potomac, and the Mall are all wonderful places to run. Flat, beautiful to look at and usually chock-a-block with runners. If you travel, you can have experiences like these too and not disrupt your training, by planning your schedule out in advance.

WHERE TO TRAIN. Beginning runners usually start out on a track, local high school or college. The surface is comfortable, the distance is measured, there is no traffic. Once you get up to 3 miles or so per workout, about 30 minutes, if you are like most of the rest of us you will find that the track experience becomes increasingly boring, then BORING, then virtually impossible to do, except for interval training (see below). The alternatives must then be considered. I live in a semirural area and find running on public roads very comfortable. I try to stay off the main ones and almost always run against traffic. Since I hardly ever run at night, the safety level is good. Biking is a bit more of a problem in terms of safety. Smooth road surface is very desirable in biking both for comfort and flat-tire avoidance. Ironically, I have found the smoother surfaces to be on the busier roads. To enhance safety, I generally stay on the shoulders, use a rearview mirror, and concentrate on the traffic at all times.

There are other options, of course. In many cities now there are parks that have special running/biking paths and/or have vehicular roads that are closed to automobile traffic at specified times. Waterfronts and riverside paths can make for great workouts, as in New York, Chicago, Washington, Philadelphia, and Fort Worth. Broad boulevards in older cities can have safe sidewalks bothered by cross streets only at infrequent intervals. City running can be done in the street, but this should be against traffic and with great care and attention. I would not recommend trying to do bike workouts on city streets, but then again I have never tried it.

Most people will do most of their swim training in a pool. As part of race preparation, as I have noted before, a few open-water swims are required, primarily for the purposes of acclimation to water temperature, salt water, tides, currents, waves, and swimming in a long, straight line. Effective pool swimming requires that lanes be set up with fixed lines. You cannot go into a community pool at general swim time and expect to do laps for 45 minutes while dealing with the constantly moving targets presented by bathers, splashers, divers, handstanders, small children, 2-lap speeders, and assorted show-offs and admirers.

Pools which provide lane swimming can be found in schools, colleges, Y's, community recreation facilities, and swim clubs. Costs vary widely. Lane swimming takes a bit of getting used to. Most pools have some kind of speed-rate pattern ranging from slow on one side over to swim-team fast on the other. After being swum over by speed demons or kicked in the face a few times by slow swimmers who won't let you pass, you will find the right lane for you. Once you do locate your niche, you will find lane swimming comfortable.

SOME TRAINING SPECIFICS . . .

BREATHING. It is easy to make jokes about breathing: "Can't live without it" and "Breathing is essential to running" are typical. It is important not to ignore it and to recognize that certain breathing patterns are more helpful than others. We can fill our lungs with air both by expanding the rib cage and by lowering the diaphragm. It is important to be able to do both. It is also important to remember that both inhalation and exhalation are important. The former brings fresh oxygen into the lungs. The latter clears wastes from the surfaces of the millions of tiny air sacs (alveoli) in the lungs through which oxygen gets into the blood stream. The more you expand your lungs in breathing in, the more sacs open up to be available for oxygen transfer and waste removal. The better you breathe out, the more surface area will be clear for waste removal and oxygen transfer on the next inhalation.

Breathing exercises at rest are found to be beneficial by many people, for both physical and psychological reasons. One approach to stress management is through breathing exercises, beginning with the old admonition to "take a deep breath" before responding to a suddenly stressful situation. I do not use formal breathing exercises myself, although I do try to remember to fully inflate my lungs and clear them out several times a day by alternately expanding my upper rib cage and raising my shoulders and then depressing my diaphragm and expanding my waist. If you are interested in formal breathing exercises, there is a good treatment of them (Book III, Chapter 1, p. 159) in Bob Johnson's and Patricia Bragg's book *The Complete Triathlon.*

Breathing while working out is a different matter. In swimming, rhythmic breathing is obviously a must. Any good swimming book will give you advice on that. (I recommend Jane Katz's book *Swimming for Total Fitness.*) In running and biking, it all depends upon how hard you are working. After almost 4 years of running, I find that when I am doing my usual workout, running at a 9:00–9:30-minutes-per-mile pace, my heart rate is up into the low end of the aerobic range but my breathing is still loose and easy, with no particular pattern. When I start going faster and must increase my oxygen intake, I like to breathe in a regular pattern, either 4 or 6 steps for a full inhalation-exhalation cycle. When I get tired, I find that a few cycles with controlled, slow exhalation for a longer period of time than inhalation is very helpful and picks me right up. This is presumably because I am fully cleaning those alveolar surfaces. Not everyone will use rhythmic breathing. But it is important to develop your own patterns, recognize them, and use them appropriately. One absolute no-no for everyone at any time is breath holding, an easy habit to fall into. Breath holding, even for an instant, slows down oxygen / waste exchange in the lungs and unnecessarily increases blood pressure. Neither is beneficial.

INTERVALS. Interval training is dividing a workout into distance or time segments with short rest periods in between them, and doing the exercise in each segment at a pace faster than you would if you were doing just one continuous workout for the total time or distance. In running, biking, swimming interval training is essential for speed. Training in the long, slow, distance (LSD) pattern popularized by Joe Henderson[9] will enable you to run (or bike, or swim) long distances slowly, not quickly. LSD is obviously the basis of my own approach. I'm not interested in winning but in participating and finishing. LSD will do that for you, in running, biking, and swimming. On the other hand, you may want to go fast as well as long, in search either of a new Personal Record (P.R.), or a trophy. You will then have to do intervals.

You can find excellent detailed advice on interval training for running in Bob Glover's *The Competitive Runner's Handbook*, for swimming in Jane Katz's book, for cycling in Fred Matheny's *Beginning Bicycle-Racing* and Dan Honig's *How to Bike Better* (see Appendix II), and for all three sports

9. Two of his best books are *Run Gently, Run Long,* and *Jog, Run, Race.* Joe keeps you up-to-date on LSD every month in *Runners World.* His column is well worth looking at.

combined in Johnson-Bragg, Book IV, Chapter 3. By the way, if you do take up intervals, take them up slowly and easily to begin with. I decided to try intervals one day, ran 4 quarters at a pace too much fast for me, totally exhausted myself, incurred several minor leg injuries, and was forced to take off from training for a week. It was a long time before I tried intervals again.

HILLS. For any endurance athlete who trains on the road, hills are a fact of life unless you happen to live out on the Great Plains. Even in swimming, you can encounter the equivalent of hills when going into an adverse current or tide. Psychologically, there are two approaches to hills. You can love 'em or you can hate 'em. Since I live in a hilly area and must train on them, it is easy for me to say this, but you will be much better off if you learn to love, or at least like them. Hill training is very beneficial for both speed and endurance. Excellent advice on the technical aspects of it can be found in the books by Bob Glover and Jim Fixx.

For myself, I find that since I train on hills I would rather race on a course that has at least some hills than one that is entirely flat, especially in biking. Coming downhill in running can create problems if you go too fast and pound too much. But downhill biking is always fun, assuming that you're maintaining control of your machine.

I find that "attacking the hills" is a very useful approach. In running, you shorten your stride, lean forward a bit, actively use your upper body, swinging your arms at your sides not across your chest, and breathe rhythmically and deeply. With some practice, you can actually glide up hills. I usually accelerate a bit going up shorter hills, although for the long ones I try to pace myself, accelerating only when the top is clearly within my reach.

In biking, you drop into a lower gear, raise your cadence, thrust the pedals forward, and stand up in the saddle when you need more power and cannot downshift because of pressure on the derailleurs. In both biking and running on steep hills I find visualization very useful. As you wind your way up think about being on the top, what it will feel like, how relaxing the downhill will be. Look up the hill. In your mind's eye see yourself at the crest. This approach does help me. It may help you too.

WEIGHT LIFTING AND TRAINING. For all sports, the thinking on this subject has changed radically over the last 10 years. Weight training is now considered to be an essential part of anyone's program by most coaches and other authorities. Virtually all the current endurance sports books have a chapter on weight training. The President's Council on Physical Fitness and Sports has a short but comprehensive guide to weight training (*Weight Training for Strength and Power*). A useful book devoted entirely to the subject is Wayne Wescott's *Strength Fitness* (Boston: Allyn and Bacon, 1983).

Weight training can be incorporated into your training program on a regular basis. Dave Scott and other elite triathletes do this. Sally Edwards recommends it in her book. If you choose this approach, you must select your weight-training exercises and schedule the sessions with care. Weight lifting requires recovery time to be effective. Thus you will probably want to plan your weight lifting to come *after* a sport workout (preferably later that same day, not immediately afterwards), and before an off-day. I do not lift weights during training season, primarily because of time limitations. I am sure that I would find it helpful if I did. I do follow the other recommended pattern, which is to make it a principal off-season activity (see below, "Winter Training").

Another choice to make is free weights vs. machine system. I have used free weights, Nautilus, and a home machine called Total Gym, which for me has proven most successful. The standard Nautilus workout improves strength, endurance, and flexibility, without doing much for bulk, unless you do a lot of it. Nautilus is a very efficient workout. Most people go through the full circuit in about 25 minutes. At that pace, the workout will likely be aerobic for you. It is for me. To gain the maximum benefit from Nautilus, you must do the circuit in the prescribed order at the prescribed pace with the appropriate weights and seat heights for the appropriate number of repetitions. Thus you should choose a Nautilus facility that is well supervised by trainers who know what they are doing and use the equipment themselves. Using Nautilus equipment in a haphazard, irregular fashion will not help and may hinder or injure you. Some centers provide little or no supervision. It may seem easier that way. You may not have to wait your turn as you often do at a well-run place. But that approach is not beneficial.

Free weights are a different ballgame. I spent my first weight-lifting winter with barbells and dumbbells. The fantasy life can be rich, as images of Mr. Universe pop into your head. You will be surrounded by men and women with bulging biceps and huge shoulders. However, bulk is not beneficial for the triathlete, and muscle definition, while very nice, is not a prerequisite to triathloning success. A great deal of time must be spent to achieve both bulk and definition. Free-weight lifting will, however, build more strength than the standard Nautilus routine will and that result may be desirable for you. Another advantage is that in a properly equipped gym, there is little or no waiting, particularly since the order of the exercises is not as critical as it is in Nautilus.

A free-weight lifting workout does require more time than does a Nautilus workout, although with Nautilus waiting time factored in, they may come out to be just about the same overall. Free-weight lifting does have to be well supervised to be effective. Exercises, weights, repetitions, and progression over time do have to be specified. But constant attendance by a trainer is not necessary. Finally, while you are weight training, regularity and consistency are as much a requirement as they are for sport-specific training, whether you do it year-round or just during the off-season.

STRETCHING. Stretching is a very important part of any training program. Stretching should be done both before and after any workout, although my observations of recreational endurance athletes lead me to believe that while almost all of them stretch before, few take the time to stretch afterwards. However, if you do not do an organized set of stretching exercises after working out, at least you should walk around and cool down some before jumping into the shower.

During my first 3 years of running, I stretched before workouts only haphazardly. At the approach of my fourth season, the first in which I would be in triathlon training for the whole of it, I decided to add regular, planned stretching to my training program. I feel that it made a significant difference. In that year, the quality of my workouts improved, my training pace picked up, and the incidence of minor leg injuries dropped. I cannot attribute all of the improvement to stretching but some of it certainly was.

I tried several programs before settling on the one I recommend, *Stretching* by Bob Anderson. (By the way, the Bob Anderson who is the editor of *Runner's World* is not the Bob Anderson who wrote *Stretching*.) I was fortunate to obtain permission from the *Stretching* Bob Anderson and Lloyd Kahn of Shelter Publications to reproduce major sections of the book for our use here. They appear in Appendix III. I highly recommend them.

OVERTRAINING . . .

I am sure that you are by now well aware of my views on this subject. I think that overtraining is more of a problem for the recreational triathlete than is undertraining. Assuming that you start the TFOMTP with your aerobic base well established and that you train consistently and regularly, if you undertrain by 25% you will still finish, only quite slowly and probably with some discomfort. If you overtrain by 25% you will not significantly increase your speed but you will significantly increase your risk of training injury and psychological stress.

One of the objectives for many recreational endurance athletes is to manage stress better. I have certainly found that since I started running my ability to handle stress has improved a great deal. But worrying about your race time and cutting more into the rest of your life in order to increase training time will increase your stress level, not reduce it. Relax, enjoy. Run your training, don't let it run you. Now if you don't believe me, listen to what some nationally known experts have to say on the subject.

Tom Bassler, M.D., has been active with the American Medical Joggers Association for many years. He is an outspoken advocate of slow, slow, slow—fun, fun, fun. He says, "Plan your rest periods with the same care that you plan your workouts! It only takes 4 hours of training per week to become a marathoner."[10]

Dick Brown, Mary Decker's coach, says:

Be conservative. You'll get there. Whether your goal is to run faster as soon as possible, to be running better in five or ten years, or to enjoy long-term health benefits, the shortest path may be the one that appears to be the longest and slowest. ... The best way to maintain an interest in running, and the fulfillment that it can bring, is to lean towards doing too little rather than doing too much.[11]

David Oja, coach of the Syracuse Chargers Track Club women's team, has Six Rules of Rest.

10. Tom Bassler, "The Child Marathoner," *American Medical Joggers Association Newsletter*, October 1983, p. 38.
11. Brown, "Running Smart," p. 12.

1. Plan your rest as seriously as you plan your running.
2. Plan your rest according to *your* needs. . . . how you feel; how injury prone you are; how long you've been running; what your goals are. . . .
3. Take days off on a regular basis.
4. Plan cutback weeks and don't be afraid to take unplanned cutback weeks if necessary. [I do both and find them enormously beneficial.]
5. Plan and take at least one month of downtime each year.
6. When judging how much rest your should have, if you err, *err on the side of too much.*[12]

Overtraining means not only not enough rest but also workouts that are too long and / or too fast and too frequent. It is easy to find triathlon training programs that provide for megamileage. They are in the sports books and magazines all the time. But they are usually written by a person who is an elite athlete or has to capability to become one or would like to become one. These people also are usually (although not always) young, have a low percentage of body fat, and have been athletic most of their lives. For them, triathlon training programs that provide for the equivalent of 60–100 miles of running per week may be suitable. But if you are not in this category, you have to think of what is suitable for *you* and what you need to accomplish your goals. Remember—those goals must be realistic ones, for you as a whole person.

I did my first marathon in 4 : 31 : 06. I ran all but about 300 yards of the race (during the 23rd mile). I ran at my planned pace of about 10 minutes per mile. I was thrilled to finish. I did it on Ardy Friedberg's *How to Run Your First Marathon* program which meant averaging less than 5 hours (28–30 miles) per week of running for 13 weeks before the

12. David Oja, "Everything You Always Wanted to Know about Rest," *Footnotes*, Spring 1984, p. 14.

race and having just one 40+ miles week. At about the same time, two friends of mine of similar age were training 50–60 miles per week for about 3 months before their race. One of them beat my time by about 8 minutes, the other by 16. In the race, they went out much too fast, had to slow way down, and all that extra training didn't help much. If you are training for a triathlon, you are training to race, not just to train. Race performance therefore means something. What you do in the race is a product of your training *and* how you run the race itself. I shall come back to this issue in Chapter 10. The point is that extra training does not necessarily mean better performance.

Extra training may well mean worse performance or non-performance. The more you train, the more you risk injury. There are injuries of overuse, usually incurred in running, and injuries from external forces (like a pothole that throws you, or a car that runs you off the road) usually incurred in biking. I have had both types of injuries. Neither is fun.

Let me conclude this section by reviewing the 10 Principles for Middle-Distance Running laid down by Bill Bowerman, in his days at the University of Oregon (1948–1972) considered one of the world's leading coaches. These principles certainly apply equally well to long-distance running.

1. Training must be regular, according to a long-term plan.
2. The workload must be balanced and overtraining, which can lead to fatigue, injury, and the loss of desire, must be balanced.
3. You must know your goals and they must be realistic ones.
4. Training schedules should be set up with a hard / easy rotation, both from day-to-day and more generally over time.
5. Moderation must be established. [Here Bowerman is really reinforcing goals 2–4. They are obviously important to him.]
6. Rest should be regularly scheduled.
7. A balanced diet is essential [see Chapter 9].
8. Working out should be fun, whenever possible.

9. Body mechanics should be such that the exercise is as efficient as possible.
10. Pace judgment in the race is vital and should be trained for.[13]

By now you may feel that I have really hit you over the head on this overtraining issue. I suppose in fact that I have. But I have done it for a reason. Articles about the dangers of overtraining appear with regularity in the endurance sports magazines. Yet many people persist in overtraining. One reason is that alongside those cautions against overtraining are articles on Alberto Salazar and his 100+ miles per week or Dave Scott and his 40+ hours of training per week. The point is that few of us are in that category. Scott and Salazar *need* that training time to do what they do. You and I *don't* to do what we do or want to do. Is your goal to comfortably participate and finish? Don't overtrain. I cannot repeat that advice too often.

WINTER TRAINING . . .

When winter is upon us in most parts of the country, that means cold, wind, snow, ice, wetness, grayness, general discomfort. Outdoor training is difficult, uncomfortable, if not plain impossible. What to do for the winter? I will make the assumption here that you have already established your aerobic base, if you have not already done a triathlon. Further, this approach to winter training is one that I recommend generally.

Your plan for the next season already includes at least 1 triathlon. You are coming off a season of regular training, whether or not you were racing. You have put in some hard

13. Chris Walsh, *The Bowerman System,* Los Altos, California: Tafnews Press, 1983, Chapter 3.

work and you want to give yourself a "reward" for doing so. On the other hand, you don't want to "lose it."

Can these seemingly contrary objectives be met in one program? The answer is yes. Yes, you can "stay in shape" while giving your body a well-deserved rest, and you can do that while doing activities which will enhance next season's performance. The key here is maintaining that 2.5–3-hours-per-week aerobic base. That is your primary goal for the winter. Your secondary goal should be dealing with areas of athletic weakness, through activities that can be done mainly indoors. The following program is the one that I have used in the winter to deal with my own areas of weekness.

I run once a week for about 45–60 minutes on Sunday mornings with my local running club, just "to keep my foot in," so to speak. I swim in the pool for a minimum of 30 minutes once to twice a week. From the technical standpoint, my weakest sport is swimming. During the season I usually do just enough swimming to make sure that I can stay afloat during the swimming leg. Now, with the aid of a good book on the subject and perhaps some coaching, is the time to work on swimming form and style. I also do some cycling on an indoor trainer. (I use the Road Machine made by Houdaille Industries, in Fort Worth, Texas. It is marvelous.) Like everyone else with whom I have spoken who has ridden indoors over the winter, I have had excellent results in terms of both leg strength and endurance.

I do 2 to 3 25–30-minute workouts per week on my Total Gym which I also like very much. Any kind of weight training which builds flexibility, endurance, and strength, rather than bulk will do. I like Total Gym or Nautilus because they are time efficient and can be done aerobically. I find weight training much easier to do when it is cold and wet outdoors rather than when it is warm and dry. Finally, occasionally I do a short stretching-only session. Having a very tight musculature, I try to improve my flexibility when I am spending less time on aerobics.

Thus I have a program which maintains my aerobic base and helps me deal with areas of athletic weakness that I tend to ignore during the season. At the same time it is less demanding than regular training and gives me a feeling of being "rewarded" for a job well done last season. It's an approach that I highly recommend.

TRAINING THE MIND . . .

A final thought, on training the mind. George Sheehan has said that the first 30 minutes of a workout is for your body, the balance for your mind.[14] A great deal of what I have been talking about in this chapter is mind training rather than body training. In fact, the two really go together very closely. The mind has to be conditioned if the body is to be properly conditioned. You must know what is realistic for you as a goal in relationship to your physical skills, your athletic experience, but most important, the balance of your life. *Could* you physically do an Ironman? Most likely. Could *I* physically do an Ironman? Most likely. But would either of us be prepared to find the necessary minimum of 15–20 hours per week of training time for 6 months before the race and do the training? Not likely, at least in my case, at least for now. It is my *mind* that is not ready, however, not my body. My mind trained to complete marathon-equivalent triathlons, but it did not train to get my body to do the training which would be necessary for me to place in my age class: more hours and lots of speed work. I set a doable goal for myself, reasonable in the context of the rest of my life—and I achieved it.

14. Quoted by Joe Henderson in "Thoughts on the Run," *Runner's World,* December 1983, p. 21.

Being consistent and not overtraining, the two points which I harp on so much, are mind matters. The essence is finding and maintaining that happy medium. Doing either too much or too little is a function of the mind, not the body. Even the keys to successful hill climbing, useful breathing, and pushing yourself to do but not to overdo intervals are to be found in the mind.

Endurance sports are not cerebral in the sense that skiing and sailing are. In those two sports the mind is constantly accumulating and processing data on wind, surface conditions, weather, rate of speed, direction, other moving objections, duration of light, steepness of slope on a hill or down a wave, and so forth. The mind then makes decisions controlling forward progress. Nor are endurance sports cerebral in the same sense that team sports are. In the latter, the mind is constantly concerned with the player's role and responsibility, the rules, the current tactical and strategic position of his or her team, what the other team is doing, and how it can be countered.

The long-distance racer generally does not have a lot of split-second decision making to do except from time to time on the bike. But the mind is central with discipline and determination, both in training and in racing. It must also be able to estimate pace and remaining energy stores, in order to appropriately regulate speed. Thus, to be successful in endurance sports, at whatever level you are competing, you must train your mind as well as your body.

6 ... *Starting from Scratch: The Basic Aerobic Fitness Program*

> *Not everyone needs to run. But everyone deserves that one hour in every 24 to make something that is his or hers alone.*
>
> Joe Henderson in *Runners World*,
> November 1984, p. 21

INTRODUCTION ...

You have decided to do your first triathlon. However, you have not yet established the "aerobic base," that prerequisite for commencing the Triathloning for Ordinary Mortals Training Program (TFOMTP). In that case, this chapter is for you. Starting from scratch, you can train to successfully complete a marathon-equivalent triathlon in 1 year from the day you make the big decision. The most important element in this journey is training your mind, along the lines that I discussed in the last chapter: consistency, realism in goal setting, and control of both undertraining and overtraining. Next, of course, is training your body. The most important physical objective is achieving fitness at a level that will enable you to exercise aerobically for up to 5 consecutive hours. Also, assuming that you will be doing a conventional triathlon, you will also have to learn how to run, bike, and swim. These goals and objectives are all achievable within a year.

Consistent with the "minutes-rather-than-miles" approach that I discussed in Chapter 5, my program is set out in minutes per day and days per week. It obviously can be undertaken using any of the sports, as long as your heart is beating in the aerobic range for the requisite number of minutes during each workout. Nevertheless, I suggest that in the beginning you concentrate on running. I discussed the reasons for this approach at some length in Chapter 1. Running is technically the easiest of the three sports. It is also the simplest to do in terms of access, place to run, time of day, weather, season of year and so forth. Of the three sports, it is also the most demanding on the body. But in order to be a successful triathlete you must get used to the trials and tribulations of running, as well as to its joys.

My full 1-year-from-scratch-to-triathlon program is divided into 3 phases. Phase I lasts for 13 weeks. With a walk / run program, you start on the road to aerobic fitness and arrive at the threshold of that state. Phase II lasts for 26 weeks. In it you firmly establish your aerobic base. You also introduce swimming and biking into your exercise program and have the time to do learning and skill training in one or both of those sports, as necessary. Phases I and II are covered in this chapter. Phase III is the TFOMTP, covered in the next chapter. Obviously, if you are not starting from scratch, you can hop into this program at any suitable point. It is essential, however, to have put in at least 6 months of work at the aerobic base, 2½–3 hours per week, before starting the TFOMTP.

MEDICAL CONSIDERATIONS . . .

Starting out on an aerobic exercise program, it is probably a good idea to have a medical evaluation done, even if you are in "good health." For persons over 35 this evaluation may include a Graded-Exercise or Stress Test (GXT). This includes working out on a treadmill while your heart rate, heartbeat pattern (as measured by an electrocardiogram), and blood pressure are measured, and several tests of the functioning of your lungs are done. Not everyone needs a GXT, however. A qualified sports-medicine physician will be able to evaluate you and advise you appropriately on this matter.

Since there is some expense involved (it can be substantial if a GXT is included), you may not want to undergo a medical evaluation until you are several months into aerobic exercise and are convinced that you are going to stick with it. Being in excellent health myself with normally low blood pressure, I did not undergo an evaluation (which included a GXT) until I had been working out for 4 months. If you take the advice given below and commence your aerobic exercise program in a gradual, paced fashion, there is little danger right at the beginning and a medical examination usually can be safely put off for a bit. However, if you have any of the following characteristics, it is a good idea to be checked out sooner rather than later:

1. High blood pressure
2. High blood cholesterol
3. Cigarette smoking
4. Pain or pressure in your chest upon exertion
5. History of heart disease in your immediate family (parents, siblings)
6. More than 20 pounds overweight
7. Completely sedentary lifestyle in recent years
8. Any history of lung problems

9. Prescribed medication used on a regular basis
10. Abuse of drugs or alcohol
11. Any chronic problems with your bones or joints
12. Any other chronic illness, such as diabetes

For a medical evaluation, you will probably want to consult your own physician in the first instance. However, many physicians do not know very much about either sports medicine or fitness and exercise. These subjects are fairly new and are taught in few medical schools. Some misguided physicians are actually anti-exercise. Even more are antirunning, because they don't understand the sport and how it can be done properly and safely. If you are not satisfied with the level of knowledge and skill and the attitude of your physician, politely, nicely, but firmly ask for a referral to someone with competence in sports medicine or health and fitness.

Alternatively, you may want to go directly to a "cardio-fitness center." These are springing up in increasing numbers around the country. They can be found both in private physicians' offices and in association with hospitals. They are usually staffed by knowledgeable medical professionals and are equipped to provide sophisticated medical evaluations. Upon your request they will always be pleased to send a complete report of their findings to your physician, thus keeping him or her both happy and informed.

GETTING STARTED: SOME SELECTIONS FROM THE LITERATURE . . .

There are many, many books on running, many fewer on cycling and swimming. I listed my own favorites in Chapter 4. Virtually all of them have a section on getting started. Before presenting my own program, I would like to review with you in some detail what I feel is the best of the work of others.

Bob Glover is an experienced runner and fitness consultant. It was his *Runner's Handbook,* written with Jack Shepherd, that I used to help me get into running. Bob's Run-Easy Method certainly worked well for me. It has two keys, the walk / run approach used by almost everyone, and the use of the heart rate as a monitor of the effectiveness of the workout.

Walk / run is really the only safe way to begin a running program. Some people go out on their first day and try to run for 10 or 15 or 20 minutes straight. Unless you are very unusual, if you do this you will only end your workout gasping for breath and feeling very uncomfortable. The next morning you will ache all over and be so stiff that you will hardly be able to get out of bed. A walk / run approach will entirely avoid gasping. It will also minimize the aches and pains, although for the first few weeks you will experience them to some degree. Bob uses two variations of walk / run. One is walk until you are ready to run and then walk again when your body tells you to stop running. This is to be done for a given period of time, usually 20 minutes per session for the first few weeks of the program. The second variation is walk 2 minutes, run 2 minutes, and so on for the set period, gradually increasing the running minutes and decreasing the walking minutes over time.

Other variants of walk / run are counting steps and going set distances, alternating walking and running. The latter is easy to do on the track, a road with utility poles spaced at regular intervals, or a city street evenly divided into blocks. The principle of all these methods is the same: to gradually ease yourself into running. Don't try jumping in with both feet even if they are shod with shiny new top-of-the-line running shoes.

Heart-rate monitoring as a measure of exercise effectiveness is an excellent concept. In previous chapters I have described the aerobic threshold, the aerobic range, and how to take your pulse. In the beginning, it is a good idea to take your pulse once or twice during every workout. After a while you will develop a feel for when you are exercising aerobically. You will then need only to confirm every once in a while that your feeling is on target.

Joe Henderson is the author of many fine running books. His *Jog, Run, Race* presents a very slow, very gradual introduction to running. It begins with a 3-month walking period, with a very small dose of jogging introduced in the third month. Running ability is then developed over another 3 months, at the end of which you are doing 1½ hours per week. This is a very gradual program. My feeling is that many people do not need to begin quite as slowly as Joe suggests. (See my own introductory program, below.) The difference between jogging and running, by the way, is nothing but rate of speed, and that's all relative. One person's run is another's jog. A friend of mine who consistently wins our age class in 10k races talks about "jogging" when he is doing a 7:30 mile. For me, that speed is about the fastest that I can do, and can only sustain it for about 4 miles.

My own program will have you up to 2½ hours per week of running by the end of the third month rather than Joe's 1½ hours at the end of the sixth. (I should point out however that Joe's program will have you doing a marathon at the end of a year just as mine will have you doing a marathon-equivalent triathlon in the same period of time.) For some people Joe's slow introduction will nevertheless be just what the doctor ordered. For some others it may indeed be just what their doctor orders! One feature of Joe's program that appeals very much to me is the precise schedule of activities and minutes per day that he provides for a 3-month walking segment, a 3-month jogging segment, a 3-month running segment, and finally a 3-month marathon-training segment.

The *American Running and Fitness Association* (ARFA) has a very nice 3-month introductory program which combines the major features of Bob Glover's and Joe Henderson's programs. It is contained in their publication *Guidelines for Successful Jogging.* ARFA uses walk / run on a minutes program, scheduled by day of week for 3 months. Like Bob and Joe, ARFA provides for rest and "hard / easy" (everything's relative). At the end of the twelfth week on the ARFA program, you will be jogging for 2¼ hours per week. Nice, neat, simple, effective.

GETTING STARTED: PHASE I . . .

In the realm of exercise prescription, originality is no longer possible. I certainly make no claim to it. Many predecessors have laid out beginning running programs. Above I have reviewed for you 3 of the best ones. Now let us look at my own program, which draws heavily on them. The basic precepts of all of them are the same: walk / run to begin, consistency, regularity, days off, hard / easy.

If you have looked ahead at the TFOMTP you will have noted that workouts are scheduled on 5 days per week, with 2 rest days. This pattern is based on the one Ardy Friedberg uses in *How to Run Your First Marathon.* Joe Henderson also recommends working out 5 days per week during the first 6 months, although he goes over to running almost every day for the second 6 months. ARFA's introductory 3-month program uses a 6-day-per-week pattern. I began using a regular 5-day-a-week schedule when I started training for my first long race (20 miles) in 1983. I have stayed with it since then, whether in training for a specific race or simply maintaining my aerobic base. I have found it to be very beneficial. As noted in the previous chapter there are few training experts today who would argue that scheduled rest is not a necessary part of training.

Phase I does require only 4 rather than 5 workouts per

week (see Tables 6.1 to 6.4). It seems to me that this sort of gradual approach is useful in the beginning. I suggest that workouts be done on Tuesday, Thursday, Saturday, and Sunday. The long workout is scheduled for Sunday to help you get into the pattern that many endurance athletes follow on a regular basis. However, you need not regard this suggested pattern as being carved in stone. Virtually any combination of days and minutes adding up to the weekly totals will do, just as long as you do not cram it all into less than 3 days per week. To avoid musculoskeletal problems and to develop aerobic fitness, you must work out at least 3 days a week. Preferably these days will be evenly spaced, but if your schedule limits you to one weekday and Saturday/Sunday, it is better to start with that than not start at all.

For each workout day, I have designated the number of minutes to be done. Note that through Phase I there is a gradual progression from a total of 1½ hours to a total of 2½ hours per week, but that it is done in waves, following the Bowerman hard/easy principle on the "macro level." The hard / easy principle is also followed within each week, at the "micro level."[1] Remember, of course, that each workout must be preceded by appropriate stretching and followed by a cooldown period.

I have divided the phase into 4 sets. In the first set of 3 weeks (Table 6.1), you should concentrate on walking, at a brisk pace, with a little running thrown in. I don't think that it is necessary to specify in detail how the time should be divided. You can find a pattern that suits you. Just as an example, in the first week in the 20 minute workouts, you might do a 6-minute walk, 2-minute run twice, concluding with walk 2 and run 2. In the second week, you could go to

---

1. "Macro level" in training refers to the overall pattern of workouts, from week to week. "Micro level" in training refers to the pattern of workouts within each week.

Table 6.1. GETTING STARTED
Phase I—Set 1   Mostly Walking

(Times in minutes per day)

Day	M	T	W	Th	F	S	S	Total
Week								
1	Off	20	Off	20	Off	20	30	90
2	Off	20	Off	25	Off	20	35	100
3	Off	20	Off	30	Off	25	35	110

Grand Total   300

(100 minutes per week)

walk 5, run 3, followed by walk 2 and run 2, and so forth. Work out a comfortable pattern, gradually but slowly increasing your running minutes. Nevertheless, by the end of the set you should still be doing more walking than running minutes.

In Set 2 (Table 6.2), you will begin to change the balance towards running. A typical 25-minute workout in this set might be run 4, walk 3, 3 times, concluding with a 4-minute run. The 40-minute workout could consist of 5 sets of run 5, walk

Table 6.2. GETTING STARTED
Phase I—Set 2   Walking / Running

(Times in minutes per day)

Day	M	T	W	Th	F	S	S	Total
Week								
4	Off	20	Off	25	Off	20	35	100
5	Off	20	Off	30	Off	25	35	110
6	Off	25	Off	30	Off	25	40	120

Grand Total   330

(110 minutes per week)

3. As you come to the end of this set, you may well find yourself running more and walking less than that. That's okay, but don't overdo it. Don't go too fast, and try to avoid the temptation to go longer. You are still new to this sport. You want to continue in it for some time, maybe for the rest of your life. Muscles are still getting used to doing tasks that they haven't been called upon to do in years, if ever. It is easy to get injured. As Mary Decker's coach Dick Brown says, it is better to err on the side of doing too little rather than too much. More often than not, quitting after 2–6 months is related to nothing more than overdoing it—injury, stress, frustration, and boredom from lack of variation. By the way, to help deal with boredom, at this stage you should begin varying your routes on the street or road. If you started out on the track, go out on the road once or twice a week.

In Set 3 (Table 6.3), the balance will definitely begin to shift to running. At the beginning of the set, you may be putting 3 or 4 2-minute walks into each workout. By the end of the set, you will probably be putting only one 2–3-minute walk in the middle of each run, if that. Notice that this set

Table 6.3. GETTING STARTED

Phase I—Set 3   Running / Walking

(Times in minutes per day)

Day	M	T	W	Th	F	S	S	Total
Week								
7	Off	20	Off	30	Off	25	35	110
8	Off	25	Off	30	Off	25	40	120
9	Off	25	Off	30	Off	35	40	130
10	Off	30	35	Off	30	Off	45	140
					Grand Total			500
					(125 minutes per week)			

lasts for 4 weeks, long enough to let you ease into the final transition from walker to runner.

Finally in Set 4 of Phase I (Table 6.4), you will become a full-time runner. For the most part, the workouts are still fairly short. At least they will feel fairly short when you get to them, even if they don't look short to you right now as you contemplate starting to run. By Set 4 you should be ready to drop the walk portion of each workout. You still should be checking your heart rate now and then to make sure that you are exercising in the aerobic range. You should be going neither too fast nor too slowly. A good rule of thumb on pace is that you should be able to talk, either to yourself or a partner, while running.

At the end of this set you are up to the aerobic base: 2½ hours per week. Congratulations! See, you did it, and it wasn't that difficult. You walked and ran for a total of 56 days over a 13-week period, 1550 minutes total. You averaged about 28 minutes per day overall. By Set 4, you were averaging 35 minutes per day.

Table 6.4. GETTING STARTED
Phase I—Set 4   Running

(Times in minutes per day)

Day	M	T	W	Th	F	S	S	Total
Week								
11	Off	25	30	Off	35	Off	40	130
12	Off	30	35	Off	30	Off	45	140
13	Off	30	35	Off	35	Off	50	150
						Grand Total		420
						(140 minutes per week)		
						13-Week Total		1550
						(120 minutes per week)		

You are now ready to commence Phase II, firmly establishing your aerobic base. In it you will be averaging about 35 minutes per day, and you will increase the number of workouts per week from 4 to 5. You will also begin adding cycling and swimming to your training program. At the end of this phase you will be well on your way to becoming a triathlete.

ESTABLISHING YOUR AEROBIC BASE: PHASE II . . .

In Phase II you will average 2¾ hours of aerobic exercise per week for 26 weeks. In the beginning, with the increase in the number of workouts per week from 4 to 5, the number of minutes per workout will decline well below what you were doing at the end of Phase I. However, it will never go below 20 minutes, the aerobic minimum established by the American College of Sports Medicine. Phase II is divided into two parts, each one containing an 8-week set and a 5-week set. Just as in Phase I, in each set there is a build-up in weekly minutes to a peak, with the next set beginning below that peak but building up to a higher one. There is a similar changing pattern of increasing and decreasing minutes within each week. Thus, as in Phase I, Bill Bowerman's hard / easy principle is followed at both the macro and micro levels.

In Set 1 of Phase II (Table 6.5), you will gradually work up to 3 hours per week, surpassing your previous high of 2½ hours achieved at the end of Phase I. Five workouts per week will come easily to you. You will begin to experience more and more the positive benefits for both mind and body of consistent aerobic exercise.

In Set 2 (Table 6.6) you drop back down and then build up once again to three hours. You are confirming your progress, firmly establishing your base. By the end of this set, you will have been exercising aerobically for 6 months. The 6-month

Table 6.5. ESTABLISHING THE AEROBIC BASE
Phase II—Set 1   Building up to 3 Hours per Week

(Times in minutes per day)

Day	M	T	W	Th	F	S	S	Total
Week								
1	Off	20	20	Off	20	20	40	120
2	Off	20	20	Off	20	20	40	120
3	Off	25	20	Off	20	25	40	130
4	Off	25	30	Off	25	25	45	150
5	Off	20	30	Off	30	20	50	150
6	Off	25	30	Off	30	25	50	160
7	Off	20	35	Off	30	40	45	170
8	Off	25	35	Off	30	40	50	180
						Grand Total		1180

(147.5 minutes per week)

plateau is considered by many running authorities to be very significant. You will have overcome the series of aches, pains, and minor injuries that plague every beginning runner. You will have trained your heart and lungs to function aerobi-

Table 6.6. ESTABLISHING THE AEROBIC BASE
Phase II—Set 2   Confirming 3 Hours per Week

(Times in minutes per day)

Day	M	T	W	Th	F	S	S	Total
Week								
9	Off	25	20	Off	25	30	40	140
10	Off	25	20	Off	25	35	45	150
11	Off	25	30	Off	25	30	50	160
12	Off	20	20	Off	30	40	60	170
13	Off	25	20	Off	30	45	60	180
						Grand Total		800

(160 minutes per week)

cally. You will have accustomed your mind to a pattern of regular exercise. You and your family will have recognized it as now part of your life pattern. Once you pass the 6-month point, the likelihood that you will stop diminishes rapidly and markedly. Also, once you reach this milestone, you are ready for another important experience: rest.

Midway through Phase II, at the beginning of Set 3 (Table 6.7), there is a complete break. One week of rest is followed by one very light week. You will not lose your aerobic base during this time. You will afford your body and your mind some time off, a chance to consolidate their gains and to recover from some very new experiences that you have been putting them through. This rest period is very important to prepare you for the challenges to come. It must not be skipped. After the rest, in Set 3 you once again engage in building up your aerobic minutes, surpassing your previous weekly high a little more than halfway through the Set.

Set 4 (Table 6.8) is designed to bring you up to the level of

Table 6.7. ESTABLISHING THE AEROBIC BASE
Phase II—Set 3   Rest and Take Off

(Times in minutes per day)

Day	M	T	W	Th	F	S	S	Total
Week								
14	Off	Off	Off	Off	Off	Off	Off	0
15	Off	20	Off	20	Off	20	Off	60
16	Off	20	20	Off	20	20	40	120
17	Off	25	30	Off	25	20	45	155
18	Off	20	35	Off	30	40	45	170
19	Off	25	35	Off	35	40	50	185
20	Off	20	40	Off	35	50	60	205
21	Off	35	40	Off	40	50	60	225
						Grand Total		1120
						(140 minutes per week)		

Table 6.8. ESTABLISHING THE AEROBIC BASE
Phase II—Set 4   Getting Ready for the TFOMTP

(Times in minutes per day)

Day	M	T	W	Th	F	S	S	Total
Week								
22	Off	30	40	Off	35	50	45	200
23	Off	30	40	Off	40	60	50	220
24	Off	35	40	Off	45	65	55	240
25	Off	45	35	Off	50	70	60	260
26	Off	45	40	Off	50	75	60	270

Grand Total   1190
(240 minutes per week)

aerobic fitness needed to comfortably begin and comfortably complete the TFOMTP itself. Also in this set, the weekly workout pattern changes. The longest one is now done on Saturday rather than Sunday, in the manner of the TFOMTP itself.

If you are a reader who is already exercising at the aerobic base level, 2.5–3 hours per week, have been doing so for at least 6 months, and do not need to carry out any of the earlier parts of the program, I would strongly recommend that you do Set 4 of Phase II or some semblance of it before starting Phase III.

INTRODUCING CYCLING AND SWIMMING IN PHASE II . . .

The organization of Phase II provides you with the opportunity to introduce cycling and swimming into your aerobic exercise program at a pace that suits you. Remember that the basis of my whole approach to triathloning is the development of aerobic fitness. Expertise and excellence in one or more of the sports, while desirable, is certainly not necessary to achievement of your major goal: completing a marathon-equivalent triathlon happily and healthily. Thus it is the total aerobic minutes done that counts, not the sports that they are done in.

Naturally you must do enough of each sport to be comfortable doing it. It is also helpful for both performance and musculoskeletal comfort to have had some work done in training by the muscle groups, different from one another, specific to each sport. And for safety's sake you must be able to swim well enough to go the required distance. But the split of time during the three sports is not at all critical in Phase II.

Assuming that you know how to swim and ride a bicycle, you can start substituting swim and bike workouts for run workouts in any pattern that is comfortable for you. Some weeks you may not run at all. You must simply be certain that you are doing the sport you are doing at a speed fast enough to get your heart rate up into the aerobic range. For me, this means an average speed of at least 14 mph on the bike and a swim speed of no slower than 44 minutes per mile, which is rather slow, I must tell you.

If you do not know how to swim or ride a bike quickly and efficiently, Phase II offers you the opportunity to learn. You may certainly count time spent in swimming lessons as a workout as long as you spend it swimming at the aerobic pace. Nonswimmers would do well to commence lessons early in Phase II. Then you can schedule them for 20- and 25-minute days. It will be easy to get both the lesson and the workout in at the same time. If you are a novice cyclist, you can also use those short workouts to begin to get a feel for your machine, learn how to sit on a racing saddle, become comfortable using bike shoes and toe clips. If you need to work on spinning (see Chapter 4) and riding in the proper gear, practice in the short workouts. Continue to devote the long ones to running. Later on in the phase, as you become more competent in the water and on the bike, you can cut back further on your running and devote some of the longer sessions to the other sports.

As you come to the end of Phase II, you will have significantly elevated your level of aerobic fitness and solidified your aerobic base. You will also be comfortable doing all three sports. You are ready to begin Phase III, the TFOMTP itself.

7 ... The Triathloning for Ordinary Mortals Training Program

> [Triathloning] represents a healthy lifestyle.... A tri-
> athlete cares about regular exercise. He or she is not
> necessarily a born-again athletic fanatic ready to mort-
> gage family and business in order to stay in the sport's
> three rings of fire. Moreover, cross-training has become
> the most sensible way to stay active and injury free....
> A few hours a week of training is all it takes to prepare
> oneself for a [marathon-equivalent] triathlon.
>
> William R. Katovsky,
> editor in chief *Tri-Athlete*,
> December 1984, p. 5

INTRODUCTION ...

You are now ready to begin triathlon training itself. You have
started down the road to the starting line of your first triathlon, from scratch, and you have completed Phases I and II,
the Basic Aerobic Fitness Program described in the last chapter. Or you are an already established recreational endurance
athlete and have been working out aerobically in your sport
for 2.5–3 hours per week on a consistent basis for at least 6

months. For the past 5–6 weeks you have been gradually increasing your workout time. You have averaged 4 hours per week over that stretch. You have achieved technical competence in swimming, biking, and running. You have clearly established your goal for your first triathlon: to finish, happily and healthily. You will not be concerned with speed, although you certainly will be pleased if you happen to do well.

You are comfortable with the minutes rather than the miles approach to working out. You realize that the faster you go in your workouts, the more miles you will cover. This kind of workout performance will perforce produce a faster race performance. But you will not push yourself to go faster than is comfortable for you in your workouts, risking injury and breakdown, just to try to improve your race time. You will be able to keep your mind firmly fixed on your goal: to finish your chosen race in a time that is right for you, your body, your experience, and your level of training. You therefore cast yourself as an Ordinary Mortal in the world of triathloning. You are ready to undertake the Triathloning for Ordinary Mortals Training Program, the TFOMTP.

HOW MUCH IS ENOUGH . . .

The TFOMTP covers 13 weeks. If followed to the minute, it will have you working out in the three sports for 3900 minutes, 65 hours, an average of 5 hours per week for that 13 week period. Although I do recommend doing the full program, you can safely miss up to 10% of it and still do just fine in the race. I know. I have done it. Also, the workouts do not have to be done to the minute. You can go over on some, under on others. Assuming that you work out at least 4 times a week, it is the total number of aerobic minutes that counts.

How did I arrive at that 3900 minute figure, you might ask. How do I know that it *will* work?

I first developed the program for myself, starting from the approach contained in Ardy Friedberg's program *How to Run Your First Marathon.*[1] I modified Ardy's program to make it suitable or so I thought, for triathloning. In the 13th week before marathon day in Ardy's program (which totals 22 weeks from scratch to marathon day) the runner is working out for 4 hours. Over the remaining 13 weeks, there is a total of 3270 minutes of workout time, 4 hours and 10 minutes per week on the average. Figuring on three sports instead of one and liking nice, round numbers, I arbitrarily upped the average weekly workout to 5 hours. I adopted the same hard/easy flow at both the micro (weekly) and macro (total program) levels used by Friedberg and recommended by Bill Bowerman and many others. I tried my program for my own first triathlon. Lo and behold, it worked for me! It can work for you too.

I have continued to use it in my own training for subsequent triathlons. I have also continued to maintain a clear vision of what is doable for me in the world of triathloning: finishing, comfortably. But you don't have to simply take my word for it. Others have used a similar approach and have found it to work for them too.

I circulated the TFOMTP privately to several fellow triathletes prior to the publication of this book. It has been used with success by a number of them. More importantly, I found out subsequently there is quite a bit of support in the literature for the 5-hour per week plan (plus or minus an hour or so) for both marathons and marathon-equivalent triathlons.

---

1. Ardy Friedberg, *How to Run Your First Marathon,* New York: Simon and Schuster, 1982. Now available from Fitness Enterprises, 175 Fifth Avenue, New York, New York 10010.

Ardy Friedberg, of course, recommends 4+ hours per week for the last 3 months for the first-time marathoner. Tom Bassler, M.D., of the American Medical Joggers Association, says that you can do a marathon on 4 hours of running per week. Ron Lawrence, M.D., president of the American Medical Joggers Association, recommends that for marathoning you do 25–40 miles per week.[2] If you train at a 9:30 pace, like I do, this works out to 4–6 hours per week (obviously fewer hours if you train faster). Joe Henderson's 13-week marathon training program calls for 4445 minutes, 5 hours and 40 minutes per week on the average.[3] However, Joe schedules 6 more workouts during that 13-week period than I do. Keeping the average workout length the same but reducing the total number of workouts to that which I recommend would lower his recommended weekly average to 5 hours and 20 minutes.

Turning to published triathlon-specific training programs, Ferdy Massimino, M.D., president of the American Medical Triathlon Association, recommends a 5-hour per week training program for a triathlon slightly under marathon-length.[4] E. C. Friederick and Stephen Kiesling recommend a 5-day, 5-hour per week program for the marathon-equivalent United States Triathlon Series events.[5] For the same event, Sally Edwards recommends 7 hours per week.[6] However, Sally also recommends working out every day. Reduce that to what many regard as a more sensible 6 or 5 days per week while keeping the workout lengths constant and again you have a program that is on the same track as mine.

2. Liz Elliott, "Interview with Ron Lawrence," M.D., *Running and Fitness,* September / October 1984, p. 22.

3. Joe Henderson, *Jog, Run, Race,* Mountain View, California: World Publications, 1977, Lessons 27, 29, 31.

4. Ferdy Massimino, "Aerobics and Fitness," *Triathlon,* April / May 1984, p. 26.

5. E. C. Frederick and Stephen Kiesling, "The Semi-Tough Triathlon," *American Health,* June 1984, p. 56.

6. Sally Edwards, "Runners' Guide to Triathlon Training," *Running and Fitness,* January / February 1984, p. 22.

THE. TFOMTP . . .

OVERVIEW. I provide four variations on the 13-week, 3900-minute, 5-hours per week theme. The first is the *generic program*. In this one, you are provided with the minutes per workout by day of week only. You decide for yourself how you want to distribute the time among the three sports. Then there are the *cycling-emphasis, running-emphasis,* and *balanced-program* variants. I do not provide a swim-emphasis program, although you could certainly develop one for yourself from the Generic Program. Swimming is almost always the shortest event in terms of time required to complete it. Also, it is almost always done first, when you are the most fresh. Therefore, it simply does not make sense to concentrate on it, when the other two sports will require more energy when you are more tired later during the race.

The two emphasis programs provide you with the opportunity to either concentrate on your weakest sport or enhance your performance in your strongest one, depending on what your personal priorities are. If you choose an emphasis program with the objective of building upon your strength, rest assured that there will still be enough minutes of workouts in the other two sports to see you through those legs of the race in good shape too. In both emphasis programs the swimming portion is admittedly minimal, 11.5 hours total. However, it is certainly enough to get you through the swim segment of the race.

Before my own first triathlon, not following my own program to the letter in this area I must admit, I did exactly 7 swimming workouts for a total of about 6 hours. Although I knew the basic strokes, I had not swum seriously since the age of 12. The race distance was 1.5 miles. The furthest I went in training was 1.2 miles on the race course 2 weeks before the event. In the pool, I was averaging 50 minutes for the mile, a very slow time indeed. But I was having no trouble with the distances because I was in aerobic shape and did not try to go too fast. Since I had plenty of aerobic minutes, I did not need too many swim-specific minutes. Under race conditions I actually average 44 minutes per mile for the 1.5 miles and had my best relative finish among the three events.

The balanced program almost doubles the allotted swim time and ends up with a fairly even distribution of time among the three sports. You can use this plan if you want to strengthen your swimming in relative terms or if you feel that your abilities in the three sports are about equal and you don't want to concentrate on any one of them.

The TFOMTP provides for a total of 6 workouts in all three sports per week. I suggest that they be done over 5 days with 2 workouts being done on 1 day each week. I recommend 2 days off per week. You may do 10–30 minutes of stretching on the off days but complete rest will be very beneficial. You may spread the 6 sessions over 6 days if need be, but 1 day off per week is mandatory. The 2-a-days are always scheduled on Tuesdays, after a rest day. Generally, biking and swimming are paired, these sports involving less total body wear-and-tear than does running. Also, for the 2-a-days the scheduled time for each workout is generally at the low end, relatively, for the week in question.

Two combined bike/runs in the same session are scheduled, 1 of them for what will be your approximate event times in a marathon-equivalent triathlon. You will note that your longest workout is 2½ hours even though you may be racing for 4 hours plus. Believe me, it will work, it *does* work. Many people facing their first triathlon will do the race distances consecutively in a workout, sometimes more than once. They are convincing themselves that they will be able to make it. Actually, by doing so in training they are probably interfering with their chances of making it in the race by expending all that energy too soon, usually without an adequate supply of drinking water on a training run.

You should be able to go the race distances individually. You certainly should be convinced in your mind that you will be able to make it through the swim. If you are afraid that you might drown, even though in most races there are plenty of swim monitors out on the course, you are going to have a tough time even getting into the water. But to go 4+ hours in a race you do not have to go more than 2½ hours in training. I have never gone more than 2½ hours in training, whether for a triathlon or a marathon. Because I am so slow in all three events, I am usually out on the course for about 4 hours, unless the event is less than marathon equivalent. Joe Henderson, in explaining his approach to marathon training, which is the same as mine is to triathlon training, puts the point about limiting your long workouts very well:

Don't bother to point out an obvious discrepancy in the program to me. I am aware of it and can explain it. The marathon . . . requires 3–4 hours of running time [4½ for me], yet the schedule hasn't called for anything longer than two hours or about 15 miles [which takes me about 2½ hours]. How are you supposed to make up the difference? Trust me. You'll make it up in the race because you have run enough total distance. *It is the total amount of running which determines how far you go, not the length of your longest runs.* . . . You'll see. [Italics mine.][7]

In each of the sport-specific programs, 3 open water swims are scheduled. As I have pointed out elsewhere, I highly recommend that all 3 be done. If the race distance is one mile or less, in the swim workouts it is not necessary to swim more than 60 minutes or the time it takes you to cover 1.5 miles, whichever is less. Regardless of what the race instructions say the water temperature will be, you must get used to cold water. Also, race water temperature is sometimes (often?) lower than advertised. If the race is to be held in salt water, you must get

7. Henderson, ibid., p. 184.

used to salt-water buoyancy. You may well encounter one or more of the following: waves, chop, surf, tides, and currents. Furthermore, I know of at least one excellent swimmer who trained very well in the pool, did no open-water training swims, panicked at the swim start of his first triathlon, and did not even begin the race.

The TFOMTP is laid out in 3 sets. The first builds slowly from almost 5 hours per week to almost 6 over a 5-week period. At the beginning of the second set, you drop back sharply to 2½ hours and then build up to peak at close to 8 hours one week before the end of this 6 week block. In the last set, you taper down for the last 2 weeks before your race. Notice that the hard/easy, build up/taper down pattern is followed over the 13-week span as well as within each week's workout schedule. This principle is based on the body's natural cycle of physical development.

THE GENERIC PROGRAM...

In Table 7.1, Set 1 of the Generic Program is presented. You will start out doing just 20 minutes more in the first week of this set than you did in the last week of Phase II, Set 4. Having built up slowly, steadily, and consistently in Phase II (or your own base building / maintenance version of it) you will easily be able to move into this more demanding schedule. You will also easily be able to add 1 workout a week to your program. Please do not regard this schedule as being carved in stone, however. There is no reason why you cannot vary the pattern even from week to week if necessary to fit your life schedule, as long as you generally follow the overall guidelines and do the scheduled minutes.

In Set 2 of the TFOMTP (Table 7.2), you begin by dropping your workout time back sharply for the first 2 weeks. This gives your body a chance to rest, recuperate, and firmly con-

Table 7.1. TFOMTP—GENERIC PROGRAM
Set 1

(Times in minutes per workout)

Day	M	T*	W	Th	F	S	S	Total
Week								
1	Off	40	45	Off	45	65	60	290
		35						
2	Off	40	50	Off	45	70	65	310
		40						
3	Off	45	55	Off	50	75	70	335
		40						
4	Off	45	50	Off	55	75	65	335
		45						
5	Off	50	55	Off	65	75	60	350
		45				Grand Total		1620
						(324 minutes per week)		

* Two separate workouts, in different sports, are to be done on each Tuesday.

solidate its gains in preparation for additional build-up. In the first 2 weeks of this set, you not only cut back on minutes per workout, but also drop back to 5 workouts per week. In the last week of the set, you cut down on total minutes and find that the weekday workouts are relatively short. However, you conclude that week, and the hardest 4-week segment of your whole training program, with your 2½ hour bike / run session. I always look at weeks 3–6 of this set as the really challenging part of my own training. I know that once I get through them I am home free and ready to race. Note that although you do have one week of close to 8 hours of work, and 3 others of 6½ you still are averaging only 5½ hours per week in this set.

In Set 3 (Table 7.3) you taper down to the race. In week 1

Table 7.2. TFOMTP—GENERIC PROGRAM
Set 2

(Times in minutes per workout)

Day	M	T	W	Th	F	S	S	Total
Week								
1	Off	40	30	Off	25	35	25	155
2	Off	30	40	Off	35	45	55	205
3	Off	55	70	Off	65	80	70	390
		50						
4	Off	55	60	Off	75	90	75	395
		50						
5	Off	65	75	Off	75	90	100*	465
		60						
6	Off	45	50	Off	55	45	150*	390
		45				Grand Total		2000
						(333 minutes per week)		

* These two workouts should be cycle / runs with the cycling segment longer.

of this set, Week 12 of the whole phase, you still have two fairly long workouts, but only 4 workouts total. If you find yourself significantly behind on total minutes coming into this week you may certainly add an extra workout or two and / or

Table 7.3. TFOMTP—GENERIC PROGRAM
Set 3

(Times in minutes per workout)

Day	M	T	W	Th	F	S	S	Total
Week								
1	Off	45	Off	60	Off	70	45	220
2	Off	20	20	20	Off	Race or Race		60
						Grand Total		280
						(140 minutes per week)		

add minutes to one of the scheduled ones. However, do not jam any extra minutes into the last week. Your body and mind are facing a big challenge on the upcoming weekend, possibly the biggest challenge they have ever faced together. You need the physical rest and the mental preparation time. Those last three 20 minute workouts should be done at leisurely pace, just to keep yourself loose. Don't neglect to stretch before doing those workouts, even if they are short and light. You don't want to risk injury at this stage of the game. During this last week you should also be planning your eating for the race with care. For expert advice on that subject I refer you to my colleague Virginia Aronson in Chapter 9.

THE SPORTS-SPECIFIC PROGRAMS . . .

Tables 7.4, 7.5, and 7.6 present the *cycling-emphasis, running-emphasis* and *balanced-program* versions of the TFOMTP. The three sets of each are presented together in one table. The choice among them is yours. My own favorite is the cycling-emphasis program. I like it best for two reasons. In terms of performance, cycling has been my weakest sport. At the same time for me cycling is physically the most comfortable sport to work out in. It is certainly less wearing than is running, and, as you may have gathered, I am not overly enthusiastic about swimming. So I will usually start off my season in early spring intending to do the cycling-emphasis program. Nevertheless, I don't always stick to it minute-for-minute. I don't like riding in the rain, in the cold, or into strong head winds. So the weather may well cause me to convert some scheduled cycling days into running or swimming days. No matter. When I get to my first race, I am still in shape to complete it since I have done the requisite number of aerobic minutes.

At the end of each emphasis table I give the approximate mileage that I would cover in each sport going at my usual training pace. The totals are not high. But at the speeds at

Table 7.4. TFOMTP—CYCLING EMPHASIS
Sets 1,2,3
(Times in minutes per workout)

	Day	M	T	W	Th	F	S	S	Total
Set	Week								
1	1	Off	40 bike 35 swim	45 run	Off	45 bike	65 run	60 bike	145 bike, 110 run, 35 swim: 290
1	2	Off	40 bike 40 swim	50 run	Off	45 bike	70 run	65 bike	150 bike, 120 run, 40 swim: 310
1	3	Off	45 bike 40 swim	55 run	Off	50 bike	75 run	70 bike	165 bike, 130 run, 40 swim: 335
1	4	Off	45 bike 45 swim	50 run	Off	55 bike	75 run	65 bike	165 bike, 125 run, 45 swim: 335
1	5	Off	45 bike 50 swim	55 run	Off	65 bike	75 run	60 bike	170 bike, 130 run, 50 swim: 350
2	6	Off	40 swim	30 bike	Off	25 run	35 bike	25 run	65 bike, 50 run, 40 swim: 155
2	7	Off	30 swim	40 bike	Off	35 run	45 bike	55 run	85 bike, 90 run, 30 swim: 205
2	8	Off	55 bike 50 swim	70 run	Off	80 bike	65 swim*	70 run	135 bike, 140 run, 115 swim: 390

Day	M	T	W	Th	F	S	S	Total
Set								
Week								
2 9	Off	50 bike 50 swim	55 run	Off	65 bike	90:50 bike/ 40 run	75 run	175 bike, 155 run, 50 swim: 395
2 10	Off	65 run 60 swim	75 bike	Off	90 run	75 swim*	100 bike	175 bike, 155 run, 135 swim: 465
2 11	Off	45 bike 45 swim	50 run	Off	55 bike	45 run	150**: 90 bike / 60 run	190 bike, 155 run, 45 swim: 390
3 12	Off	45 bike	Off	60 run	Off	70 bike	45 swim*	115 bike, 60 run, 45 swim: 220
3 13	Off	20 bike	20 swim	20 run	Off	Race	Race	60

Grand total minutes: 1755 bike, 1455 run, 690 swim, 3900 total
Approximate mileage: Cycling at 16 mph: 468 total, 36 per week
Running at 9.0 minutes per mile: 161 total, 12.5 per week
Swimming at 40 minutes per mile: 17 total, 1.3 per week

*These are open-water swims.
**Alternatively, you may want to do the bike and run race distances regardless of time. Do not go over 3 hours, however.

Table 7.5. TFOMTP—RUNNING EMPHASIS

Sets 1,2,3

(Times in minutes per workout)

Set	Week	Day	M	T	W	Th	F	S	S	Total
1	1		Off	40 run 35 swim	45 bike	Off	45 run	65 bike	60 run	145 run, 110 bike, 35 swim: <u>290</u>
1	2		Off	40 run 40 swim	50 bike	Off	45 run	70 bike	65 run	150 run, 120 bike, 40 swim: <u>310</u>
1	3		Off	45 run 45 swim	55 bike	Off	50 run	75 bike	70 run	165 run, 130 bike, 40 swim: <u>335</u>
1	4		Off	45 run 45 swim	50 bike	Off	55 run	75 bike	65 run	165 run, 125 bike, 45 swim: <u>335</u>
1	5		Off	45 run 50 swim	55 bike	Off	65 run	75 bike	60 run	170 run, 130 bike, 50 swim: <u>350</u>
2	6		Off	40 swim	30 run	Off	25 bike	35 run	25 bike	65 run, 50 bike, 40 swim: <u>155</u>
2	7		Off	30 swim	40 bike	Off	35 run	45 bike	55 run	90 bike, 85 run, 30 swim: <u>205</u>
2	8		Off	55 bike 50 swim	70 run	Off	80 bike	65 swim*	70 bike	150 run, 140 bike, 115 swim: <u>390</u>

Day	M	T	W	Th	F	S	S	Total
Set								
Week								
2 / 9	Off	60 bike / 50 swim	55 run	Off	65 bike	90:45 bike / 45 run	75 run	240 run, 105 bike, 50 swim: <u>395</u>
2 / 10	Off	65 bike / 60 swim	75 run	Off	90 bike	75 swim*	100 run	175 run, 155 bike, 135 swim: <u>465</u>
2 / 11	Off	45 bike / 45 swim	50 run	Off	55 run	45 run	150**: 90 bike / 60 run	210 run, 155 bike, 45 swim: <u>390</u>
3 / 12	Off	45 run	Off	60 bike	Off	70 run	45 swim*	115 run, 60 bike, 45 swim: <u>220</u>
3 / 13	Off	20 bike	20 swim	20 run	Off	Race	Race	<u>60</u>

Grand total minutes: 1860 run, 1350 bike, 690 swim, 3900 total
Approximate mileage: Running at 9.0 minutes per mile: 206 total, 16 per week
Cycling at 16 mph: 360 total, 28 per week
Swimming at 40 minutes per mile: 17 total, 1.3 per week

* These are open-water swims.
** Alternatively, you may want to do the bike and run race distances regardless of time. Do not go over 3 hours, however.

Table 7.6. TFOMTP—BALANCED PROGRAM
Sets 1,2,3

(Times in minutes per workout)

Day	M	T	W	Th	F	S	S	Total
Set								
Week								
1 1	Off	40 run 35 swim	45 bike	Off	45 run	65 swim	65 bike	105 bike, 90 run, 95 swim: 290
1 2	Off	50 run 40 swim	50 bike	Off	45 run	65 swim	70 bike	110 bike, 95 run, 105 swim: 310
1 3	Off	55 run 40 swim	45 bike	Off	50 run	70 swim	70 bike	120 bike, 105 run, 105 swim: 335
1 4	Off	45 bike 45 swim	50 run	Off	55 swim	75 bike	65 run	120 bike, 115 run, 100 swim: 335
1 5	Off	45 bike 50 swim	55 run	Off	65 run	60 swim	75 bike	120 bike, 120 run, 110 swim: 350
2 6	Off	25 run	30 bike	Off	25 run	35 bike	40 swim	65 bike, 50 run, 40 swim: 155
2 7	Off	30 run	40 bike	Off	35 bike	45 run	55 swim	75 bike, 75 run, 55 swim: 205
2 8	Off	55 bike 50 swim	70 run	Off	80 bike	65 swim*	70 run	135 bike, 140 run, 115 swim: 390

Day	M	T	W	Th	F	S	S	Total
Set								
Week								
2 9	Off	50 bike 50 swim	55 run	Off	65 swim	90:50 bike/ 40 run	75 run	110 bike, 170 run, 50 swim: <u>395</u>
2 10	Off	65 run 60 swim	75 bike	Off	90 run	75 swim*	100 bike	175 bike, 155 run, 135 swim: <u>465</u>
2 11	Off	45 bike 45 swim	50 run	Off	55 bike	45 swim	150**: 90 bike / 60 run	190 bike, 110 run, 45 swim: <u>390</u>
3 12	Off	45 swim	Off	60 run	Off	70 bike	45 swim*	70 bike, 60 run, 90 swim: <u>220</u>
3 13	Off	20 bike	20 swim	20 run	Off	Race	Race	

Grand total minutes: 1415 bike, 1305 run, 1180 swim, 3900 total
Approximate mileage: Running at 9.0 minutes per mile: 145 total, 11 per week
Cycling at 16 mph: 377 total, 29 per week
Swimming at 40 minutes per mile: 29.5 total, 2.3 per week

* These are open-water swims.
** Alternatively, you may want to do the bike and run race distances regardless of time. Do not go over 3 hours, however.

which I train I am doing the equivalent in the three sports of about 33 miles of running per week, on the average. However, in three of the 4 heavy weeks of Set 2, I am doing the equivalent of over 40 miles of running, and in Week 10 I am doing over 50 miles equivalent.[8] Thus I say again, do not worry. You will have enough training under your belt to enable you to achieve your goal. And obviously, the faster you happen to train in any of the sports, the more miles you will cover. But don't pick up your training pace just to add miles. You just have to train in each sport at a pace fast enough to get your heart rate up over that aerobic threshold of 70% of your theoretical maximum heart rate, which is 220 minus your age.

By now I am sure that you know the principles of this approach to training and the keys to making it work for you: consistency, regularity, hard / easy, scheduled rest, balanced training, not overtraining, and most importantly a clear concept—with which you are entirely comfortable—of the goal that you are trying achieve: completing a marathon-equivalent triathlon. Bearing the principles in mind, following the TFOMTP variant most suited to you, your needs, and your abilities, you will be able to achieve that goal.

8. The conversion ratios for the speeds at which I train are as follows: cycling miles divided by 2.5 = running miles, swimming miles multiplied by 4.5 = running miles.

You can easily work out your own conversion ratios. First determine your average training rate of speed in each event in miles per hour. Dividing your running rate into your cycling rate will give you the figure to divide into cycling miles to derive the running miles equivalent. Dividing your swimming rate into your running rate will give you the figure by which to multiply the swimming miles to derive the running-miles equivalent.

8 . . . Equipment

Why tri? Why indeed, mother of four and grandmother of two? It's easy-chair and soap-opera time, right? Wrong! First it was jogging, that last-ditch defense against corrugated thighs. Then it was a two-mile fun run, a 10k, a ribbon, firmish-looking legs, and a few half-marathons. Then the race flyer. "Carson City Mini-Triathlon," it said. "Three-mile run, 10-mile bike, half-mile pool swim." As a kid you swam across the pool. And remember bicycles? Balloon tires and coaster brakes. . . . [Now,] how many grandmas do you know [who] want a new bicycle for Christmas?

Kitty Brown of Carson City, Nevada,
quoted in "Triathlete Profile Contest Winner"
by William R. Katovsky,
Tri-Athlete, March 1985, p. 46.

INTRODUCTION . . .

An important element of triathloning is equipment. Not that super equipment will make a winner out of somebody who with ordinary stuff runs at a 9-minute pace, rides at 16 mph, and swims 40-minute miles. But good equipment can help significantly to make the sport more comfortable, safe, healthy, and enjoyable. Triathloning, since it requires buying and maintaining a bike, and paying not insignificant travel costs to participate in the races, is not the cheapest of sports. But compare it to downhill skiing. The equipment package easily costs as much as a good bike. Then you have to pay $75.00 a day or more for lodging and lift ticket. Worse yet, compare it to sailing, for which the cost of the central piece of equipment can run in the tens of thousands of dollars, not to mention several thousands per year in upkeep. In this context, triathloning can hardly be considered expensive. Starting from scratch, you can get into the sport, with a decent bike, for $1200.00 (1984) (see Table 8.1). The bulk of that cost is for cycling equipment. On the other hand, while equipping yourself may not be overly expensive, if you start from scratch it can seem somewhat complicated, particularly where the bike is concerned.

In this chapter I will offer you some basic advice on clothing and equipment for the three sports. But the most useful advice I can offer is to locate the best bicycle shop and the best running-shoe store in your area, before you buy anything. Some people are in the sporting goods business just to make money and will sell you anything you ask for. But the better shops will take your interests and needs as well as their own desire to make a sale into account. Among other things, they know that in the long run attention first to your needs is good business and will likely make a loyal customer of you.

A good running-shoe store will be owned and/or staffed by people who are runners. It will carry a limited number of running-shoe brands and not every model in every line. The staff will have carefully evaluated the myriad number of makes and models on the market and will have preselected a good range from which you can choose. They will make sure that the shoes fit, and will stand behind their products. They will also be knowledgeable about clothes, socks, and other accessories.

Likewise a good bicycle shop will be owned and / or staffed by cyclists. Do not buy your bike in a department store. They

Table 8.1. A Basic Triathlon Equipment Budget
(In 1984 prices)

RUNNING

Shoes	$ 75.00
Shorts, singlets, T-shirts, (2 sets)	50.00
Socks (4 pair)	25.00
Sweatbands (4)	5.00
Warm-up suit, nylon	75.00
Polypropylene underwear (1 set)	30.00
Woolen hat	10.00
Athletic supporters / support bras	25.00
Subtotal	$ 295.00

CYCLING

10- to 12-speed bike, good quality	$ 400.00
Bike computer, pump, water bottle, other on-the-bike accessories	100.00
Helmet	40.00
Bike shirt and shorts (2 sets)	100.00
Gloves	15.00
Touring shoes	35.00
Tools, floor pump	50.00
Subtotal	$ 840.00

SWIMMING

Suits, two	$ 30.00
Goggles, top quality	25.00
Noseclip, ear plugs	5.00
Subtotal	$ 60.00
Grand Total	$1195.00

generally carry only the cheapest equipment, will not be equipped to handle ongoing service, and will rarely have knowledgeable sales people. At the same time, take note that not all bicycle shops are the same. Those that do a high volume in BMX's and Christmas 10-speeds may well know little or nothing about racing and high-performance machines. One way to judge a bicycle shop is by the most expensive bike it carries. A decent bike for the beginning triathlete will cost somewhere between $250.00 and $400.00. If a $400.00 model is the most expensive one in the shop, look elsewhere.

Really good bikes cost $1000.00 and up. Really good bike shops will carry at least a few bikes of that type in inventory. They will also be staffed by bike racers or tourers who can speak to you from experience about the bike you are buying. The mechanics in such a shop should also be knowledgeable and willing to spend time talking with you. Another good measure of a bicycle shop's quality is the number of people there, in season, who are wearing those long black cycling shorts and the funny little cycling caps that say "Campagnolo" or "Ciocc" or "Guerciotti" on the brim. Experienced cyclists know the good bike shops from the not-so-good ones.

There is a very large mail-order business in both running and cycling gear. I have made very good use of it. The prices are usually lower than those found in the stores, for obvious reasons. The reputable mail-order sellers make returning items as painless as possible. But I feel that the mail-order business must be used with care. You should certainly not make your first purchases through the mail. Find those good, local shops. Develop good relationships. Get educated. Buy your first round of equipment from them. (The exception to this rule is swim gear. It is simple and straightforward. It can be successfully bought through catalogs right from the start. Personal counseling is of little import in its selection.) After you become somewhat knowledgeable, then you can intelligently buy some of your equipment by mail. But continue to spend money locally, especially on major items, even if the cost is a bit higher. Personal advice and counsel and continuing personal service are invaluable and you do want those shops to stay in business.

RUNNING GEAR . . .

The most important part of running equipment is, of course, the shoes. The most important aspect of shoes is fit and comfort. There is no one "best brand." The best shoe for you is the one that fits, that provides good cushioning, and provides good stability both for the forefoot (the flat part behind the toes) and the rearfoot (heel). Buying from a running-shoe store, you should count on spending at least $45.00 (list) for a decent pair of shoes. I would not spend less than that, and usually spend considerably more. Running shoes come in a wide variety of colors, but any one model usually comes in only one color. The uppers on the better shoes are usually made of a combination of nylon and suede leather. To help keep your feet cool, look for at least some mesh material in the upper. A molded inner sole is helpful both for cushioning and stability. If your foot has a very high or a very low arch; if you overpronate (bend in sharply at the ankle); or if you frequently get shin splints, knee pain, or minor nagging aches in your feet or legs, you may need custom-made inserts called orthotics. Consult a well-recommended sports podiatrist or orthopedist.

Running-shoe technology is advancing rapidly in the mid-80s. New cushioning and stabilizing materials and combinations of materials are being developed all the time. The major shoe companies spend a great deal of money doing research. The best way to keep up with the progress being made is by reading articles in such magazines as *Runners World* and *The Runner*.

The most important part of equipment after shoes is socks. Invest in several pair of good-quality running socks. They will help to keep your feet cool and protect against blisters.

As far as clothing is concerned, the most important rule is to wear as little as possible for any given temperature. In winter, if you are warm before the start of a run, you have too much clothing on. On summer mornings, if you are slightly chilly in nylon running shorts and singlet before starting out, that's good. You will get warm quickly enough.

For year-round running, you will need the following clothing items: nylon running shorts, singlets (those tops cut like men's undershirts that racers wear), T-shirts (you will accumulate these rapidly as you race), athletic supporter / support bra, sweat bands, warm-up suit, polypropylene long underwear, a woolen hat, and gloves. In the winter, if it is too cold to be comfortable after running for a mile or so in anything more than a set of polypropylene long underwear, shorts, and a T-shirt under a nylon windbreaker warm-up suit, plus woolen hat and gloves, it is probably too cold to be running. In really cold weather, even if the bulk of you warms up, you risk frostbite, penile-tip irritation, nipple burn, and other assorted nuisance ailments. For a little more protection from the cold and a lot more protection from the rain (if you like running in the wet stuff), you can purchase a Gore-Tex suit. This breathable fabric makes very nice running gear, but the suits made from it are considerably more expensive than the conventional nylon ones.

It will not take you long to work out the clothing combinations that are right for you in various temperature and weather conditions. I find having an outdoor thermometer mounted outside my bedroom window to be very helpful in making the correct clothing selection for a workout. Remember, unless you are going out for over an hour, you will always be better off if you are a bit underdressed rather than a bit overdressed.

CYCLING: THE BIKE . . .

Obviously, the most important piece of equipment is the bike itself. A great deal has been (and will continue to be) written about selecting the right bike. Thom Lieb's and Fred Matheny's books each have a good chapter on the subject. There are both general articles and specific ones on the different components that appear constantly the cycling magazines. I find the article that usually accompanies *Bicycling*'s annual winter buyer's-guide feature to be helpful. Information can also be gathered from friends, experienced cyclists whom you may meet, and bike shop staff. I offer you some helpful hints based on my own experience.

PRICE. For your first triathlon bike, buy a ready-made machine. You can buy a very suitable stock bike for $250.00 to $400.00, designed and equipped to meet the criteria that I set out below. The best bicycles are ones for which you buy separately a frame set and all the various bits and pieces, called components in cycling terminology (wheels, gear shifters, brakes, seat, etc.), exactly to your liking and put them together. However, custom-built bikes usually cost a minimum of $1000.00 and can be quite a bit more expensive than that. You should have some miles under your seat and know what you like and dislike in frames and components before you go spending that kind of money.

FRAMES AND WHEELS. The bike you buy should have a chrome-molybdenum steel alloy (cromoly or cro-mo for short) frame. This material combines strength and rigidity with light weight. As bike prices go up, frame weights go down, but not by much. At this stage, it is not worth spending an extra two to three hundred dollars to save a pound or two on the frame. It is much cheaper, and healthier, to lose that weight on you. The important place to save weight is in the wheels. The bike you buy must have aluminum alloy rims on the wheels. (In this price range, any bike with steel rims is definitely over-priced). It is at the edge of any rolling circle that weight is multiplied by centrifugal force. Thus small weight gains at the wheel rims are magnified in terms of less rolling resistance. A well-balanced aluminum rimmed wheel with correctly tightened spokes is just as strong as a steel wheel.

Frames come in several different sizes, measured in inches or centimeters of the height of the *seat tube* (the one connecting the seat to the *bottom bracket,* the short transverse tube through which the pedals are mounted). There are various rules of thumb for picking the correct size. A good first approximation for correct frame size is that when straddling the frame, wearing bike shoes, you should have at least 1 inch, and better 2, of clearance between you and the *top tube,* the one that connects the *seat post* to the *head tube,* (the one on which the handlebars are mounted).

Frames also come in a variety of configurations. The three

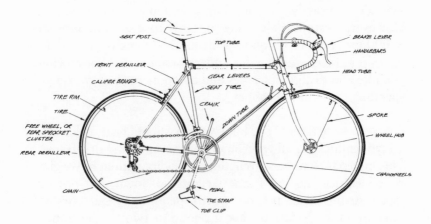

10-SPEED BICYCLE

principal definers of frame configuration are the seat angle, the head angle, and the wheel base. Racing bikes tend to be short and compact upright machines. The two angles are usually in the 74°–75° range and the wheel base is generally under 39″. Racing bikes are stiff and highly maneuverable but tend to give a relatively rough ride. Touring bikes are longer and more resilient. They are less responsive but more comfortable to ride. The two angles are usually in the 71°–72° range and the wheel base is generally over 41″. These dimension differences seem rather small, but in practice the differences in ride and handling characteristics between racing and touring bikes are noticeable.

For triathlon bike racing a combination of characteristics not found in either the out-and-out racing or the out-and-out touring bike is needed. The bike leg of a marathon-equivalent triathlon is 20 miles or more. You want a comfortable ride akin to that needed for touring because you will be on your bike riding hard for an hour or more. You do not need the high maneuverability of the racing bike. With the no-drafting rule[1] that is in force in most triathlons, you will be neither pack riding nor pace lining (riding in a close single-file group) the two situations in which precise control is critical. However, you will be riding at high speed, so the flexibility of the touring bike is a disadvantage. You want a rigid frame so that the thrust you apply to the pedals is converted into forward motion, not into twisting the bike's frame.

Many bicycle manufacturers responded to the triathlon explosion by producing a "triathlon bike." Generally this bike is a compromise, which seems logical and sensible. The wheel base is in the 39″–40″ range while the head and seat angles hover around 73°. The objective is produce a bike that is comfortable to ride at high speed for long stretches without

---

1. Drafting in bike racing is the practice of following closely behind another rider in order to reduce wind resistance.

being too flexible, and that is maneuverable enough for triathlon bike racing without being unnecessarily twitchy. For the nontriathlon market, this type of bike is called the "sport tourer." That was where the state of the art was in 1985. You would certainly be very safe buying such a bike in $250.00–$400.00 price range. However, I am not at all certain that the last word has yet been written on the triathlon racing bike. With the improvements in frame materials (aluminum is becoming increasingly popular), and cromoly tube cross-sectional structure, it may be possible to produce a rigid frame (for high energy efficiency) with a longer wheel base and lower angles (for improved riding comfort). Only maneuverability and handling are sacrificed here, and they are not that critical for most situations in triathlon bike racing.

BIKE FIT. Aside from frame height, wheel base, and tube angles, there are other parameters of bicycle fit which are important for efficiency, safety, and comfort. These include seat height and angle, and handlebar height. These are best adjusted for you by the dealer at the time you buy the bike. If the seat that comes with the bike is not right for you, your dealer should be able to change it for you at little or no cost. Pedal cranks (the arm to which the pedal is attached) vary in length. Most bikes are equipped with 170mm cranks. If you need longer or shorter ones, your dealer should be able to help you. Handlebar widths also vary. Should you need something out of the ordinary, your dealer should be able to help you with that too.

TIRES. There are two types of bicycle tires, "clinchers" and "tubulars" (also called "sew-ups"). Clinchers are like old-fashioned automobile tires. They are U-shaped in cross-section, attach snugly to the rim with a bead, and contain an inner tube. The inner tube is easy to repair when punctured but it takes some doing to get clinchers off and on the rim.

Tubulars are O-shaped in cross-section. The two longitudinal edges of the tire are sewn together to form an "O", and the tube is contained inside the tire, forming an integral unit. Tubulars are relatively easy to get on and off the rim, to which they are attached with a rubber-cement-like glue. However, when punctured, the tubes are hard to get at within the sewn-up tire and are difficult to repair. With comparable materials, tubulars are quite a bit more expensive than clinchers.

For clinchers, a small patch kit and even an extra tube can be easily carried in a seat bag making roadside repairs easy, once you become proficient in removing and replacing the tire on the rim, that is. For tubulars, you carry one or more spare tire-tube tube sets, ready to go on the rim and inflate with the small hand pump every cyclist must carry on the bike.

Tubulars can be built lighter and narrower in tread than clinchers and thus have less rolling resistance. They are thus the choice of bike racers. In triathlon bike racing as well as in training rides, puncture avoidance is all-important, however. Clinchers, usually heavier, tend to be somewhat more puncture resistant than high-performance tubulars. They also can be repaired on the road. If you have a flat tire on the bike leg of a triathlon and cannot fix it (or replace the tire in the case of tubulars) the only alternative to dropping out is walking or carrying your bike over the course. In any case, there are some clinchers now on the market which have a rolling resistance approaching that of the good tubulars.

Tire manufacturers have enhanced the puncture resistance of both clinchers and tubulars by adding either steel or kevlar belts under the tread. There is also a high-tech plastic strip called Mr. Tuffy, which can be placed (by your dealer, please) between the tube and the inner surface of a clincher tire. It provides a protective shield against most causes of tube puncture. I have a great aversion to flat tires. Tire irons and I don't get along too well. At the beginning of the 1984 season, I installed kevlar-belted tires *and* Mr. Tuffy on my wheels. I carried a little extra weight, but I did not have one flat all season.

HUBS. Most hubs on the medium-quality bikes we are talking about are of good quality. Quick release on the front wheel is very nice for transporting your bike, either on a rack or inside a car. This feature should be standard in this price range. Rear-wheel quick release is almost a necessity if you contemplate any on-the-road-flat repair work. Most bikes in this price range have it too.

CRANK SETS AND GEARING. The crank set is the whole apparatus to which the pedals are attached. I explained front and rear cogs, gearing, and gear ratios in Chapter 4. For triathlon bike racing, you do not need more than two different chain rings (sets of cogs) on the crank set. Usually, you will have a 52-tooth cog and a 42-tooth one. Five different cogs on the rear wheel gives you ten different combinations, a "10 speed." (The rear-wheel cogs and special hub taken together are called the "free wheel.") Six rear-wheel cogs gives you a "12 speed." Except in certain special applications, anything over 12 speeds supplies only redundancy in gearing.

I happen to use a special kind of crankset called the Powercam. It is manufactured by Houdaille Industries. The powercam is a device which converts the regular circular motion of bicycle pedaling to more of an up-down, runninglike motion.[2] Whereas in conventional pedaling the up-pull backstroke is as important as the downstroke, in Powercamming only the downstroke matters. I find the device very helpful. I am able to pedal at lower rpm. in a higher gear, conserving energy. In the triathlon, the bike-run transition is much easier with the Powercam than it is with a conventional bike. I need

2. Susan Weaver, "Powercam," *Bicycling,* September / October 1984, p. 39.

use none of the special bike-run transition routines that I describe in Chapter 10 and tend to run faster and certainly more comfortably.

DERAILLEURS. Except for a few exotic titanium-containing models, neither front nor rear derailleurs (the mechanisms that move the chain from cog to cog) are big-ticket items. Whereas ordinary-quality rear derailleurs run $15.00 to $20.00 (1984 prices), you can get all but the very best for $35.00. For front derailleurs the difference is between a $10.00 unit and one costing no more than $20.00. The extra few dollars are well worth the difference in shifting ease and position. On a stock bike, most dealers will be happy to make the upgrade just for the cost differential.

SHIFTERS. Shifters can be mounted on top of the head tube, just behind the centerpoint of the handlebars, or on the *down tube* (the lower, diagonal tube that connects the lower end of the head tube to the bottom bracket). In the price range we are talking about, both variants appear. Although all out-and-out racing bikes have down tube mounted shifters, there is nothing wrong with stem-mounted ones. When just learning to ride, down-tube mounted shifters seem a long way away. However, it is inefficient to sit up each time you want to shift. Nevertheless, for comfort as a beginning cyclist you can have stem-mounted shifters. Later on they can always be moved to the down tube, at nominal cost.

BRAKES. There can be much discussion over the relative merits of centerpull and sidepull brakes. However, both the cheapest and the most expensive brakes are found in the side-pull design. It is obviously the quality of materials, workmanship, and engineering that makes the difference. Most bikes in the $250.00–$400.00 range are equipped with good brakes. If you want to upgrade to a more expensive model of the same basic design found on the bike, most dealers will be happy to do that at cost.

There can be no discussion, as far as I am concerned, over the utility of auxiliary brake handles, horizontal bars attached to the brake bodies that allow you to brake with your hands on the handlebar tops. I spent 2 years riding with them.[3] I got used to them. It was less than 3 months before the accident described in Chapter 4 that I got a bike that did not have them. It was only then that I discovered how comfortable it was to ride with my hands resting naturally on the brake hoods, something you cannot do when auxiliary handles are in the way. However, when I went slowly through that intersection with my hands on the tops, I was unconsciously thinking that I still had auxiliary brake handles. (If I had had them, I could have stopped the bike when the front-wheel wobbling began, put my leg instead of my arm out, and I would not have suffered that shoulder dislocation.) I did not have them. My hands should have been on the drops, with my fingers on the main brake handles. I would have been able to stop easily in that case. There are obviously two possible solutions to this problem: always use auxiliary handles or never use them. My recommendation is firmly to adopt the latter approach.

It is not possible to ride correctly a drop-handlebar bike equipped with auxiliary brake handles. You simply cannot properly place your hands on the hoods. This you must be able to do for comfortable long-distance riding. The presence of auxiliary brake handles just encourages bad habits. If the bike you choose comes with auxiliary handles, have the dealer remove them and install hoods on your brake handles. If you never have auxiliary handles, you can't get used to them! By the way, if you already own a bike and it has auxiliary brake

3. This section on auxiliary brake handles is drawn from an article in the January, 1985 issue of *The Beast*. The material is used with the permission of the publisher of *The Beast*.

handles, have them taken off and quickly get used to riding without them.

SADDLES. Like running shoes, the best saddle (seat) is the one that fits you and is comfortable. No saddle will keep your bottom from getting sore forever but some do a better job of it than others. Most bikes in the $250.00–$400.00 range come with a decent racing saddle. Men's and women's saddles do differ. Saddles can be interchanged easily. There are a number of gimmick saddles on the market. None have been well reviewed. I tried one twin-seat type and was not at all happy with it. A good pad can help quite a bit. The traditional sheepskin cover is popular. I have had good luck with the Spenco saddle pad.

ACCESSORIES. A water bottle is a must for triathloning. In the race, you should use the provided water stops, of course, but have your own bottle as a spare. I have tried several different mounts, and have found the traditional cage to be the best. You should always carry a bike-mounted air pump. You will want some kind of under-the-seat saddlebag in which to carry your tire/tube spares, a small tool kit, and a tire-pressure gauge. Although the purists gasp, I like to have a kickstand on the bike. It makes leaving the bike a breeze. In aluminum it doesn't weigh much. If you are not planning to ride at night, certainly remove the orange reflectors on the wheels and consider removing the fore-and-aft body-mounted red reflectors.

Shock-absorbing handlebar padding is a nice, inexpensive extra to have. Spenco makes little shock-absorbing covers for the brake bodies. I am happy using them. Rearview mirrors, an important safety item, come in several different configurations.

I highly recommend that you buy an electronic speedometer / cadence counter. Several makes are now available in the $60.00–$100.00 price range. Most of them will also tell you the time, the elapsed time, elapsed distance in a particular ride, total distance done, and one or two other bits of information. The most important feature to look for beside the computer functions is how the pickups on the front wheel (for speed and distance) and the crankset (for cadence) mount. You want them to attach securely, preferably with a nut-and-bolt-tightened bracket, rather than with friction-tightened wires, glue, or some similar item.

CLOTHING. Unless you are planning to do cold-weather riding (which I do not recommend), your bike wardrobe will be very simple. Cycling shorts have long legs to prevent chafe and a seat pad, usually made of chamois, to provide some cushioning. They usually come in basic black but, especially in form-fitting lycra, are also available in colors. Bike shorts are usually made of either polypropylene or wool. Their principal function is to wick away moisture from your body. Both materials work well. Bike shirts usually have two or three pockets on the back at the waist which can be used for carrying an extra water bottle and other paraphernalia. Bike shirts also come in form-fitting lycra. A pair of padded gloves will make your hands feel more comfortable.

PEDALS, TOE CLIPS, AND SHOES. Pedals come in a variety of configurations. In the $250.00–$400.00 bike price range you will get good quality but not exotic design pedals. Racing pedals are designed with toe clips and straps. Together with the shoes, they form a system for attaching your feet to the bike. I strongly recommend against using your running shoes for cycling. Cycling shoes have stiff soles for a reason: to prevent the diversion of downward thrust from the pedal to flex in your foot. Running shoes are made to flex in the foot. Furthermore, running shoes tend to be bulky and thus can easily get caught in the toe clip, especially when you need to get your foot our fast.

There are two kinds of bike shoes. Racing shoes have totally inflexible bottoms, cannot be walked in easily, and attach to the pedal with an adjustable cleat on the sole. They are intended to be tightened into the toe-clip / pedal assembly with the toe-clip strap. They provide the most efficient attachment for rider to bike. They also take a lot of getting used to and can be dangerous in sudden stops because of the potential difficulty getting them out of the toe clips quickly. Touring-bike shoes have a sole that is rigid in the rear, but can be walked in. They do not have cleats but rather fixed grooves for positioning the sole on the pedal. They can be used with the straps loose enough so that you can get your feet out quickly in panic situations. I highly recommend them.

HELMETS. Finally, on helmets. You must have one. Most races now require that you wear one and that it must be of the hard-shell variety. Those Italian "hair nets" look great but offer zero protection. You might as well be wearing nothing. I recommend strongly that you wear your helmet wherever you ride. There are a variety of good brands. Get one that is well recommended by your bike store and / or cyclists that you know. You are looking for a combination of comfort, coolness, and good protection. But first and foremost, as with running shoes and bicycles, you must make sure that the helmet you buy fits you and is secure on your head. Your head will then be secure in it.

CONCLUSION. Just as in the case of running shoes, the bike that fits you best is the one for you. Just as with running shoes, there is no one make or type that is clearly superior to all of the rest. Just as with running shoes, there is a certain minimum amount of money that you should spend to assure that the item you buy will be of decent quality. Even more than with running shoes, it pays to spend some time talking, shopping, and reading cycling books and magazines. However, if you buy a bike that has a cromoly frame and aluminum-alloy rims, is the proper size, and for a price in the $250.00–$400.00 range, from a shop with a good reputation, you will be getting a bicycle that will be very suitable for entry into the marvelous world of triathloning.

SWIMMING . . .

Swim equipment is by far the simplest and cheapest of the three types to acquire and maintain. You will need 1 or 2 suits, briefs not boxers for men, and one-piece racing—not any other design—for women. Plan to wear the suit throughout the race. The modern suits dry quickly and provide good support for both sexes. There is no need to change out of them after the swim, a time-consuming process. For the bike and run legs you simply put the appropriate specialized clothing on over the swimsuit. I cannot comment from personal experience on the one-piece triathlon suits designed to be worn throughout the race. However, I have never used one myself for two reasons. I like the seat padding that comes in regular bike shorts but is not included in most tri-suits because it doesn't help too much when wet. I also like to be as cool and unencumbered as possible on the run. I think that I would find tri-suits rather confining for running.

Goggles are a necessity for swimming. You must be able to see clearly at all times. I found the inexpensive swim goggles that are readily available for under $5.00 to work reasonably well in keeping the water out but to hurt my face after 30 minutes or so. An investment of $20.00 to $25.00 for a well-padded set like the Barracudas that I use is well worth it in terms of both effectiveness and facial comfort. I use a nose clip, a matter of personal preference. I highly recommend earplugs, of the easily removable "pine-cone" variety.

In salt water, if there is any threat of jellyfish (they sting),

I suggest using vaseline on the forward-facing surfaces of your body. It helps those unfriendly little fellows to harmlessly slide by you. It is also generally washed off by the end of the swim so that you do not have to worry about skin-pore blockage and interference with sweating on the bike and the run from its use.

CONCLUSION . . .

Good equipment will help make your first triathlon experience a good one. However, aside from a well-fitted pair of running shoes, an effective, comfortable pair of swim goggles, and a hard-shell cycling helmet, there is no one piece of equipment that you must buy new. You can train and ride round the bike course on any bike, even one borrowed for the purpose from a neighbor or a teen-ager. You may use your running shoes for biking if your budget rejects cycling shoes as a priority. Run, bike, and swim clothing does not have to be purpose bought. The most important thing is to assemble an equipment set that you are comfortable with, and please, do remember to take it all with you when you set off for your first race!

9 ... The Triathlon Training Table: Nutrition for Ordinary Mortals

Virginia Aronson, R.D., M.S.

INTRODUCTION ...

Just as training for a triathlon can be accomplished by the Ordinary Mortal with a minimum of physical stress and a maximum of psychological enjoyment, eating for optimal health and strength can also be painless and fun. All that is required for optimizing nutrition to meet training (and everyday) needs is the motivation to alter your individual lifestyle in order to eat well, eat wisely, and eat wonderfully. Any Ordinary Mortal can do it!

Food serves as a tasty source of both nutrients and energy. Like an automobile, we need the proper array of well-greased parts to ensure optimal engine performance, as well as a continual and ready supply of fuel to keep us running smoothly. If you learn how to take adequate care of your car, you can then depend on it (for the most part) to get you where you want to go. And if you feed yourself adequately, your body can usually be relied upon to lead you down desired paths. Yet, with high-octane fuel and extra attention, your car will *really* run well. And with the appropriate diet (and training), you can fine-tune your body for optimal triathlon performance.

Despite lucrative advertisements and promising claims, there are no magic dietary potions for maximizing sports performance. Athletes serve as one of the population groups most vulnerable to food fads and frauds. Americans are currently wasting billions of dollars on nutrition nonsense and useless (sometimes dangerous) diet gimmicks. Therefore, it is wise for Ordinary Mortals to learn to avoid health quackery and fad diets in favor of common-sense fitness advice. Nutritionally speaking, this simply means amassing some basic nutrition know-how and instituting practical applications on a daily basis.

Fortunately, there is no need to suffer from dietary deprivation when following the triathlon training table diet. Training is supposed to be fun, and so is eating! After all, food is certainly one of life's greatest pleasures. Thus, a healthful diet, like a sensible overall training program, should enhance physical status while providing psychological pleasure. With some nutrition know-how, Ordinary Mortals can eat for optimal triathlon performance—and actually enjoy themselves in the process!

NUTRITION BASICS FOR ORDINARY MORTALS . . .

How well do you eat? When asked this question, most Americans would reply (rather guiltily) that their diets are less than perfect. However, national surveys reveal rather surprising statistics. In a country where a wide variety of nutrient-rich foodstuffs is available and affordable, and during an era of keen interest in the importance of good nutrition, Americans *are* eating well. The biggest dietary drawback is that too many of us are eating *too* well, which has led to a state of overweight for about ⅓ of the population. Yet, true nutrient deficiencies are rare, and most of us are eating better than we think.

Take the following eating-habit quiz in order to evaluate just how well you tend to eat. For each statement below, fill in the numbers which most closely approximate your typical dietary habits:

1) I usually include _____ servings of whole-grain or enriched cereal, bread, pasta, rice, or other grains everyday.

2) I usually include _____ servings of oranges, grapefruit, tomatoes, or their juices everyday.

3) I usually include _____ servings of dark green leafy vegetables (collard greens, kale, mustard greens, spinach, Swiss chard, etc.) or bright yellow fruits or vegetables (apricots, carrots, pumpkin, squash, etc.) each week.

4) I usually include _____ servings of other fruits and vegetables everyday.

5) I usually drink _____ cups of milk every day; I eat _____ servings of cheese daily; I eat _____ cups of yogurt each day.

6) I usually include _____ servings of meat, poultry, or fish every day; I eat _____ eggs each week; I eat _____ cups of dried beans or peas (black-eyed peas, cowpeas, lentils, navy beans, pea beans, soybeans, etc.) each week.

7) I usually include _____ servings of 1 or more of the following each week: cake, candy, cookies, donuts, jams, jellies, gum, pastries, pies, soft drinks, sugar, syrups.

8) I usually include _____ servings of 1 or more of the following each week: chips, crackers, dips, dried or smoked meats, salted nuts, pickles, pretzels, soups.

9) I usually drink _____ alcoholic beverages each week.

10) I usually drink _____ cups of coffee, tea, or cocoa every day.

11) I usually at at fast-food restaurants (fried chicken or seafood,

hamburgers, hot dogs, pizza, tacos, etc.) _____ times each week.

12) I consider my own diet to be:

_____ well balanced and varied.

_____ unbalanced.

_____ repetitive.

_____ generally poor.

If your answers are as follows, your diet is probably quite well balanced: 1) 4 or more; 2) 1 or more; 3) 3 or more; 4) 3 or more; 5) Total = 2 (adult), 4 (teen or pregnant); 6) 2; 3 or less; 1 or more; 7–11) In general, the lower the numbers, the better; 12) Your answer may inspire you to read on!

If your own answers to the eating-habit quiz differed greatly from the above, you may want to read up on basic nutrition in order to revamp and revitalize your present diet. Even if your answers appeared to be quite accurate, you may choose to further enhance your nutrition know-how with a good sound review of the nutrition basics. After all, even Ordinary Mortals deserve to know how to feed themselves extraordinarily well!

Nutrient Know-how

With 10,000–15,000 different items available in the typical supermarket, it may seem like a confusing chore to select foods wisely in order to eat a balanced diet. Actually, a well-balanced (and tasty!) diet can be achieved very simply, with a little nutrition know-how.

Nutrients are the chemical substances we obtain from foods. Nutrients are essential for:

the growth, upkeep, and repair of body tissues
the regulation of body processes
energy for the body.

No single food contains the 50 or so nutrients that the body requires in amounts adequate for proper growth and health. However, all of the nutrients we need can be provided by foods. A well-balanced diet contains the proper array of nutrients, and since foods vary in the kinds and amounts of nutrients they provide, it is important to include a variety of foods in the diet each day.

Nutrients are separated according to their chemical compositions into six categories:

proteins
carbohydrates
fats
vitamins
minerals
water.

Nutritionists have incorporated both the bodily needs of individuals and the nutritive values of foods into what is known as the "Basic Four." This grouping system separates foods in accordance with the similarities of their individual nutrient contents. Each of the four groups includes a variety of different foods with similar nutrient compositions. You can ensure an adequate intake of the needed nutrients by including in your diet the recommended number of daily servings of various foods from each group in the Basic Four:

fruit and vegetable group
grain group
milk and cheese group
meat and alternates group.

Then there are the "other" foodstuffs, those items for which the overall nutrient content is outweighed by the caloric content. These foods typically contain appreciable amounts of one or more of the following:

fat
sugar
salt
alcohol.

Your body does not require a specific number of servings of "other" foods. If you choose to include some of these foods, serving sizes should be moderate. After all, Ordinary Mortals enjoy eating, and "other" foods can serve to enhance dining delight: an ice cream cone on a weekend jaunt, a few chips 'n' dip at a party, and a cold brew on a hot afternoon can certainly add psychological pleasure without deriving devastating dietary damages—as long as portions are moderate and the rest of the overall diet is well balanced.

The chart on pp. 176–7 illustrates the appropriate number of daily food group servings required for a well-balanced dietary intake.

Protein Know-how

Protein is required for life itself and is found in the cells of all plants and animals. To most Americans, "protein" means "meat," but high-quality protein is also provided by poultry, fish, eggs, cheese, milk, yogurt, and specific plant combinations.

Excluding water, protein is the most abundant substance present in our bodies, contributing around 50% of dry body weight. Protein helps to form hair, nails, skin, bones, and muscles. Protein is essential to oxygen transport in the bloodstream, blood-sugar regulation, clotting mechanisms, and systems for protection against infection. Protein also forms enzymes which speed up body processes and the hormones which regulate these body processes.

Protein is composed of some 22 building blocks known as "amino acids," linked together in various combinations. In

Basic Four Food Group	Number of Servings Per Day	Serving Size	Food Sources
Fruit and vegetable	4	½ cup juice	Citrus fruit or juice daily
		1 cup raw or ½ cup cooked	Dark green leafy vegetable or bright yellow fruit / vegetable 3–4 times per week
			Starchy vegetables are included in Grain Group
Grain	4	1 slice	Bread—whole grain or enriched
		½–¾ cup	Cereal—cooked, dry, flours, grains
		½ cup	Pasta—macaroni, noodles, spaghetti
		⅓–½ cup	Starchy vegetables: corn, lima beans, peas, potato, pumpkin, winter squash
Milk and cheese	3 (adult) 4 (teen, pregnant)	1 cup 1½ oz.	Milk—buttermilk, skim, whole Cheese (calcium contents are higher in harder varieties)
		1 cup	Yogurt
Meat and alternates	2	1½–2 oz. cooked 2 2 oz. ½ cup	Meat, poultry, fish Eggs Cheese Cottage Cheese

Basic Four Food Group	Number of Servings Per Day	Serving Size	Food Sources
"Other" foods	—	4 Tbsp.	Peanut butter, nuts
		1 cup	Dried beans or peas
		Sweets	—candy, cake, cookies, donuts, gum, jams, jellies, pastries, pies, soft drinks, sugars, syrups
		Fats	—butter, margarine, oils, salad dressings, shortening, bacon, cream, olives, avocado
		Alcoholic beverages	—beer, wine, liquors, liqueurs, cordials

order to build body protein efficiently, a well-balanced mixture of amino acids must be present. If the amino acids available are not properly balanced (i.e., certain amino acids are low or missing), protein cannot be built and the amino acids are wasted.

Some of the necessary amino acids can be manufactured by our bodies, but 9 cannot be synthesized at a rate sufficient to meet our needs. These 9 so-called essential amino acids must be provided by foods.

A high quality protein provides all of the essential amino acids in the proportions required by the body. Because the composition of the animal body is similar to that of the human body, the amino-acid balance of animal foods (meat, poultry, fish, eggs, cheese, milk, yogurt) is of higher quality than that of plant foods. Plant proteins do not contain the proper assortment of amino acids in the amounts sufficient to support bodily growth. Therefore, plant foods should be combined with animal foods in order to improve the quality of the available protein. Also, so-called complementary plant foods—which balance each other out by providing adequate amino acids when eaten together—can contribute high quality protein to the diet:

Plant Foods ⟷ Animal Foods
(meat, poultry, fish, eggs, cheese, milk, yogurt)

Legumes ⟷ Grains
(dried beans and peas) (barley, buckwheat, corn, oats, millet, rice, rye, wheat)

Legumes ⟷ Nuts and Seeds

Despite the popular myth, athletic training does *not* require increased dietary protein. Training will build muscles, and any excess protein will be stored as body fat. Many athletes are actually consuming 3 times their protein needs, a financially wasteful and quite unhealthy dietary pattern.

Carbohydrate Know-how

Carbohydrates in our diets come in two major forms:

sugars
starches.

The simple sugars (monosaccharides) are the building blocks for most common carbohydrates. They double up to form double sugars (disaccharides) and connect in chains of 3 or more to form the more complex starches (polysaccharides). In order for the body to be able to use them, carbohydrates must be broken down during digestion into simple sugars. In storage form, carbohydrates (glycogen) in muscles and liver are ready forms of energy for physical activity.

The carbohydrate material which the human body is unable to fully break down is known as fiber. Although it does not provide us with either energy or nutrients, fiber is an important dietary constituent. Fiber is essential to the proper functioning of the gastrointestinal system, assisting in digestion, elimination, and in the prevention of certain diseases.

The major function of carbohydrates is the provision of energy, but carbohydrate foods also serve as carriers of other nutrients and fiber. The world's major carbohydrate sources are:

cereal grains
potatoes
fruits and vegetables
legumes
cassava (tapioca)
sugar cane
sugar beet.

Many of our processed foods are also rich in carbohydrates, including such products as:

breads and other baked goods
pastas
dried fruits
jams and jellies
molasses, honey, syrups
sweet desserts.

Many carbohydrate foods contain a combination of sugars and starches, but the most desirable are the "complex" carbohydrates, the starch-rich foods which also contain a combination of essential nutrients and / or fiber.

From sugar cane and sugar beet we derive refined table sugar (sucrose), which is basically pure carbohydrate. Table sugar provides calories without any accompanying nutrients. Brown sugar, "raw" sugar (which is actually refined), and honey provide, in addition to carbohydrate, only trace amounts of a few nutrients.

Our bodies do not require any refined sugar. We can obtain all of the energy we need, plus various nutrients and fiber, from the natural sugars and starches available in milk, fruits, vegetables, and whole-grain breads and cereals. The complex carbohydrate foods are especially important for endurance athletes, particularly during training and after an event.

Fat Know-how

Food fat is important for health as it provides us with the following:

calories for body energy
palatability to enhance the flavor of food
satiety value to aid the feeling of "fullness"
fatty acids essential for growth
transport for certain vitamins.

Evidence now exists, however, which links various diseases with high blood levels of certain types of fat. The kinds of fat included in the diet appear to influence the levels of fat in the blood. Thus, you may want to keep in mind the following concepts:

Heart disease is the number one killer in America today, accounting for more deaths than all other diseases combined.

Most cultures which follow a diet rich in "saturated" fats demonstrate a high rate of heart disease.

A high-fat diet produces heart disease in many species of laboratory animals.

Recent studies indicate a possible relationship between a high-fat diet and certain cancers.

Most sources of "saturated" fat are of animal origin and are usually solid at room temperature. Because they spoil less rapidly than most liquid fats, saturated fats are often included in processed foods. Some common foods which are high in saturated fats include:

fatty meats
whole milk and its products (such as cheeses, ice cream, and puddings)
cream, butter, shortening
fried foods
and—surprisingly—the highly saturated vegetable oils, palm and coconut.

"Unsaturated" fats come from plant sources and are usually liquid at room temperature. Unlike saturated fats, "polyunsaturated" vegetable oils and other unsaturated fats do not contribute to heart disease. However, an excess of any type of fat is undesirable—especially from a caloric standpoint.

It may surprise you to learn that fat actually provides more than twice as many calories per gram (or ounce) as either protein or carbohydrate. The latter two nutrients each provide approximately 4 calories per gram (or 115 calories per ounce), while fat provides a whopping 9 calories per gram (or 260 calories per ounce). And it is quite easy to misjudge and underestimate the amount of fat in food because fat is such a concentrated source of energy. What appears to be only a "dab" of fat may turn out to be worth over a hundred calories!

The average American diet contains 15% of the total calories as protein and more than 40% as fat. It has been recommended, however, that the amount of fat we eat (the amount of saturated fat in particular) be reduced to comprise only 30% of the total calories. This would leave 55% of our total caloric intake to be supplied by carbohydrate. And since high carbohydrate eating is a plus for the training triathlete—as well as the nontraining mortal—reduction in overall fat intake is doubly important, as such alterations make more room in the diet for the starchy, nutrient, and fiber-rich foods.

Although technically not a fat per se, cholesterol is a fatlike substance found only in foods of animal origin. Most of our cholesterol does not come from the diet, however, but is manufactured in the body, mainly by the liver. An essential component of all cells and important in the production of certain hormones and vitamin D, cholesterol is required by the body in specific amounts. However, like saturated fats, excesses can prove detrimental to heart health; simply by keeping fat intake to a moderate level dietary cholesterol can be controlled. And since eggs are the most common source, while the less popular organ meats (liver, kidney, sweetbreads) and shrimp, an expensive food, are also rich in cholesterol, intake of these items should be moderate as well. Remember that athletes are not immune to heart disease. Exercise does help to reduce the overall risk, and regular physical activity can reduce blood fats and total cholesterol while elevating blood levels of the more desirable fat-clearing "HDLs" (high density lipoproteins). However, physical activity alone cannot be relied upon to offset dietary imbalances.

Vitamin Know-how

Americans spend well over a billion dollars each year on self-prescribed vitamin supplements. Yet, for the majority of individuals, supplementation is unnecessary. Because of common vitamin misconceptions, many Americans continuously succumb to sales pitches and "health with vitamins" promotions. Let's take a look at some of the popular myths about vitamins, and then examine the facts.

MYTH: Vitamin supplements serve as an insurance policy for guaranteed health, even for those consuming an unbalanced diet.

FACT: Minute quantities of the known vitamins are required in the regulation of body processes. The normal, healthy individual who eats a wide variety of foods can easily obtain from them all of the necessary vitamins. Vitamin supplementation cannot make up for an inadequate intake of other nutrients. After all, vitamin supplements do not provide the protein, carbohydrate, fat, or minerals needed for growth and health. Nor does a vitamin supplement supply fiber. Also, our foods may provide certain essential factors that science has not yet identified. Thus, the surest, simplest guide to adequate nutrient intake is the selection of a variety of foods from the "Basic Four" food groups. Because vitamins occur in differing amounts in the vast array of foods now available, variety in food selection is essential.

MYTH: Foods available in our supermarkets cannot provide us with adequate amounts of the necessary vitamins.

FACT: We now know more than ever before about the nutrient content of our food supply and about our individual nutrient needs. The problem is not that our foods are vitamin deficient. Rather, our food choices are inappropriate, and methods of home preparation are vitamin destructive. Commercially available foods can easily meet all of the nutrient needs of the wise shopper and cook. You may want

to use the following chart as a helpful guide toward more
selective shopping and in the proper preparation of vitamin-
rich foods.

MYTH: Our soil is nutritionally deficient, making the foods grown
in it low in vitamin content.

FACT: Only very slight variations in the nutritive value of crops
are due to soil quality. The nutritive value of plants is influenced more by genetic makeup than by the fertility of the
soil. The protein, carbohydrate, fat, vitamin, and fiber content of a plant is controlled by the plant's particular genetic
composition, rather than by the soil. On the othei hand, a
high mineral content in the soil may be reflected in the crops,
but this is usually of little significance.

MYTH: Vitamins supply extra energy, vim and vigor to cure "that
run-down feeling."

FACT: Energy is supplied by food in the form of calories. Protein,
carbohydrate, and fat provide calories, while vitamins, minerals, and water are all calorie-free. Since vitamins do not
provide calories, they do not furnish the body with energy.
Some vitamins aid in the conversion of foods to usable energy,
but "that run-down feeling" is rarely caused by a vitamin
deficiency. To be energetic and full of vigor usually requires
more than a vitamin supplement can provide.

MYTH: Since a certain amount of vitamins will provide health benefits, huge dosages will offer an added boon to health and
well-being.

FACT: The accepted guide for vitamin intake is based on the actual
amounts used in the body. Extra doses of vitamins are useful only in documented deficiencies. Unneeded vitamins are
either excreted, which puts a strain on the kidneys, or
stored—even up to toxic levels. A disproportionate amount
of any one nutrient tends to alter the function of other
nutrients, and an unhealthy imbalance can occur with indis-
criminate self-dosages of vitamins. Vitamin supplements may
be medically prescribed for growing children, pregnant
women, and individuals with specific illnesses, but for the
average, healthy individual, a well-balanced diet supplies
sufficient vitamins to insure nutritional health.

Vitamin	Best Sources	Additional Tips
A	Fish-liver oils, liver, margarine, butter, whole and fortified milk, cheese, cream, egg yolk, dark green leafy vegetables, bright yellow fruits and vegetables.	Cooking vegetables increases the availability; deeper color in vegetables indicates richer amounts.
D	Fish-liver oils, fortified milk.	Exposure of skin to sunlight creates this vitamin; milk should be labeled as "fortified with Vitamin D."
E	Vegetable oils, margarine, nuts, dried beans and peas, wheat germ.	Destroyed by light, air, and in bleaching of flour; avoid excessive intake of vegetable oils.
K	Dark green leafy vegetables, cauliflower, cereals.	Destroyed by light, acids, and antibiotic drug therapy.
C	Citrus fruits, tomatoes, strawberries, cantaloupe, cabbage, broccoli, potatoes, green peppers.	Destroyed by contact with copper, iron, heat, air; dissolves easily in cooking water and if food source is finely chopped.
B_1 (Thiamin)	Lean pork, organ meats, whole grains, wheat germ, dried beans and peas, milk, peanuts.	Destroyed by heat and air; dissolves easily in cooking water.

Vitamin	Best Sources	Additional Tips
B₂ (Riboflavin)	Milk, organ meats, lean meats, eggs, dark green leafy vegetables.	Destroyed by ultraviolet light (sunlight); store in cool, dark place.
Niacin	Lean meat, poultry, fish, organ meats, whole grains, dark green leafy vegetables, peanuts, milk.	May be lost with excessive heat, air, light exposure.
B₆ (Pyridoxine)	Wheat germ, lean meat, organ meats, milk, whole grains, legumes, corn.	Destroyed by heat; use of oral contraceptives increases requirement.
Folic Acid	Organ meats, dark green leafy vegetables, legumes.	Destroyed by heat during long storage; lost in acid medium, as when cooked in vinegar.
B₁₂	All foods of animal origin (meat, milk, dairy products), specially prepared fermented yeasts and soy products.	Destroyed by air and light; strict vegetarians must include the special yeasts and/or soy products.

MYTH: Massive doses of vitamin C are effective in treating both physical and psychological stress, including symptoms of the common cold.

FACT: There is no evidence to suggest that vitamin C in amounts exceeding the recommended dietary allowances can be of physical benefit—in coping with stress or preventing the common cold. The claims for increased vitamin needs during stress have yet to be substantiated by studies on normal, healthy humans. Stress is currently a popular health issue, one upon which many "health with vitamins" promoters have successfully cashed in. The possibility of a relationship between vitamin C intake and the common cold has been the subject of public controversy for many years. However, most nutritionists and physicians do not believe that large doses of vitamin C are effective in decreasing the incidence of the common cold and related infections. The safety of prolonged ingestion of excessive doses of vitamin C is questionable. This is true for excessive intakes for most of the other vitamins as well. In excess, vitamins act as drugs in the body and can be harmful.

Final Fact: A well-balanced diet can provide the normal, healthy individual with all of the essential vitamins required for optimal health and well-being—including those nutrients important during periods of increased physical and psychological stress—even with the rigors of triathlon training for Ordinary Mortals.

Mineral Know-how

The 17 minerals now known to be essential for good health perform two basic functions:

building the skeleton and all soft tissues
regulating body systems (e.g., heartbeat, blood clotting, oxygen transport, nerve conduction, etc.).

However, the essential minerals are separated into two categories not by function, but by size:

Macrominerals are needed by the body each day in amounts
greater than 100 milligrams—calcium, sodium, potassium, sulfur, phosphorus, chloride, and magnesium.
Microminerals are needed by the body in daily amounts no
greater than a few milligrams, and are also called "trace"
elements—iron, copper, zinc, chromium, selenium, man-
ganese, iodine, cobalt, fluoride, and molybdenum.

Mineral supplements are often expensive and, unless prescribed for a diagnosed deficiency, are usually unnecessary.
Excessive doses of minerals, like megadoses of vitamins, do
nothing to enhance health. Foods supply us with a combination of nutrients (protein, carbohydrate, fat, vitamins, minerals, and water) as well as fiber, but minerals supplements
do not. And our food supply may even provide essential minerals which are still undiscovered. It is best to avoid self-prescribed mineral supplements. They can be as detrimental to
health as they are to the budget. Instead, use the information
in the chart to help in the selection of mineral-rich foodstuffs.

Water Know-how

Perhaps because it is not thought of as a food per se, water is
the nutrient category which is most often overlooked. Yet,
our bodies actually contain more water than anything else;
water accounts for about 60% of total body weight, even
more in individuals (like athletes) who have a high percentage
of lean tissue (muscle vs. fat). Water is present inside all body
cells, bathes the outside of body cells, and comprises the fluid
portion of the blood.

All of the body's chemical reactions for energy production
and tissue formation require water. Water evaporation is the
body's best technique for ridding itself of heat. Flushing away
body wastes would not be possible without water. Water per-
forms all of the following functions quite adeptly:

Mineral	Best Food Sources
Calcium	Milk and milk products Sardines and salmon (eaten with bones)
Phosphorus	Meat, poultry, fish, eggs Whole grains
Sodium	Table salt Most processed foods
Chloride	Table salt Most processed foods
Potassium	Bananas, citrus fruits, melon, strawberries, tomatoes, potatoes Lean meats, low-fat milk
Magnesium	Legumes and nuts Green leafy vegetables
Sulfur	Eggs, meat Milk, cheese
Iron	Liver and other organ meats Meats and poultry Clams, oysters
Manganese	Bran Coffee, tea Nuts, legumes
Copper	Organ meats Shellfish Nuts, legumes
Iodine	Iodized table salt Seafood
Zinc	Meat, poultry, fish Egg yolk
Cobalt	Meat Eggs

Mineral	Best Food Sources
Chromium	Liver Whole grains
Fluoride	Fish Tea Fluoridated water
Selenium	Foods grown in selenium-rich soils Seafood Whole grains
Molybdenum	Meat Whole grains and legumes

acts as the body's transportation system
helps to absorb shocks to the body
lubricates joints
carries digestive juices
cools down body and maintains body heat
removes body wastes.

Athletes have special hydration needs, a critical factor in performance and for optimal endurance, safety, and health. It is advisable to consume at least 1–2 quarts of water daily, more during hot-weather training. This need not entail forcing down 8 big glasses of water everyday, however, because there are many good sources in addition to the kitchen tap. In fact, we can obtain a large percentage of the water we need from our foods.

Dietary Guidelines

In February of 1980, the U.S. Department of Agriculture and the U.S. Department of Health, Education, and Welfare released a landmark report entitled "Nutrition and Your

Health—Dietary Guidelines for Americans." This report was later revised with the input of the public and an expert scientific advisory committee. The general gist of the original guidelines remains the same, however, and includes the following sensible suggestions:

Eat a variety of foods.
Maintain a reasonable body weight.
Avoid too much fat, saturated fat, and cholesterol.
Eat foods with adequate starch and fiber.
Avoid too much sugar.
Avoid too much sodium.
If you drink alcohol, do so in moderation.

In practical terms, this means modification of the usual American diet in the following ways:

Increase consumption of fruits, vegetables, and whole grains.
Reduce consumption of meat, and substitute high-protein low-fat alternates such as poultry and fish.
Reduce intake of high-fat foods (whole milk, cream, butter, fried foods, fatty meats), and partially substitute polyunsaturated fats (vegetable oils, salad dressings, margarine) for saturated fats (hydrogenated / solid fats, coconut and palm oil, butter).
Reduce consumption of sugar and foods high in sugar content (soft drinks, pastries, presweetened cereals, candy, desserts, sweets).
Reduce consumption of salt and foods high in salt content (pickles, chips, crackers, condiments, soups).
Moderate intake of alcoholic beverages to 1–2 drinks a day (i.e., wine, beer, or spirits).

It is especially important to insure that the diet is quite varied by selecting many different foods from within each of the Basic Four food groups. By expanding your dietary selections, you have a better chance of obtaining adequate amounts of the 50 or so nutrients your body needs, and less of a chance of consuming too much of any particular constituent. Plus, variety is the spice of life!

Rules and guidelines regarding optimal dietary patterns tend to change and conflict, often causing confusion for health-conscious consumers. Media announcements regarding cancer-causing foodstuffs and dietary factors in heart disease are often exaggerated and sensationalized. Sometimes, one wonders if *anything* is safe for the Ordinary Mortal to eat! The professional nutrition community advises the public to simply eat a well-balanced diet based on the Basic Four, keeping in mind the dietary guidelines, and to avoid food fads and ignore diet scares. After all, no one wants to suffer a heart attack from the stress of constant worry over the supposed cancer-causing agents lurking in the food supply!

Utilizing the Basics

Using the EATTTT (Eating at the Triathlon Training Table) log at the end of this chapter, record your food and beverage intake for one day. You may want to try to recall yesterday's meals and snacks as a typical sample day, rather than utilizing your new nutrition know-how to adhere to a "perfect" diet plan for record-keeping purposes.

First, complete the log as instructed and evaluate your overall diet. Next, complete the questionnaire below to further evaluate your intake in respect to the dietary guidelines. Do you need to alter your diet in order to achieve a better (Basic Four) balance and adhere more closely to the dietary guidelines?

YES   NO

——   ——   1. Did you have 2 or more servings of fruit?
——   ——   2. Did you have 2 or more servings of vegetables?
——   ——   3. Did you have 4 or more servings of whole-grain products?

YES   NO

——— ———   4. Did you select poultry or fish in preference to red meat?

——— ———   5. Did you include any of the following high-fat foods: butter, cream, whole milk, whole-milk cheeses, fatty meats, ice cream, fried foods, coconut or palm oil?

——— ———   6. Did you include any of the following high-cholesterol foods: egg yolk, organ meats, shrimp, fatty meats, butter, cream, whole milk, whole-milk cheeses?

——— ———   7. Did you include any of the following high-sugar foods: donuts, pastries, sweet desserts, candy, presweetened cereals, jams, jellies, honey, syrups, sugars, soft drinks, chewing gum?

——— ———   8. Did you include any of the following high-salt foods: smoked / dried meat or fish, canned fish, bacon, luncheon meats, salted nuts, pickled vegetables, sauerkraut, salted crackers, olives, condiments, salted chips or snackfoods, prepared soups, seasoned salts, table salt?

——— ———   9. Did you consume more than 1 or 2 alcoholic beverages?

——— ———   10. Is your overall food intake varied, or does your diet tend to be quite similar in content nearly every day (e.g., cereal every morning, meat and potatoes every evening)?

If you do note some definite aspects of your typical diet pattern which may need alteration, avoid the urge to attempt a rapid dietary overhaul. Your current lifestyle has been gradually developing over a number of years, and dietary patterns—like exercise patterns—are difficult to change. Thus, the best approach to diet modification is via the gradual adoption of wise dietary habits. By slowly adding improved food selections to your present diet plan, you will eventually find that your diet more closely approximates the Basic Four pattern and incorporates more of the dietary guidelines. Remember: Ordinary Mortals need not strive for perfection, just self-improvement!

In order to shop wisely, plan your menus ahead of time and make a shopping list—then, try not to fall for the lures of appealing advertisements and tempting displays by procuring only the preplanned healthful and affordable foodstuffs. By reading food labels carefully, you can evaluate the ingredients, nutrient information, freshness, and cost. Watch out for misleading terminology such as "natural," "organic," "light," or "diet" which is often meaningless but usually indicative of inflated prices. No need to "race" through food shopping sojourns, since careful selection can ensure nutritious and delicious menus for future eating enjoyment.

Dining-out situations—such as restaurant meals, eating at work or school, and social functions—only present problems for those who fail to eat moderately and/or to choose foods wisely. Even fast-food fare can provide nutrients as well as eating enjoyment for those who limit portions and make choices carefully. Salad bars are currently available in many restaurants, while lean-meat selections, fruit juices, low-fat milk, and even whole-grain breads can also be found. By using some nutrition know-how in every dining situation, dietary balance can easily be maintained. For triathlon trainees consuming increased calories, occasional indulgences will not ordinarily result in dietary devastation or loss of weight control.

KEEPING WEIGHT IN CONTROL . . .

Are you overweight and overfat? Underweight but overfat? Or within a reasonable weight range but with a more-than-adequate body fat content? Perhaps, like many Americans and an increasing number of athletes, you are merely overconcerned about your body weight status. Although optimal athletic performance does depend on a high proportion of muscle to fat, it can prove unhealthy to become obsessed with weight and fat percentages. After all, performance is a far better indicator of fitness than body fat levels. For both training and dietary intake, the key to success and health for Orindary Mortals is moderation.

Body fat serves as a storage form of energy, insulation from cold, and protection from injury. Fat is inactive, while well-developed muscles are active—contracting and relaxing efficiently to power the body's movements. Excess fat is extra weight to be carried around, causing increased work for over-fat individuals. Obviously, it is wisest to maintain fat stores which are adequate to meet bodily needs but not excessive, causing extra work and hampering athletic ability.

In order to estimate your own reasonable weight range and desirable body fat percentage, use the body-build charts at the end of the chapter. Then weigh yourself—on a doctor's scale or reliable home digital mode—and have your body fat measured. A visit to a local sports-medicine clinic, registered dietitian, or professional nutritionist can provide you with a caliper reading of your body fat stores; the more time-consuming and cumbersome method of "hydrostatic" (underwater) body weighing is utilized at a number of universities and human-performance laboratories.

For at-home body fat estimation, use the following general assessment techniques:

1) Midriff-Bulge Test—Use a tape measure to compare your chest / bust line to your waistline. Is the former smaller than the latter?
2) Pinch-an-Inch Test—Pinch the skin on the back of your upper arm halfway between the shoulder and elbow, pulling the skin away from the muscle. Is the distance between the pinching fin-

gers greater than an inch? Repeat this test by pinching your side
in the rib area, 1–2 inches above your waist.
3) Mirror Test—Examine your naked body in a full-length mirror.
   Are there any areas of flab requiring toning? Jog in place: does
   anything jiggle?
4) Is your body weight and/or fat percentage more than 10% above
   the levels given in the body-build charts at the end of the chapter?

If your answers were affirmative in each of the above tests,
you are probably overfat. If you are significantly overfat, your
athletic skills may be markedly improved with a simultane-
ous increase in muscle tissue and reduction in body-fat stores.

Crash Diet Losses

Which of the methods below would you be most apt to select
(or have you elected to follow in the past) in attempting to
lose excess body fat:

1) High protein, low carbohydrate diet (e.g., Dr. Stillman's, Dr.
   Atkins's, Scarsdale, etc.)
2) Liquid-protein diet sold door-to-door or in pharmacies (e.g.,
   Cambridge Diet Plan, Last Chance Diet, Herbalife, etc.)
3) Fasting
4) "Crash" or "quickie" diet provided by paperback books or in
   "health-food" stores
5) Diet clinic (e.g., Weight-Loss Clinic, Nutri / System, etc.)
6) Nutrition counseling with a registered dietitian or professional
   nutritionist
7) Eating less and exercising more

Except for the last two methods, adherence to any of the
above will only achieve temporary results at best, causing
dehydration, fatigue, loss of lean tissue including muscles, and
decreased performance skills. Weight is rapidly regained once

such unbalanced "crash" diets are forsaken, with an increase in body fat stores replacing muscle tissue losses. Thus, ex-dieters actually become fatter by attempting to short-cut nature with "quickie" weight loss regimes.

The two recommended weight loss methods, however, can be successful means for achieving safe and permanent weight control. Professional diet counseling encourages the lifestyle adjustments of eating less food (but maintaining a well-balanced diet) and becoming physically active in order to gradually deplete body fat stores as muscles are simultane-ously toned and strengthened.

Reduced caloric intake coupled with daily physical activity results in the breakdown of body-fat stores to supply needed energy. Thus, excess fat is gradually depleted from the stor-age depots throughout the body. Despite popular claims, "spot reducing" is impossible. As weight is lost, fat for energy is derived from all over the body, not just from trouble spots such as hips, midriff, thighs, and buttocks. Specific exercises, however, *can* help to tone the muscles in these problem regions, as the caloric restriction / physical activity reduces the total amount of body fat.

Regular exercise can regulate appetite, burn up calories, and increase metabolism so that the body runs at an elevated rate. Following strenuous exercise, appetite is usually dimin-ished, possibly due to an increase in body temperature and / or an elevated level of appetite-suppressing hormones. Physi-cally fit individuals also tend to display an elevated degree of "dietary-induced thermogenesis," that is, the rate and dura-tion of their postmealtime digestive processes are more exten-sive than those of their sedentary peers. Also, exercise appears to exert a fat-mobilizing effect which persists for a significant time period following physical activity, increasing the body's working rate by 25% or more for 4–24 hours (depending on the intensity and duration of the specific activity and the indi-vidual level of fitness of the participant). Thus, exercise itself not only utilizes calories, but the overall metabolism of an active person uses more calories—after meals, and even when the body is at rest.

Since muscles are active, these tissues use more calories than inactive body fat stores, so an increased proportion of energy-burning muscle to the heat-conserving fat results in an elevated caloric expenditure. By increasing activity, lean tissue is conserved, even increased while fat is lost; with low-calorie intakes without physical activity, ⅓–½ of any weight lost is lean tissue, only to be replaced by more fat once the low-calorie diet is abandoned. Obviously, the key to weight control lies in eating a bit less and exercising a lot more. NOTE: A caloric intake below 1000 for women and 1200 for men is apt to be nutritionally inadequate and can be maintained only temporarily. Over 95% of all Ordinary Mortals who attempt to lose weight with "crash" diets are doomed to failure in their attempts. And for triathletes in training, such arduous and unbalanced weight loss endeavors can cause extraordinary physical and psychological problems.

Disordered Eating

Take a careful look at your body-build test answers (under "Keeping Weight in Control," earlier): If you answered only yes in the mirror test, your body image may be distorted, that is, you may be viewing yourself as "fat" when your actual build is acceptable, or thin, or even too thin. In severe cases, victims of such disordered thinking starve themselves into a state of emaciation, malnutrition, and serious illness while continuing to live under the illusion that they are excessively fat. Anorexia nervosa, as the syndrome is now known, is one type of eating disorder in the overall spectrum to which athletes seem highly predisposed.

For the Ordinary Mortal in training for a triathlon, moderation rather than obsessive-compulsive behavior will enhance performance. Rigid and restrictive diet patterns—just like excessively demanding training schedules—are neither healthy nor enjoyable. And the results can be deadly. If you think your eating / exercise behaviors border on or have become disordered, you should be aware that, if left untreated, the damage may be permanent. The wise Ordinary Mortal will choose a sensible training schedule and a sound, well-balanced diet plan to guarantee physical and emotional health as well as optimal performance. If you are either too thin or too fat and cannot remedy the situation easily on your own, consult a registered dietitian or knowledgeable physician.

THE TRIATHLON TRAINING TABLE . . .

You may be an Ordinary Mortal who is eagerly reading this chapter in hopes of discovering a dietary miracle to provide the ever-elusive "competitive edge," that special something one can simply swallow in order to guarantee outstanding sports performance. Unfortunately, such unrealistic expectations only lead to the purchase of diet gimmicks and useless food fads. "Health" products now constitute a multibillion-dollar business—and are only to the advantage of those doing the marketing.

Just as there is no fountain of youth but only realistic lifestyle patterns that can truly support health and longevity, a secret dietary formula for superathletic prowess has yet to be found. Claims to the contrary are just misleading sales hype. However, there *are* specific dietary guidelines which can help to ensure optimal nutrition, good overall health, and satisfactory athletic performance. With a bit of nutrition know-how, Ordinary Mortals can learn to set their own triathlon training tables with delicious, nutritious, and energy-enhancing foodstuffs.

Diet Myths

Although a well-balanced and nutritionally adequate diet is essential for optimal performance, all of the required ingredients can be obtained simply by eating a wide variety of foods from each of the Basic Four food groups. An adequate diet is not improved with supplementation, and an inadequate diet cannot be redeemed by supplementation. There are no super-foods or special nutrient supplements which can override poor dietary intake or directly improve performance. Such dietary fads are a waste of money at best, while some can damage health and diminish performance.

Yet, despite the absence of any supportive evidence, claims based on nutrition myth-information are constantly circulating amongst athletes in training who are willing to believe nearly anything in the search for new tactics for self-improvement. Some of the various dietary claims are derived from the ancient tales of our ancestral athletes and others are touted by the misinformed but successful athletes who are in competition today. The majority of sports-nutrition myth-information, however, emanates from the misleading advertisements and sensationalism promulgated by the media. No wonder the Ordinary Mortal suffers from so many dietary dilemmas!

A close look at the facts behind some of the common diet myths shared by many of today's athletes can help to enlighten you and may protect your health and performance. For each of the statements which follow, indicate whether you believe it to be factual or mythical. Once you understand the facts behind your own diet myths, you can then alter them in order to improve your nutritional status and triathlon training.

FACT   MYTH

_____   _____   1. Vegetarian athletes find it more difficult to build muscles than their meat-eating peers.

_____   _____   2. Honey is a good source of quick energy for athletes.

FACT	MYTH	
———	———	3. Drinking milk before training bouts causes "cotton mouth."
———	———	4. Allergies to common foods are quite common and often impair athletic performance.
———	———	5. Drinking water during athletic events can cause stomach cramps.
———	———	6. Salt tablets are advisable after heavy workouts in hot weather.
———	———	7. Beer is a good choice for fluid replacement following vigorous physical activity.
———	———	8. Caffeine intake may aid performance in endurance events.
———	———	9. It is safer and equally effective to carbohydrate load without first depleting muscle stores (via adherence to a low-carbohydrate diet).
———	———	10. Carbohydrate loading is only effective in preparing for endurance events.
———	———	11. Steak and eggs, buttered toast, and tea with milk is *not* a good menu for a preevent meal.
———	———	12. Pasta with vegetable sauce, tossed salad, fresh fruit, low-fat milk and oatmeal cookies *is* a good menu for a postevent meal.

Diet Facts

Contrary to popular belief, eating large amounts of protein will not assist in muscle building. Only heavy muscular workouts can stimulate muscle growth and increase muscular strength. High intensity exercise—plus proper rest and an adequate diet—will produce the desired results. In order to gain muscle weight extra calories are needed, but most protein sources are too costly to use for that purpose. Since building muscles occurs with training and does not necessitate the intake of extra protein, vegetarians who follow well-balanced diets can certainly excel in a variety of sports.

Although there is no need to completely avoid eating meat, overall health and performance *can* be enhanced with a low-fat diet which emphasizes carbohydrate-rich foodstuffs.

The "complex" (starchy) carbohydrates provide athletes with the most nutrients (and fiber) in addition to fuel for energy stores. Ingestion of "simple" carbohydrates (sugars) just prior to athletic activity does not aid performance. The energy for athletic activity is mainly provided by the muscle fuel stores which have been built up by the meals eaten during the *weeks* before the event, not from any food intake *hours* (or minutes) beforehand.

Often eaten for "quick energy" purposes, honey (or other concentrated sugars and sweets) actually have the opposite result, acting to reduce blood-sugar levels and cause the symptoms of "hypoglycemia" (i.e., fatigue, lightheadedness, shakiness, poor coordination). By drawing fluid into the gastrointestinal tract for dilution purposes, concentrated sweets taken before exercise can also cause stomach upset. However, exercise which lasts for 3 hours or more can itself cause hypoglycemia, although this is uncommon in well-trained individuals. Dilute sugar drinks (2.5% sugar in cold water) will not upset the stomach, but can take 2–3 hours to reach the working muscles, so can be consumed early in an endurance event by those prone to activity-induced hypoglycemia.

Although drinking milk just before exercising is not advisable as it, too, may cause some stomach distress, there is no need to avoid milk altogether during training. A combination of stress and anxiety with dehydration can cause "cotton mouth," whereas low-fat milk contributes calcium and other essential nutrients to the diet.

Milk intolerance (actually "lactose intolerance," inability to properly digest the milk sugar, lactose) is not an allergy per se, but does commonly afflict American adults. Drinking small amounts of milk with meals and substituting fermented milk products such as yogurt can provide the essential nutrients with a minimum of side effects. And special products (e.g., Lact-Aid, Sweet Acidophilus milk) are now marketed to lactose-intolerant milk drinkers. True food "allergies," however, are relatively rare, usually appearing during childhood and often outgrown. Special "elimination" diets and expensive foods allergy tests are merely another "health" gimmick currently promoted to athletes as a method for improving performance. The restrictive "allergy" diets, however, are often unbalanced and can actually impair athletic performance due to energy / nutrient inadequacies.

Hydration

Perhaps even more important for athletes than the food they eat is the fluid they drink. Inadequate fluid before, during, or after physical activity can significantly hamper performance, leading to dehydration and muscle cramps. It is important to consume a glass of cold water prior to physical activity, to continue to drink about ½ cup every 10–15 minutes during the event—this does *not* cause stomach cramps, contrary to popular myth—and to fully replace fluid losses afterward. Since the feeling of thirst is not an accurate indicator of total fluid needs, it is important to drink enough water to quench thirst— and then some. After exercise, we tend to replace only ⅔ of our actual fluid needs. Cold water helps to cool the body and is emptied rapidly from the stomach.

Stomach cramps *can* occur, however, if salt tablets are taken. These tablets also make users more prone to heatstroke due to the dehydration effects. A simple shake of the salt shaker at the dinner table will easily replace the body's sodium (salt) losses from the exercise-induced perspiration. And since most Americans tend to consume salt in amounts 10 or more times that required by the body, sweat losses of sodium are usually inconsequential.

Despite the appealing advertising claims for "electrolyte

replacement drinks" developed specifically for thirsty athletes, typical losses (of potassium, calcium, chloride, magnesium, phosphorus, and sulphur) are insignificant and—like the slightly more significant losses of sodium—are easily replaced during postexercise meals. Some of these drinks are relatively high in sugar content (which can cause gastric upset and low blood sugar if consumed just before or during exercise), and all are significantly more expensive than the best replacement drink: cold water. Beer is not a wise fluid replacement choice either, since alcohol actually causes dehydration rather than the desired rehydration.

Ergogenic Aids

Ergogenic aids are substances which are work producing. Such aids can be mechanical (e.g., massage), psychological (e.g., music or hypnosis), pharmacologic (drugs, including steroids), and nutritional. There are numerous dietary "aids" marketed for performance enhancement, including such items as bee pollen, brewer's yeast, fructose, garlic, ginseng, honey, S.O.D. (superoxide dismutase), spirulina, vitamin E and derivatives (wheat-germ oil, evening primrose oil), and raw eggs. These items are generally ineffective and some can be harmful.

There are a few effective ergogenic aids which can maximize performance by enhancing energy production / availability, decreasing fatigue, and / or helping in the maintenance of optimal body weight. Use of ergogenic aids cannot, however, overcome inadequate diet and training. Caffeine may prove to be an ergogenic aid for endurance events. Although it can dehydrate the body by inducing a diuretic effect, a moderate amount of caffeine (e.g., 4–5 mg/kg body weight or 1–2 cups of regular-to-strong coffee) taken 1 hour prior to participation in an endurance event appears to aid in work performance. Research is still under way, however, and caffeine-sensitive individuals will suffer physical side effects (e.g., nausea, rapid heartbeat, gastrointestinal upset, nervousness) which can offset any potential benefits from use of this product.

Loading Up

A more popular means for enhancing exercise endurance in long-distance events is by use of the method known as "carbohydrate loading." Devised by Scandinavian researchers in the late 1960s, the original method entailed a 7-day regimen which began with a "depletion" phase (exhaustive exercise for a day, then 3 days of low-carbohydrate eating to reduce the muscle glycogen stores), followed by 3 days of a high-carbohydrate diet. It was believed that the depleted muscles would soak up carbohydrates more rapidly than normal for conversion into glycogen, thus boosting glycogen stores to provide the extra energy needed in endurance events to avoid "hitting the wall." Most trained athletes store enough glycogen to support at least an hour of exercise. When the stored glycogen is used up with the muscular demands, the body's other principal energy source—fat—is called into play. However, fat cannot be broken down to meet energy needs very quickly. Muscles may begin to stiffen and become unable to work efficiently. Damage to muscle tissues can then occur. Carbohydrate loading, however, can double (perhaps triple) glycogen stores to significantly enhance endurance and thus prevent the "wall hitting" which competitors so dread.

To deplete muscle glycogen, a training run of 15–20 miles, or several hours of either swimming or bicycling is required. The accompanying depletion diet should be high in protein and fat, but low in energy-promoting carbohydrates. Fortunately, recent research indicates that there is no need to include the depletion stage, which is uncomfortable and unhealthful—initially causing low blood sugar and fatigue, followed by the bloatedness of water weight gain with the potential for long-term, unknown health consequences, as well as known dangers for those individuals prone to diabetes, heart disease, and other ills. There is actually little advantage to be gained from the depletion phase, and the desired benefits can accrue simply with the adoption of a high-carbohydrate regime for the 3 days prior to an endurance event. In practical terms, this means adhering to the normal (well-balanced) diet, but adding in more carbohydrate-rich foodstuffs—such as breads, cereals, pastas, legumes, fruits and vegetables—for the 3 days preceeding a triathalon. Thus, the normal dietary intake of 50%–60% of total calories as carbohydrate should be increased to 70%–80% for these 3 days. Resting up during the week preceeding the event—that is, tapering activity levels as recommended in the TFOMTP—produces additional benefits.

Many athletes are under the illusion that carbohydrate-loading is beneficial for all sports, but this dietary practice can only yield results with endurance (that is, 1½–2 + -hour) events. Also worthy of note is that athletes are often mistakenly *fat*-loading instead of loading up with carbohydrates: greasy fried foods, high-fat meat or cheese dishes, ice-cream concoctions, and fatty desserts should be replaced with whole grains, low-fat milk products, various fruits, and vegetable dishes. The menus below illustrate carbohydrate-loading versus undesirable fat-loading:

FAT-LOADING MENUS

Pizza with extra cheese and pepperoni
Spaghetti with meat balls
French fries, potato skins, or baked potatoes (loaded with butter, sour cream, cheese, or bacon)
Garlic bread (soaked with butter)
Tossed salad with croutons and creamy dressing

Ice-cream sundae
Carrot cake with cream-cheese frosting
Potato chips
Beers (no fat, but alcohol contributes much of the calories)

CARBOHYDRATE-LOADING CHOICES

Pizza with low-fat mozzarella cheese
Spaghetti with vegetable sauce
Baked potato (with low-fat yogurt and sprinkled with herbs)
Whole-wheat rolls (without butter)
Steamed mixed vegetables with lemon
Baked apple with dollop (small) of ice cream
Angelfood cake with fresh strawberries
Popcorn, unbuttered
Fruit or vegetable juice, skim milk, or—okay, okay—a glass of ale
   (high carbohydrate) or "light" (low-calorie) beer

Preevent Eating

As in the preevent carbohydrate loading process, the preevent
meal itself should emphasize "complex" (starchy) carbohydrates. Eaten around 3 hours prior to the event, this meal
should be light, relatively low in protein and quite low in fat,
and nonirritating to the individual's digestive system. The meal
should also be psychologically appealing.

The food eaten during the preevent meal only contributes
energy for the physical activity which is ongoing after the first
45 minutes of exercise. A meal rich in rapidly digested and
absorbed carbohydrates, therefore, may prove to be advan-
tageous. Fats and proteins, however, are digested so slowly
they cannot contribute to immediate performance. In fact,
preevent meals which are high in protein and/or fat can actually
hamper performance by causing gastric distress and fatigue

due to competition between the stomach and the muscles for the body's blood supply. Dehydration may occur with a high-protein intake since protein metabolism can strain the body's temperature-regulating abilities and cause excessive fluid losses in flushing out the proteinous waste products.

Most of the carbohydrate foods included in preevent meals should be rich in starch rather than high in sugar content. Too much bulk and fiber, however, can cause uncomfortable bloating and may induce an ill-timed laxative effect. Unfamiliar carbohydrates should be avoided in favor of those foods which can serve as psychological palate pleasers. Eating strange new foods at a time of intense anxiety—such as before a triathalon—may hamper performance.

The classic steak-and-eggs preevent meal is only of benefit to the restaurant owner who serves it! Pretriathlon menus of benefit to Ordinary Mortals should resemble the following samples:

BREAKFAST

Fruit juice
Shredded, puffed, or flaked cereal with sliced banana and low-fat milk
Whole-wheat English muffin with
margarine or jam (lightly spread)
Coffee or tea with low-fat milk

LUNCH

Fruit juice
Turkey, cheese, chicken, or tuna sandwich
(thick bread, thin spread!)
Raw vegetable sticks
Low-fat milk
Oatmeal or peanut-butter cookies

SNACK(S)

Banana bread, date-nut bread, or bran muffin, with low-fat milk
Low-fat yogurt with fresh fruit
Celery stuffed with low-fat cottage cheese

Whole-grain toast with peanut
butter (lightly spread) and fruit
juice

During a marathon-equivalent triathlon event, only fluids
need to be replaced, and cold water—with small amounts of
sugar (1–2 grams / 100 milliliters) for those prone to activity-
induced hypoglycemia—should meet the body's needs.

After the event, the muscle glycogen needs to be restored.
The first 4 hours constitutes an important period of recovery,
a time during which the fluid and carbohydrate losses should
be replaced. A high-protein, high-fat diet will not produce
complete glycogen replacement in the depleted muscles.
Nutrient-rich "complex" carbohydrates should be empha-
sized in the postevent diet for a period of several days which,
when coupled with proper rest, will result in refueled muscles, revamped energy levels and an overall feeling of good
health.

EAT WELL TO TRIATHLON WELL . . .

Now that you have a basic understanding of the rudiments
of no-nonsense nutrition and the dietary needs of the triathloner in training, it should be quite simple to integrate these
food facts into your own lifestyle patterns. The essential dietary factors for you to remember to include in your
triathlon-training eating plan are:

Eat a well-BALANCED diet based on a wide VARIETY of foods from
  each of the BASIC FOUR food groups.
The optimal dietary balance for training includes 50%–60% carbohydrates, 12%–15% protein, and 25%–30% fat, mostly in

the unsaturated forms. Emphasize "complex" CARBOHYDRATES such as fruits, vegetables, legumes, and whole-grain products, and select LOW-FAT sources of PROTEIN such as lean meats, poultry, and fish, legumes, and low-fat milk products.

Control portion sizes to keep body weight within a REASONABLE weight range: Eat sensibly and exercise regularly to stay fit not fat, but be careful to avoid unhealthfully obsessive-compulsive diet / exercise regimens.

Be sure to consume adequate fluids before and during training, and to reHYDRATE beyond simply quenching thirst following strenuous exercise.

There is no need to deplete prior to CARBOHYDRATE-LOADING during the week before an event, and the preevent meal should be light, low in fat and bulk, and psychologically pleasing; emphasis on "complex" carbohydrates in the postevent meals will gradually replenish depleted fuel stores.

There are no magic elixirs, superfoods, or special dietary supplements which can improve athletic performance. Avoid the financial (and health) drains of food fads and fitness frauds in favor of a SENSIBLE diet plan and a careful training schedule.

Food is not only a source of fuel, but provides eating enjoyment as well. Food is for fitness—and FUN!

By completing the EATTTT log occasionally in order to examine your dietary habits, you may uncover specific eating patterns which are not conducive to good health and optimal performance. With the nutrition basics in mind, you may then want to alter your diet in order to enhance your training. It is surprising how beneficial some simple dietary changes can prove to be for those in training—and in competition. Although food is not magic and diet is not the only training factor, optimal nutrition can lead to optimal performance . . . even for the Ordinary Mortal.

FURTHER READING . . .

The following references can provide interested readers with additional information on eating well for optimal athletic performance:

The American Alliance for Health, Physical Education, and Recreation. *Nutrition for Athletes: A Handbook for Coaches*. 1201 Sixteenth Street, NW, Washington , D.C., 1971. (An old standby with easy-to-read information on dietary balance, food and energy, eating for athletic events, and diet myths.)

N. Bayrd, and C. Quilter. *Food for Champions*. New York: Pocket Books, 1983. (A helpful paperback with common-sense nutrition information backed by scientific facts.)

Haskell, Scala, and Whittam (eds.). *Nutrition and Athletic Performance*. Palo Alto, California: Bull Publishing Co., 1982. (The proceedings of the 1981 Conference on Nutritional Determinants in Athletic Performance, with good discussions on substrate utilization, hydration, body composition, and sports anemia.)

National Dairy Council. *A Guide to Food, Exercise & Nutrition for You*. (Two informative booklets—one for females, one for males—on teenage dieting for health and athletic ability; much practical information in an appealing format.) *Food Power: A Coach's Guide to Improving Performance*. (An informative package with nutrition guidelines for specific sports including running, jogging, bicycling, and swimming; although aimed at high school coaches, diet guidance is readable and sound.) 6300 North River Road, Rosemont, Illinois.

M. *Williams (ed.). Ergogenic Aids in Sport*. Champaign, Illinois: Human Kinetics Publishers, 1983. (A text on the practical and health aspects of increasing energy / stamina via nutrition, drugs, oxygen / blood doping, hypnosis, and other techniques.)

These texts have more in-depth information on the topic of general sports nutrition for students, coaches, and studious athletes:

P. Eisenman and D. Johnson. *Coaches' Guide to Nutrition & Weight Control.* Champaign, Illinois: Human Kinetics Publishers, 1982.
F. Katch and W. McArdle. *Nutrition, Weight Control, and Exercise, 2nd Edition.* Philadelphia: Lea & Febiger, 1983.
M. Williams. *Nutrition for Fitness and Sport.* Dubuque, Iowa: William C. Brown Company Publishers, 1983.

These books provide general nutrition guidance including nutrient/caloric information and specific food values:

Virginia Aronson. *Thirty Days to Better Nutrition.* New York: Doubleday & Co., Inc., 1984.
C. Marshall. *Vitamins and Minerals: Help or Harm?* Philadelphia: George F. Stickley Co., 1983.
U.S. Department of Agriculture. *Nutritive Value of American Foods in Common Units.* Handbook 456, Superintendent of Documents, U.S. Government Printing Office, Washington, D.C., 20402.
J. Stern, and R. Denenberg. *The Fast Food Diet.* Englewood Cliffs, New Jersey: Prentice-Hall, Inc., 1980.

The following newsletters can also provide accurate sports-nutrition and general diet information for health-conscious athletes:

Environmental Nutrition. 52 Riverside Drive, Suite 15A, New York, New York 10024.
Sports Nutrition News. P.O. Box 986, Evanston, Illinois 60204.
The First Aider. Cramer Products, Inc.. P.O. Box 1001, Gardner, Kansas 66030.
Nutrition Forum. The George F. Stickley Publishing Co. 210 West Washington Square, Philadelphia, Pennsylvania 19105.

EATTT LOG...

The Eating at The Triathlon Training Table log can be used to record your daily food intakes on an occasional basis in order to follow your progress and pinpoint areas requiring attention. You might want to keep track of your eating activities for several days just prior to your first triathalon, during the day of the event, and for a day or two afterward. Then, try this again for your next event to see if your diet and performance can both be improved.

In the EATTT log below, list everything you eat and drink: be sure to record your intake immediately after consumption in order to be as accurate as possible. Try to estimate portion sizes and, for mixed dishes, record the probable constituents of such foodstuffs (e.g., broccoli with cheese sauce = vegetable + milk + other foods—fats). At the end of each day, determine the number of servings per meal / snack which you included from each group of the Basic Four, and total the day's number of servings: Are you missing out on any particular food group(s)? Is your diet repetitive and unvaried? Are you concentrating too many of your calories in the other-foods group? Is your total food intake too high? Or too low?

By occasionally keeping track of your eating habits for a period of several days, you may note individual dietary patterns which need to be altered in order to improve your nutritional status. Changes in body weight can also be attributed to specific dietary indulgences or lapses. Thus, your EATTT log should become a helpful health tool which you can use regularly to examine your nutritional intakes and adjust your diet as indicated. Any Ordinary Mortal can do it!

EATTTT Log

Day: Date, Time, Meal/Snack	Food and Amount	Basic Four: Number of Servings				Other Foods		
		Fruit & Vegetable Group	Grain Group	Milk & Cheese Group	Meat & Alternates Group	Fats	Sweets	Alcohol

Day's Total Number of Servings

BODY-BUILD CHARTS

Desirable Weights for Men and Women of Age 25 and Over

Height (in Shoes)	Weight in Pounds (in Indoor Clothing)		
	Small Frame	Medium Frame	Large Frame
Men 5' 2"	112–120	118–129	126–141
3"	115–123	121–133	129–144
4"	118–126	124–136	132–148
5"	121–129	127–139	135–152
6"	124–133	130–143	138–156
7"	128–137	134–147	142–161
8"	132–141	138–152	147–166
9"	136–145	142–156	151–170
10"	140–150	146–160	155–174
11"	144–154	150–165	159–179
6' 0"	148–158	154–170	164–184
1"	152–162	158–175	168–189
2"	156–167	162–180	173–194
3"	160–171	167–185	178–199
4"	164–175	172–190	182–204
4'10"	92– 98	96–107	104–119
11"	94–101	98–110	106–122
5' 0"	96–104	101–113	109–125
1"	99–107	104–116	112–128
2"	102–110	107–119	115–131
3"	105–113	110–122	118–134
4"	108–116	113–126	121–138
Women 5"	111–119	116–130	125–142
6"	114–123	120–135	129–146
7"	118–127	124–139	133–150
8"	122–131	128–143	137–154
9"	126–135	132–147	141–158
10"	130–140	136–151	145–163
11"	134–144	140–155	149–168
6' 0"	138–148	144–159	153–173

(Source: Metropolitan Life Insurance Company. Data are based on weights associated with lowest death rates. To obtain weight for adults younger than 25, subtract one pound for each year under 25.)

Net Energy Expenditure per Hour for Horizontal Running*

Body Weight kg	lbs	km.hr.*	8	9	10	11	12	13	14	15	16
		mph	4.97	5.60	6.20	6.84	7.46	8.08	8.70	9.32	9.94
		minutes per mile	12:00	10:43	9:41	8:46	8:02	7:26	6:54	6:26	6:02
		kcal per mile									
50	110	80	400	450	500	550	600	650	700	750	800
54	119	86	432	486	540	594	648	702	756	810	864
58	128	93	464	522	580	638	696	754	812	870	928
62	137	99	496	558	620	682	744	806	868	930	992
66	146	106	528	594	660	726	792	858	924	990	1056
70	154	112	560	630	700	770	840	910	980	1050	1120
74	163	118	592	666	740	814	888	962	1036	1110	1184
78	172	125	624	702	780	858	936	1014	1092	1170	1248
82	181	131	656	738	820	902	984	1066	1148	1230	1312
86	190	138	688	774	860	946	1032	1118	1204	1290	1376
90	199	144	720	810	900	990	1080	1170	1260	1350	1440
94	207	150	752	846	940	1034	1128	1222	1316	1410	1504
98	216	157	784	882	980	1078	1176	1274	1372	1470	1568
102	225	163	816	918	1020	1122	1224	1326	1428	1530	1632
106	234	170	848	954	1060	1166	1272	1378	1484	1590	1696

*The table is interpreted as follows: For a 50 kg person, the net expenditure for running for 1 hour at 8 km.hr.[1] or 4.97 mph is 400 kcal. This speed represents a 12-minute-per-mile pace. Thus, in 1 hour 5 miles would be run and 400 kcal would be expended. If the pace was increased to 12 km.hr.[1], 600 kcal would be expended during the hour of running.

**Running speeds are expressed as kilometers per hour (km.hr.[1]), miles per hour (mph), and minutes required to complete each mile (minutes per mile). The values in boldface type are the net calories expended to run 1 mile for a given body weight, independent of running speed.

From William McArdle, et al, *Exercise Physiology: Energy, Nutrition and Human Performance*, Philadelphia: Lea and Febiger, 1981.

Body-Fat Percentages

Athletes		Nonathletes		
Male	Female	Male	Female	
6	12	12	22	Lean
7–15	13–23	13–21	23–28	Acceptable
15 +	23 +	21 +	28 +	Overweight
10–12	18–20	13–15	23–25	Ideal

10 ... The Race

I felt so good when I crossed the finish line. People who saw me on TV thought I was spaced out. ... All I did was go beyond [my previous] limit.

Julie Moss,
after the February 1982 Hawaii Ironman Triathlon

INTRODUCTION ...

You have completed your training. You have become aerobically fit. You have learned how to run, bike, and swim. You have accumulated the various bits and pieces of equipment that you need for triathloning. You are eating properly, you may have lost some weight, and you have certainly redistributed some of your body mass. You have taken proper concern to check your overall health, steps to prevent injury, and care if you have become injured. You have chosen a suitable triathlon, entered it, and received your entry confirmation and race instructions. You have made your travel plans and accommodation arrangements. You are ready to achieve the goal that you have been pointing towards all of these months: completion of your first triathlon.

Doing your first triathlon is an experience that is unique. It cannot be duplicated. There can never be another first time for you in this sport. If you are like most of the rest of us you will be nervous for up to several days before the race. You will be wondering if you really will be able to do it. Will you make it through the swim? Will you be able to ride your bike up all the hills? Will you be able to finish the run without walking or indeed will you be able to finish all? Will the pain level be tolerable? Has all the time and energy that you put into training really been worth it?

The answer to all these questions is yes. If you have done the training program, not necessarily to the minute, but necessarily following the basic principles, yes you will finish, happily and healthily. The principles first and foremost and the training program itself will enable you to achieve your goal. And you will be in for one of the great experiences of your life: the exhilaration, the high, the feelings of self-worth, self-esteem, and accomplishment that come with the achievement of that goal. The feelings are magnificent, worth every step of your training program.

On the specifics, will you make it through the swim? Yes you will, for several reasons. The swim almost always comes first, for good reason. Of the three sports, it is potentially the most dangerous one. But since it is first, you and all the other triathletes are at your freshest. You have been training to be able to exercise aerobically for up to 5 hours straight. You will certainly have plenty of energy in storage to enable you to finish the swim, even if you run into trouble later on in the race.

Furthermore, the race organizers are just as interested in safety as the competitors are. You will be required to wear a brightly colored swim cap. You can expect the course to be well marked and well monitored. There will be people on a variety of small boats watching you all along the course. In many races, you will be told that resting in the water while holding onto a boat monitor is permitted, as long as you do not try to move forward. If you have any fear at all, just make sure that you don't try to go too fast. If you do run out of breath, just turn over on your back for a blow.

Will you have to walk your bike up the hills? You should
have become used to your bike, know how to shift, and be
able to maintain a proper cadence by selecting the correct
gears. With the training you have had, you will do just fine
on any hills you will find on a triathlon course. The key to
successful long-distance cycling is riding in a gear that is low
enough to permit you to pedal at 80 rpm or more regardless
of incline. This will prevent kneestrain and early energy
exhaustion. You will be okay.

Will you have to walk in the run? I always recommend a
2–4-minute planned, vigorous, purposeful walk at the beginning of the run in order to aid the bike-run transition which
can be wobbly, awkward, and disconcerting. A second planned
2-minute walk at around the 12-minute mark can also be
very helpful in completing the transition and really getting
your legs stretched out. Other than that, you will only end up
walking later on in the run because you can't run anymore
and must walk, if you have not paced yourself and have gone
out too fast. If based on your training paces you have accu-
rately estimated the race paces of which you are capable and
have stuck to then, you will be just fine. If you find that you
have a lot left with a mile or two to go, great. You can pick
it up then, pass some faltering folks in front of you, finish
strong, and feel like even more of a hero than you will be just
for finishing.

How much will it hurt? It will hurt. You cannot do long-
distance aerobic events and expect not to hurt unless you are
a very unusual person. However, it should hurt no more than
training did, even though you are going further. It is conceivable that with your adrenalin level up, as it will be during the
race, you will hurt less than you did in training—again as
long as you don't try to overdo it and go too fast. In any case,
if you do get pain the memory of it will fade very quickly
after you finish. You will remember the race, but not the
hurting. I do hurt during races, but within a day or two while

I remember the course, water stops, race anecdotes, and the weather, I have forgotten the specifics of any pain that I did suffer, in the golden glow of accomplishment.

You must continue to keep your objectives in mind: to finish, to have fun, and to feel good. As I noted in Chapter 1, at a meeting of the Big Apple Triathlon Club in New York City on June 6, 1984, Dave Horning, elite triathlete and race organizer, was talking about the 1984 Liberty to Liberty Triathlon. (This one requires a 2-mile swim through New York Harbor to the Statue of Liberty, a 90-mile bike ride to the outskirts of Philadelphia and a 10k run to Independence Hall.) He said that his principal goal for the race was for everyone to have a good time doing it. He encouraged the Ordinary Mortals in the audience who would be doing the race to treat the bike ride more like a tour or a rally than a road race. He welcomed the use of support crews. "Stop and have a picnic— enjoy yourselves", he suggested. He pointed out that although triathlons, at least the name races, are won by the elite athletes, the sport would not, and indeed could not exist without the participation of the thousands of us Ordinary Mortals who contribute our sweat—and our entry fees—to it.

In the next section of this chapter, I am going to take you through my own first race with me. Then I am going to share some other thoughts and racing tips with you.

DOING THE 1983 MIGHTY HAMPTONS TRIATHLON[1] . . .

My first triathlon was the 1983 Mighty Hamptons event. Since my name is not Dave or Mark (or Marc) or Scott (first or last), I obviously had no chance to finish at or near the head

1. This description of my first race was first published in part in *The Beast*, in the July and September 1984 issues. It is used with the permission of the publisher.

of the men's division. I was actually 456th out of 489 finishers overall. I was 2 hours and 10 minutes behind the winner. But I was 1 hour and 10 minutes ahead of the last person to finish, and he was younger than me. I did have a race and I did have a good time. Most important to me, by the next day when I had physically recovered, I experienced feelings about myself and my abilities that I had never experienced before. They were worth the whole ballgame.

Most articles that you read in the triathlon publications about races concern the winners and near-winners. And so they should. But people like you and me, who will never win, and will most likely not even ever place in our age class, race too. Our view is just different. It is the view from the back of the pack.

THE NIGHT BEFORE THE RACE. I am all registered. My bike is numbered. I am numbered. I have all the race paraphernalia loaded into the three plastic bags, one each for swim, bike, and run gear, that each entrant is given. I have double-checked, triple-checked the bags and all my stuff to make sure that forgetful-me hasn't forgotten anything, this time. By golly, it's all there, the several varieties of shoes, socks, shorts, shirts, headgear, glasses, gloves, undergarments, and watches that one needs for triathloning. The race numbers are pinned on in the appropriate places. I really am an ATHLETE.

I have eaten well, very well at the carbo-loading dinner. I have felt so good that I have broken all the rules and had a big, rich, gooey hot-fudge sundae from a purveyor of home-made goodies of that sort on Main Street in Sag Harbor, New York, where the race is held. It was wonderful. I worry a little bit about insulin overshoot and reactive hypoglycemia (but in the event I suffer no ill effects). I go to my room and fall comfortably asleep.

THE MORNING OF THE RACE. I arise early, intentionally. I am staying in a guesthouse with a shared bathroom. I am known to be slow in the morning and I don't want to hold everyone else up. Feeling virtuous and considerate, I am out of the bathroom before anyone else awakens. I do not feel tired. My adrenalin level must already be up because I have had less than 7 hours sleep.

I eat my breakfast: pita bread, an apple, a banana, and Gatorade. I check my equipment out once more, hop in the car, and drive over to the race. My bike is already there, having been left in its numbered stall the night before under the watchful eye of the race committee. I am early and get a good parking spot, near the changing area.

I fetch my bike and top off the air in the tires with one of those little 12-volt air pumps. I don't look as much of a real cyclist as do those using their Zefal and Silva hand pumps for topping off, but I do need to save my energy. Anyway, my tires are only 1⅛″ clinchers, not 1″ sew-ups. (But at least I have a 10-speed. One of my fellow age-group members, whom I never did meet but later corresponded with, actually raced on an almost-antique ladies' Raleigh with a 3-speed Sturmey-Archer gear shifter, a full steel chain case, and a wicker basket on the handlebars. Marvelous!) I put my bike back in its place, check my gear once again, and start walking at a leisurely pace to the start of the swim. Although I could have gone over on the bus which was provided, I thought that the walk would be a good way to stretch out and warm up. I was right. I recommend it. (If you do this, be sure to remember to take along a plastic bag to put your footgear and shirt in, and make sure that the race committee will collect the bags and bring them back to the bike / change area.) As I reach the swim area, I am starting to relax.

THE START OF THE SWIM. I have brought Vaseline and start smearing it on. I am really going to do this, I keep telling myself. I go down to test the water, thankful of pleasant temperature. I stand towards the back of the assembled throng. I think about the swim. Based on my (minimal) swim training,

I estimate that my pace will be about 50 minutes per mile. (In the event I do 44. Race psychology is a powerful force.) I take off my shirt and deck shoes, place them in the numbered bag, and put on my goggles, ear plugs, and swim cap. I am ready.

THE SWIM. The gun goes off. The water is suddenly white with splashing and churning swimmers. I walk slowly to the water's edge and wade in. I take seriously the admonition to let the bulk of the traffic get out in front to avoid risking a kick in the face. I look around for an open space, adjust my goggles, and dive in. I am racing.

The swimmer's world is a strangely isolated one. It is not quiet, but the only noise you hear is that of your own breathing and swimming motion. Goggles tend to fog quickly (the following winter I began using an antifog solution, a great idea), so it really becomes you and the water. The beach is on the left and the course is laid out along it. There are big red buoys marking the course and I swim from one to the next. I am in the water swimming for distance for the eighth time in my life, over a 1.5 mile course.

I have convinced myself that I will make it if I just take it easy. And I do. I swim a leisurely crawl. When I need a blow I just turn over and do a comfortable elementary backstroke. In the crawl, I breathe on my right side. Waves happen to be coming in from that side. Being a sailor and knowing something about wave action, I time my stroke so that I will breathe at the top of each wave, Fortunately, the wave pattern fits my swimming pattern.

As I breathe to my right I keep looking for other swimmers, and see none. Well, I think, I thought that I would be at the back and indeed I am. Finally, I look over to my left. It turns out that there is a fairly substantial number of swimmers back there, some of them way back there. Since the lead swimmers seemed to be halfway to the finish line when I entered the water, this turn of events gives my ego a big boost. I pick it up a bit.

The end is now in sight. I will make it. There is a swimmer on my right shoulder, coming up. I am not going to let her by. All of a sudden I am racing, not just finishing. I swim as fast as I can towards the finish line. She does not pass me. I make it. I didn't drown. Indeed I have my best relative finish in the swim of the three events, finishing ahead of nearly 100 people.

I trot up the ramp towards the changing area. I am told to take it easy, I am handed a cup of Gatorade, and I am spritzed down with fresh water courtesy of the local volunteer fire department. Although I don't know what a problem it will turn out to be for me, I am heading for my first really slow segment of the race: the change of clothes from the swim to the bike.

THE FIRST CHANGE. The changes, taken together, turn out to be my slowest events, relatively speaking. I am certain that no one took more time than I did: 23 minutes *in toto*. And in the 1983 Hawaii Ironman, Dave Scott, the winner, spent a total of 90 *seconds* in the change area. Ah well, what can I say?

First, there is the matter of my earplugs. I am using a pair of flat-topped ones and cannot manage to extract the right one with my wet, water-ridged fingers. But standing near my bike is Dave Horning (self-same of the Liberty to Liberty Triathlon), not racing in the Mighty Hamptons due to injury. At the prerace conference the night before Dave had seemed like a very friendly fellow so I tried my luck. Could he help me with my earplug? He comes right over, with a big smile, and seconds later has deposited the offending rubber object in my hand. What a wonderful sport this is. In what other sport does the Ordinary Mortal play on the same field with the best? Not only that, in what other sport is the Ordinary

Mortal able to enlist the personal assistance of the top athlete in solving an equipment problem? A memorable moment. By the way, I now use those little pine-cone shaped earplugs. They work better and are very easy to remove.

Second, my prerace plan included a complete change of outfit for each event. Feeling good about my swim performance, I take a leisurely stroll over the the changing tent. I note in passing that it is not very busy, but that fact doesn't really register with me. I take off my boxer swim trunks (the equivalent in swimming, I find out later, of using a 3-speed bike for the bike race) and put on a complete, fresh bike outfit. I find out later that I am one of very few people to do this. I not only wear socks which not everybody does, but I even change my socks twice, using anklets for the bike and my customary over-the-calf support socks for the run. At any rate, after a leisurely change, which affords me a nice rest and the opportunity to eat a banana, I buckle on my helmet, and take off on the bike leg.

THE BIKE. I am feeling good. It is not yet too hot so the self-generated breeze of a brisk ride is enough to keep me feeling comfortable. The course is a hilly one for the first half, but since I train on hills I am not too uncomfortable on them. By the time I get out on the course, the field is fairly well strung out. I pass an occasional cyclist. In turn, I am passed too. On the whole, this segment is uneventful for me until mile 22 or so of the 25-mile circuit.

I am pedaling at a decent pace across a flat stretch of farmland heading towards what is a fairly steep descent to the end of the bike route. I am overtaken by a petite woman wearing a smart red and black one-piece tri-suit who sings out gaily as she passes me, "I like your form." "What form or which form?" I think to myself. I have not been biking for very long and have had no coaching. She couldn't be referring to my cycling form, could she? Could it be my body? Being more of an A-shape than a V-shape I doubt that. I accelerate a bit and draw even with her. I see that I have been hailed by a delight-ful little woman with muscular legs and sparkling eyes, who looks to be in her mid-50s. Perhaps she was referring to my biking form after all, or perhaps she likes younger men. At any rate I begin talking with her.

We pedal along and engage in some pleasant chit-chat about cycling. She has a very good bike (I do not) and she tells me how she is becoming part of her machine. She has been cycling seriously for 2–3 years. Her experienced cyclist friends have told her that in another 10 she will be pretty good. What are the implications of that statement for me, a rank novice, I wonder. The conversation lapses. Suddenly, she pulls ahead of me. I have been suckered, I think. I accelerate as fast as I can and go charging past her, calling out "You are in a race, madam!" About half-a-minute later a small red and black blur goes screaming by me, just as we begin the descent to the bike finish. I pedal hard, but I do not see her again until the run.

THE SECOND CHANGE. Following the advice of the few triath-lon articles I had read, I start slowing down about half-a-mile from the end and glide comfortably into the changing area. Again, I do a leisurely, complete change from bike to run outfit. My color coordination is perfect, but boy am I slow. How slow is indicated by the reaction of my 10-year-old son who is standing with the rest of my family in the spectator area as I start out on the run. I am thrilled to see them. I run over to say hello, give and get kisses. My boy is waving at me, no, no, don't stop, get out there, you are so far behind! He is right.

I later learn that my wife and kids had arrived in time to see the race winners finish the whole event before I came in from the bike. Then they see me come in from the bike (I do not see them at that point), but see people who are behind me on the bike get out on the run before I do. My boy is very impatient. Dawdling while dressing again, Daddy, just like you do in the morning! I am so slow in the changes that the next 15 people who finished ahead of me in the race spent more time actually swimming, cycling, and running than I did, but less time changing. Nevertheless, I am reinvigorated by seeing my family and trot out onto the run course.

THE RUN. The run will prove to be the toughest event for me. It is 11:10 AM and very hot by the time I start. I go slowly and am all right for the first mile or so. I pass the little cyclist in red and black. She is really going slowly. (Seven months later, I would meet her at the 1984 Long Island Half-Marathon and remind her of the episode. She would remember it well, and she would tell me that my "You are in a race, madam" challenge ruined her for the run.) Soon thereafter, however, the heat and the problems of the bike-run transition begin to get to me. I am suffering. But I keep on running, however slowly. Mistakenly, I believe that it is somehow wrong to stop running and walk. I do not learn, in this race at any rate, from the example of a woman walking whom I pass but who later overtakes me running and leaves me far behind.

It is hot. Water stops are adequate but mile markers are not. Ten minutes apart I pass two people who tell me: "Only 6 miles to go." I am struggling. Everything hurts. I am going very slowly. "I will never, never, never do a marathon," I tell myself. (In the event, I did another triathlon 3 weeks later and my first marathon less than 3 months later.) With 3 miles to go I see some friends sitting on a shaded bench in downtown Sag Harbor. I sit down for a brief chat. Revitalized, once again I pick up my pace a bit, heading for the finish.

With about 2 miles to go, I pass a man in my age group. I get about 30 yards ahead of him, figuring that I have him. "Why are you racing, when you said that all you wanted to do was finish?" the persistent little voice says. "Because, I'm racing. Now keep quiet and concentrate," I retort. I keep going. With 1 mile to go, I look back. I am losing my lead, ever so slowly. I try to pick it up. I cannot. I have given it everything I've got. I am running on empty. With about half-a-mile to go, I am hearing footsteps. I can do nothing.

I think about the experience I have had many times in sailboat racing going downwind, being blanketed, hearing the splop-splop-splop of the little waves on the other boat's bow as she catches up and goes by, with me powerless to do anything about it. With a quarter mile to go I am passed by the man I had passed before. I cannot go any faster. But within 2 minutes, as I cross the finish line myself, the thought of defeat is replaced with the overwhelming thought of victory—my victory for myself in finishing. What a feeling!

AFTERMATH. I am tired, sore and stiff, but absolutely flying. My family is there—a great feeling. I take it real easy. I strip off my wet running gear very slowly. I drink—water, Gatorade, and drink some more. I pack up my things and walk off to the car. We go over to the pool at the race headquarters motel. The kids go for a swim. I sit, reflect, bask in my own private glow. I did it, I really did it. I have seen a new me and I really like what I see. When is the next race?

SOME TIPS ON RACING . . .

I am hardly either an expert or a fast triathlete. I do not have secrets on winning from my own experience to share with you. Nor am I an expert on technique or form in any of the sports. For that kind of information I refer you to some of the books mentioned earlier and listed in the bibliography. I do know something about racing in comfort and finishing happily and in good health. In no particular order of importance, I will share with you some of my observations and experience in racing.

HOW TRIATHLONS ARE USUALLY LAID OUT. In the traditional swim-bike-run triathlon, there is a transition area which is literally and figuratively at the center of the race. It is here that you will place your bicycle, usually in a specific area assigned to you by your race number. With your bike, you will leave your biking gear and your running gear, prepared for changing. The race organizers will usually provide you with two or three bags, for swim, bike, and run equipment.

If the swim starts from the triathlon area (an out-and-back course) then you do not need a separate bag for swim stuff. You get fully prepared for the swim at your bike stall. When you come back from the swim you just dump your swim stuff (which is not very much anyway) into your soon-to-be-empty bike bag.

In some races the swim is point-to-point, starting at some distance from the transition area and going to it in a straight line. In this case you will have to walk to the swim start, or go on the bus if one is provided. You will usually wear a shirt to keep warm (triathlons generally start early in the morning) and shoes or sandals. You may also want to carry, not wear right away, your goggles, cap, nose clip, and earplugs. You may also have Vaseline. Thus you will need a bag in which to leave this paraphernalia. Make sure that it is numbered and that the race organizers will pick it up and bring it back to the transition area.

The bike course will either be a single loop starting and finishing at the transition area or several laps around a loop that begins and ends just outside the transition area. The run in the marathon-equivalent events is usually a single loop, although it could be laps as well. The race then is simple: swim, out-and-back or point-to-point; transition area, change to bike stuff; bike, single loop or laps; transition area, change to run stuff; run, single loop or laps; and finish.

In most races your time is your overall time, changing time included. If you are at all concerned about time, do a little changing practice. In that first race I spent 23 minutes changing my clothes. I looked great. All of my outfits were color coordinated. However, if I had dressed a little less stylishly and had spent only 13 minutes changing (the average changing time for people who finished towards the end like I did), I would have moved up 23 places on the list!

EQUIPMENT AND CHECK-LIST.[2] Even though I have a poor memory and am compulsive at the same time, I don't use a written check list to inventory my equipment before a race. I probably should and after writing this section I may very well do so in future races. I do lay my stuff out very carefully the night before the race, however. Further, before leaving home, I check over my equipment bag or bags right after packing and then once again before I walk out the door. I really don't want to be setting up my stuff the night before a race and find that I left my swim goggles or bike helmet home.

The basic equipment lists are as follows:

> General (leave in car)
>> Full-size bicycle pump
>> Warm-up suit
>> Fresh clothes for after the race
>> Extra safety pins for race numbers
>> Bandaids
>> Tape
>> First-aid cream
>> Muscle salve

2. See Chapter 8 for thoughts on specific types of equipment.

Swim
    Swimsuit[3]
    Goggles
    Nose clip
    Earplugs
    Vaseline
    Waterproof stopwatch
Bike
    Towel (for drying off and removing sand after the swim)
    Sunscreen, if you need it
    Bucket with water (for rinsing off sand if no hose or showers
        are available)
    Food (bananas do very nicely)
    Bicycle
    Bike shoes
    Gloves
    Hard helmet
    Water bottle (1 or 2)
    Bike shorts, with chamois padding
    Bike shirt with pockets in the back to carry extra water bottle
        and / or food
    Socks (the same as you will use in the run)
    Sunglasses
    Sweatband (if your helmet does not have one built in)
Run
    Singlet or T-shirt, depending on the weather
    Shorts
    Running Shoes
    Fresh sweatband
    Hat or sun visor (optional)

It sounds like an awful lot of stuff but it really isn't, at least
after the first race. But do make sure that everything is there.

3. You may, of course, wear a tri-suit. See Chapter 8.

You will be nervous enough without having to worry about mislaid or missing equipment.

PACING. Just as consistency is the way to successful training, it is also the key to successful racing. You should work out at a comfortable pace in each event and get used to it. You should then estimate how long it should take you to complete each event at your comfortable pace. As you get into each leg you should get onto your planned pace and stick to it. The number one rule of racing to finish is: don't go out too fast. If you overdo it in the swim and bike, you may end up walking for most of the run.

There are no split-distance markers for the swim. (On an out-and-back course you will, of course, know when you have reached the halfway mark.) You really have to feel the proper pace. For the bike there are usually splits, but I find that the little electronic speedometer / timer / cadence counter that I have on the bike really keeps me on track very well. In the run there are likely to be markers every mile. Use them. In comparison with my training speeds in the race I usually go a bit faster on the swim and the bike and a bit slower on the run. You may have a different pattern. But once you find the right one, stick to it.

RACING. Related to pacing is racing, that is competing directly with one or more fellow triathletes in some portion of the event rather than competing solely with the clock. I did it for a short time in each segment of my first triathlon, as I described above. I tend to to it at some time or another in each event that I enter. But I do it for fun. I don't let racing take over, I don't do it for too long at any one stretch, and I don't let it wear me out. I keep my eye on my main event: finishing the race.

THE SWIM. This is the one mass start you will be in. It can be a mess. Some races start on the beach. With the gun, everyone charges into the water, usually with some degree of noise. Other races start with the swimmers in the water. The start is more in slow motion here, but there is still plenty of clamor. For the swim start you will be asked to seed yourself by your expected time. The faster swimmers will be asked to move towards the front of the throng. Be smart and be honest. If you are not a fast swimmer and start too far up front you will only be in the way. As swimmers climb over and go around you, you stand a good chance of being grabbed on the leg or kicked in the face. If you don't pick just the right spot in the seeds it is certainly better to start too far back than too far forward. From the back at least you are in full control of any passing situation.

An increasing number of races, especially the bigger ones, are adopting staggered starts. This is a boon to the racers. You will start in groups of 50 or 100 at 1-minute intervals. The organizers will have seeded you by a predicted swim time that you put down on your entry blank. Your overall finish time will be appropriately adjusted. There will still be some clamor, confusion, and kicking, but it is nothing like what happens in a total mass start.

As a first-time triathlete you may well want to use alternating strokes in the swim. Although I now generally swim all crawl, in that first race I spent about a third of my time doing elementary backstroke. Breast, back crawl, and sidestroke are also used. If you need to keep your head out of the water for extra breathing, because the water is cold, or for psychological reasons, by all means do it. You will slow down a little bit, (crawl being the fastest stroke), but you will feel more comfortable. For finishing, that is what counts.

It is very important to stay on course and swim in a straight line. There are no white lines on the water so this may take some doing. But any deviation from the true course just adds unnecessary distance to your swim. You will have to be able to get your head out of the water and look straight ahead from time to time. Breast stroke or lifesaving crawl are good for this. Most swim courses will be marked by buoys or patrol boats or both. Buoys are the best. They stay in place and you can just go from one to the next. You can also sight on the turning mark of an out-and-back and/or the finish line.

In the swim it is best to try to find a little niche for yourself with no one passing you and you passing no one. Once in the niche, get into a nice steady rhythm and stay there. It will usually take at least a quarter of the leg to do this however, and sometimes takes me up to half.

Salt water is a pain if you swallow some, but the added buoyancy is a nice plus. Lake swimming is nice because there are no tides, usually no waves of any consequence, and usually no currents. But lake bottoms can be mucky and swimming through lake grasses, which I have done, can be a bit disconcerting. In tidal salt water, hopefully the race organizers will have worked the timing out so that any tides or currents are going with you. However, if you have thought that swimming uphill is an impossibility you should have been at the 1983 Mighty Hamptons. In that race, we swam against an incoming tide *and* a headwind with waves. On the other hand, in the 1983 Ricoh East Coast Championships at Ship Bottom, New Jersey, ⅓ of the swim was with a 2-mph current. Everyone had a wonderful ride and set a swim P.R.

SWIM-BIKE CHANGE. Coming to the end of the swim leg, I try to swim as far in as I can before standing up. It is really easier than trying to wade quickly in waist-deep water. Coming out of the water, stay in line through the exit chute. Race officials must get your number and record your time. If there is a traffic jam here, just be patient. You will be losing much less time than you think. For salt-water races, showers, usually courtesy of the local fire department, will be provided. Don't skip

the shower. It is really important to get that salt off before
the bike and the run. Dried salt can really chafe. The shower
will also get the sand off your feet. There is nothing like sand
in your socks for producing blisters. For fresh-water swims,
showers may not be provided. In this case a bucket prefilled
with water can really be a big help should there be sand or
mud to remove. Otherwise you must wipe your feet off with
a towel, a time-consuming endeavour.

Drink some water if available and jog gently from the end
of the swim chute over to your bike. I suggest planning to
keep your bathing suit on for the whole race. Women almost
have to do this. The one-piece swimsuits used for racing take
a long time to remove. If they are going to change, most women
will want to use the enclosed disrobing area provided. However, that all takes lots of time that you don't have to spend.
Some women, and men too, do strip to the buff in the transition area. Everyone else is so preoccupied with their own
changes that no one really has a chance to look anyway. In
my own first race, however, I wore a boxer swimsuit and
went to the disrobing area to modestly change. I now wear a
brief and just keep it on for the whole race. It provides excellent support in both the bike and the run, obviating the necessity of wearing an athletic supporter.

Your bike water bottle should be filled and ready to go.
During the change is a good time to eat a banana. Some people ride and run sockless. If every second counts for you, that's
fine, but I like to protect my feet. After my time-wasting experience in my first race, I put on one pair of socks for the bike
ride and keep them on for the run.

Some people bike in their running shorts and shoes. This
maneuver will save considerable transition time, but I do not
recommend it for the beginner triathlete. Bike shorts with a
chamois pad cushion your bottom and protect your thighs
against seat chafe. They are well worth wearing. You can get
lightweight ones and leave them on for the run if you wish.

But again, I will trade a bit of time here for comfort in both segments and change to nylon running shorts.

I definitely recommend against cycling in your running shoes. They have a flexible sole which robs energy from the down-stroke. Bike shoes have a firm sole which keeps your heel straight and funnels all your downthrust onto the pedals. Running shoes also have thick and nobby soles which are difficult to get into and out of toe clips and straps. For speed lacing, you can get quick-tie gadgets or you get shoes with velcro straps. I don't bother with either, but they will save some seconds.

THE BIKE RIDE. In most triathlons, the bike race is an almost pure time trial. You are out to cover the distance as quickly as you can, on your own. Drafting, riding closely behind another racer to take advantage of the windbreak provided, is usually prohibited. Thus the pack riding and / or pace lines to facilitate drafting that serious bike racers are used to do not appear. You will ride your own race. Make sure that you carry at least one water bottle. If you have only one water bottle bracket on your bike, you can carry a second bottle in the pocket(s) on the back of your bike shirt if you use one. It is very important to drink on the bike leg. There will usually be water stops. You may well be offered a full water bottle. Take it, drink as much as you can, and then discard it along the side of the road. It will be picked up later. If there are water stops, use them. Save your own water bottles for a later time when there may be no race-provided water.

Ride your own race. Try to get into that steady, smooth, regular cadence that you practiced in training. Spin your way up the hills in a low gear. Power your way down the hills. Downhills provide a real opportunity to pick up time. They should be taken advantage of. However, if the road surface is not smooth, don't try to go too fast. A flat or an unexpected bump on a fast downhill could prematurely end your participation in the race as well as cause serious long-term injury. A minute or two off your time is not worth that risk. Speaking of bike safety in general, it is a good thing to keep in mind during the race, for your own sake and that of your fellow competitors as well.

BIKE-RUN CHANGE. Most women will still have their swim-suits on and will run in them. If you had put on bike shorts, you will probably want to remove them for the run. Running shorts are optional, but can help limit chafe. For the men, you will probably have your swimsuits on too, and the same recommendations apply. If you did not keep your swimsuit on for the bike ride, you will want to get an athletic supporter on for the run. You will change your shoes here. Spend a few extra seconds and make sure that you have laced up your running shoes properly. No need to risk foot blisters now. You may want to eat another banana while changing. This change is easier than the swim-bike routine because you don't have to dry off, remove sand, and put on socks. Move through this change purposefully and methodically, but don't forget anything. I always put on a fresh sweatband here. I also change glasses. Being farsighted, for the bike I wear bifocals with flip-up sunglasses so that I will be able to see up close if I have to change a tire or put a chain back on. For the run, where close-up vision is not likely to be necessary, I switch from the heavier bifocals-plus-sunglasses to lighter unifocal prescription sunglasses.

THE RUN. At the beginning of this leg, you are likely to encounter the most difficult physical transition of the triath-lon. For most people, going from the bike to the run, at least the first time out, provides a most peculiar sensation. Your legs feel rubbery, your stride is short, you cannot get stretched out, you cannot get moving. This may last a mile or two, or more. In the 1983 Ricoh East Coast Championships it took me about 45 minutes to painfully shuffle the first 3 miles. I finally stopped trying to run, walked about a quarter of a mile, got stretched out, and ran the last 7 miles at a sub-9-minute pace.

If you are riding a conventional bike, I suggest starting off the run with 2–4 minutes of purposeful walking. You may well find walking for another 2 minutes or so at the 12-minute mark to also be helpful. This routine helps get everything stretched out, making the run more comfortable and faster. You can also try a bit of static stretching before starting out on the run, either in addition to or in place of the walking. Even the great Allison Roe had to do this in the 1982 Mighty Hamptons Triathlon, her first. For myself, as I noted in chapter 8, I now use the Powercam bike which makes the transition significantly easier.

Drinking is ever so important on the run. If you are slow like I am, even in an early-starting triathlon, it is likely to be pretty hot by the time you get out on the run. Keeping yourself well-hydrated is the single key to finishing at this point. Remember well the old but true adage of the long-distance runner; if you get to the point of feeling thirsty, it is already too late for you to catch up on water intake. Keep drinking enough so that you simply do not get thirsty. After trying the fortified drinks in several races, I found that water is the best drink for me. Also, if it is hot at each water stop pour a cup of water over your head, and splash another on your face. One poured down the back of your neck helps too. If spectators are offering garden-hose rinses, take one, but make sure not to get your socks wet. Running in squishy socks is a distinctly uncomfortable feeling. If I am in a hurry for one reason or another, I do drink on the run. I take small sips to avoid swallowing air and developing that bloated, uncomfortable feeling. Belches always seem to come slowly when I am running. If I am taking it easy in a particular race, I will stop for water to drink and make sure that I liberally splash water on my head, face and neck.

If shade is available on the run, go to it, even if it means crossing the road more than once. The temperature in the shade can be 10°–15° degrees cooler than in direct sunlight. On an out-and-back course, running in the shade on one side of the road out-bound may mean that you are running against in-bound runners ahead of you. If so, just make sure that you stay out of their way, but stay in that shade.

"Hitting the wall," simply running out of gas due to glycogen depletion is a common experience among marathoners, usually occurring, if it does, around the 20-mile mark. I have never heard a competitor in a marathon-equivalent triathlon complain of hitting the wall. This is not to say that it does not or could not happen. But it is rare. I don't have a ready explanation for that fact. However, it is a fact and its existence does give first-time triathletes one less thing to worry about.

If at some point during the run leg you feel that you must engage in an unplanned walk to recoup some energy, by all means do it. Better to finish on your feet walking than to persist in running to the point of exhaustion and then not be able to finish at all. But if you have paced yourself properly and if you have stretched out at the beginning of the run, you should not find it necessary to engage in unplanned walking. Remember, your overall performance is the product of your training *and* how you run the race.

POSTRACE RECOVERY. At the end of your first triathlon, you will probably feel like I did: very tired, rather stiff, but very proud of yourself. Just take it easy. Drink. Get in the shade if you can. Get into some fresh clothes if possible. At least change your shoes and socks. Walk around a bit. Stretch out gently. Sit down and rest for a bit. Then carefully gather up all of your stuff, check the contents of your race bags, collect your bike, load the car, and go back to your room for the much-deserved shower. If you are going home right after the race, the night before see if your motel will give you a late check-out time. In conjunction with a triathlon, many will do so.

The next morning, go out for a light jog or an easy spin on the bike for 20 minutes or so. This will help get the pain and stiffness out of your muscles. But most of all, bask in the glory of self-satisfaction. You deserve it. You did what you set out to do: finish your first triathlon.

11 ... What's Next?

When I now wear a triathlon T-shirt and someone asks me if I've competed, I look them in the eye and say, "Yes, I have." But, I add to myself, "You ain't seen nothin' yet."

Neil Feineman, after completing his first triathlon,
a training-length event, in his article,
"I Did It! How I Conquered My First Triathlon,"
Triathlon, February 1985, p. 40.

INTRODUCTION . . .

You have completed your first triathlon. You are basking in that golden glow of feelings of accomplishment. You feel really good about yourself. You are proud of what you have done. Your mind and your body both reflect your sense of pride. You have trained your cardiovascular and respiratory systems to work aerobically for an extended period of time. You have trained your musculoskeletal and nervous systems to do aerobic work in three different sports. You have achieved your objective of finishing a marathon-equivalent triathlon happily and healthily and you have done that with a training program that does not require you to turn the rest of your life upside down. The logical next question is "What's next?"

RECOVERY...

In my experience and that of most other triathletes recovery from a marathon equivalent triathlon takes very little time. Usually by the next day you are feeling just fine physically. (You will very likely have felt just fine mentally within minutes of finishing the race.) This is in marked contrast to the postrace experience of most people who do marathons. For myself, the good mental feelings of accomplishment postmarathon begin right away, but physically it is another story. My muscles ache, a lot. I walk around rather stiffly for several days. Stair climbing and descending present a bit of a problem for my thighs. In terms of postmarathon exercise, I find that I cannot do anything more than 10–20 minutes of very easy jogging for 4–5 days after the race. Full recovery takes me about a month. This is a figure that you will hear commonly from marathoners. You will not feel like doing much distance or much speed work during that period.

Post-triathlon recovery is an entirely different matter. After my first triathlon I was feeling fine physically by the next day. Mental state was a different matter. I was not just feeling fine; I was flying. I felt that I had just had one of the truly great experiences of my life. I immediately began casting around for another race that I could do before the season was over. I found one, almost as long, and did it—3 weeks later, again happily and healthily. In the interim, 2 weeks after the first race, I did a 100k (metric-century) ride on my bike at close to race pace in an American Heart Association cyclethon. Eight weeks after that second triathlon I ran my first marathon.

In my second season of triathloning I did three races over a 4-week period, 2 weeks between events. Again no problems. Each race became the long workout to be done 2 weeks prior to the next race. Between races I just maintained an easy 4 hours or so of aerobic work per week. I felt good in and after all three races and maintained a pretty consistent, if fairly slow, performance level throughout. My race paces are about 38 minutes per mile in the swim, 17–19 mph on the bike (depending upon how hilly the course is), and 9–10 minutes per mile on the run (depending upon how hot a day it is). Thus I do a true marathon-equivalent race like the Mighty Hamptons in a bit over 4 hours.

Three weeks after my last triathlon of the 1984 season, I did a half-marathon in what for me was a fast time: 1:52:17. That was to be my last good race of the season. Unlike my experience with triathlons, I did not recover quickly. During the subsequent 3 weeks leading to my last race of that season, the Marine Corps Marathon, on training runs my legs more often than not felt like lead. Although I could easily do triathlons every 2 weeks with no effect on performance, such was not the case for the long-distance running events. While I started well enough in the Marine Corps Marathon and actually held myself back to run at my planned 9:30–9:45 pace, by the 18th mile I was beginning to slow down. I did not hit the wall, but by mile 20 my legs and feet were really hurting. I then had to slow way down and walk some considerable distance towards the end. I set a Personal record of 4:28:45 but I missed my objective of 10-minute miles and a 4:22 clocking. I concluded that doing that fast half-marathon had a lot to do with my difficulty, a difficulty that rarely occurs in frequent triathloning.

THE NEXT RACE . . .

After your first race, then, if it is early enough in the season you can look around for one or more additional races to do. I myself wouldn't try to race on consecutive weekends but there are some recreational triathletes who do that without any problem. Many of the young, very fit, very well trained, professional triathletes do a race every weekend for the season—and they are out to win. Assuming that you have used the TFOMTP as is, I wouldn't try to do anything longer than a marathon-equivalent event right away. Certainly, if you successfully completed a training-length triathlon for your first event, you can go right out and do a marathon-equivalent race next time. But to go that next step up, to a half-Ironman, I would want another 13 weeks of training and I would want to add an average of 3 hours per week to my schedule, mostly in cycling.

If you decide that you want to try a marathon after triathloning, I suggest that you make it your last event of the season. You should probably allow at least 6 weeks after your last triathlon before doing a marathon. For your training schedule, you can use the Generic Program of the TFOMTP. You do not need to do the second Tuesday workout. You can still devote two of the scheduled training sessions per week to swimming or cycling in preparation for the marathon, just as long as those workouts are aerobic.

THE NEXT SEASON AND BEYOND . . .

Once you get over the psychological hump of doing your first race, your horizons will expand rapidly. You will look forward to the appearance of the race schedule for next season in the one or more triathlon publications to which you have probably become a subscriber. I know that I plan my season very early. I also get my race application requests and my race applications in early since the popular and well-run races fill so far in advance.

Completing any triathlon is a wonderful experience of course. You may, however, look for new challenges. The most important consideration here is to make sure that any goals you set for yourself are achievable ones. Nothing turns off an endurance athlete faster than frustration. Since you set your own goals, you are entirely in control of your own frustration level.

The two types of challenges that you can consider are "going faster" and "going longer." If you want to go faster in a race, you will have to go faster in your training. One day a week of the TFOMTP should then be devoted to interval training. Good advice for interval training is swimming, cycling, and running can be found in the books by Jane Katz, Paul Matheny, and Bob Glover and Pete Schuder, respectively. If you want to go significantly longer in a race, you will have to go longer in your training. As I said above, to go from a marathon-equivalent to a half-Ironman triathlon, the next step up, you should need to add about 2.5 hours per week over 13 weeks to the TFOMTP. Since the big difference between the two classes of events, in addition to total aerobic exercise time, is the length of the bike ride, I would devote the bulk of the additional training time to cycling.

You can also look at doing different kinds of events. Going into my 1985 season, I planned to do three or four triathlons plus several events in the International Masters Games scheduled for Toronto, Canada, in August. There was no triathlon to do there, but there were plenty of challenges in separate swimming, cycling, and running endurance events.

Once you are into this wonderful world of triathloning your boundaries are limitless. You have added a marvelous new dimension to your life. Continue to make the most of it and it will remain with you forever.

Appendix I
National and Major Regional Triathlon Publications

The Beast. A monthly national triathlon and ultrasport newspaper published on Long Island in New York State. Box 789, Wainscott, New York 11975 (516)324–2027.

Midwest Triathlete Quarterly. A quarterly magazine focusing on the Midwest. Box 14842, Chicago, Illinois 60614. (312)528–2893.

Running and Triathlon News. A monthly newspaper concentrating on the West Coast and Southwest. Box 2822, La Jolla, California 92038 (619)270–4974.

The Tri-ing Times. A regular newsletter published by the Big Apple Triathlon Club, 301 East 79th St., #30D, New York, New York 10021. (212)288–5661.

Tri-Athlete. A full-color national monthly magazine. 1127 Hamilton St., Allentown, Pennsylvania 18102. (215)821–0390.

Triathlon Magazine. A full-color national monthly magazine. Box 5901, Santa Monica, California 90405. (213)558–3321.

Tri-Fit. A quarterly newspaper emphasizing coverage of Canada and the Pacific Northwest. 575 Burns Street, Penticton, British Columbia, V2A1W9, Canada. (604)493–5181.

Ultrasport. A glossy national bimonthly magazine. Box 27938, San Diego, California 92127. (619)227–1988.

Appendix II
Books

RUNNING . . .

American Running and Fitness Association. *Guidelines for Successful Jogging*. 2420 K Street, NW, Washington, D.C., 1977.

Jim Fixx. *The Complete Book of Running*. New York: Random House, 1977.

Ardy Friedberg. *How to Run Your First Marathon*. New York: Fireside / Simon and Schuster, 1982. As of 1984 distributed by Fitness Enterprises, 175 Fifth Avenue, New York, New York 10010.

Jeff Galloway. *Galloway's Book on Running*. Bolinas, California: Shelter Publications, 1984.

Bob Glover and Jack Shepherd. *The Runner's Handbook*. New York: The Viking Press, 1978.

Bob Glover and Pete Schuder. *The Competitive Runner's Handbook*. New York: Penguin Books, 1983.

Joe Henderson. *Jog, Run, Race*. Mountain View, California: World Publications, 1977.

Dan Honig. *How to Run Better*. New York: Ballantine Books, 1984.

George Sheehan. *Dr. Sheehan on Running*. Mountain View, California: World Publications, 1975.

Joan Ullyot. *Running Free*. New York: G. P. Putnam's Sons, 1980.

BICYCLING . . .

Ray Adams. *Serious Cyling for the Beginner*. Mountain View, California: Anderson World, 1977.
Dan Honig. *How to Bike Better*. New York: Ballantine books, 1984.
Thom Lieb. *Everybody's Book of Bicycling Riding*. Emmaus, Pennsylvania: Rodale Press, 1981.
Fred Matheny. *Beginning Bicycle Racing*. Brattleboro, Vermont: Velo-News, 1983.
Denise de la Rosa and Michael Kolin. *The Ten-Speed Bicycle*. Emmaus, Pennsylvania: Rodale Press, 1979.

SWIMMING . . .

Jane Katz. *Swimming for Total Fitness*. Garden City, New York: Dolphin / Doubleday, 1981.

TRIATHLONING . . .

Sally Edwards. *Triathlon: A Triple Fitness Sport*. Sacramento, California: Fleet Feet Press, 1982.
Bob Johnson and Patricia Bragg. *The Complete Triathlon Distance Training Manual*. Santa Barbara, California: Health Science, 1982.

Appendix III
Stretching

INTRODUCTION . . .

The following material is reprinted from *Stretching*, by Bob Anderson. This is a complete guide to stretching all parts of the body and shows stretches for each sport. The complete book, which I highly recommend owning, is available in bookstores for $8.95. *Stretching* the book, as well as wall charts and other educational material related to stretching, is also available by mail from Stretching, Inc., Box 767, Palmer Lake, Colorado, 80133. I am grateful to both Bob and Lloyd Kahn, editor of Shelter Publications, for the grant of this permission. In this appendix the material is organized as follows:

Section I is the general instruction, "How to Stretch." You must read this section with care before doing any of the exercises detailed in the following pages.

Section II presents the specific before-and-after exercise sets for each of the principal triathlon sports. The exercises in these sets are keyed to a detailed description and illustration of each one that appears in Section III. Do not attempt to do any of the stretches before reading those detailed explanations. Do stretch. It will make your training program that much better.

SECTION I—HOW TO STRETCH . . .

Stretching is easy to learn. But there is a right way and a wrong way to stretch. The right way is a relaxed, sustained stretch with your attention focused on the muscles being stretched. The wrong way (unfortunately practiced by many people), is to bounce up and down, or to stretch to the point of pain: these methods can actually do more harm than good.

If you stretch correctly and regularly, you will find that every movement you make becomes easier. It will take time to loosen up tight muscles or muscle groups, but time is quickly forgotten when you start to feel good.

The Easy Stretch

When you begin a stretch, spend 10–30 second in the *easy stretch*. No bouncing! Go to the point where you feel a *mild tension,* and relax as you hold the stretch. The feeling of tension should subside as you hold the position. If it does not, ease off slightly and find a degree of tension that is comfortable. The easy stretch reduces muscular tightness and readies the tissues for the developmental stretch.

The Developmental Stretch

After the easy stretch, move slowly into the *developmental stretch*. Again, no bouncing. Move a fraction of an inch further until you again feel a mild tension and hold for 10–30 seconds. Be in control. Again, the tension should diminish; if not, ease off slightly. The developmental stretch fine-tunes the muscles and increases flexibility.

Breathing

Your breathing should be slow, rhythmical and under control. If you are bending forward to do a stretch, exhale as you bend forward and then breathe slowly as you hold the stretch. Do not hold your breath while stretching. If a stretch position inhibits your natural breathing pattern, then you are obviously not relaxed. Just ease up on the stretch so you can breathe naturally.

Counting

At first, silently count the seconds for each stretch; this will insure that you hold the proper tension for a long enough time. After a while, you will be stretching by the way it feels, without the distraction of counting.

The Stretch Reflex

Your muscles are protected by a mechanism called the *stretch reflex*. Any time you stretch the muscle fibers too far (either by bouncing or overstretching), a nerve reflex responds by sending a signal to the muscles to contract; this keeps the muscles from being injured. Therefore, when you stretch too far, you tighten the very muscles you are trying to stretch! (You get a similar involuntary muscle reaction when you accidentally touch something hot; before you can think about it, your body quickly moves away from the heat.)

Holding a stretch as far as you can go or bouncing up and down strains the muscles and activates the stretch reflex. These harmful methods cause pain, as well as physical damage due to the microscopic tearing of muscle fibers. This tearing leads to the formation of scar tissue in the muscles, with a gradual loss of elasticity. The muscles become tight and sore. How can you get enthused about daily stretching and exercise when these potentially injurious methods are used?

Many of us were conditioned in high school to the idea of "no gain without pain." We learned to associate pain with physical improvement, and were taught that "the more it hurts, the more you get out of it." But don't be fooled. Stretching, when done correctly, is not painful. Learn to pay attention to your body, for pain is an indication that something is *wrong*.

The easy and developmental stretches, as described on the previous page do not activate the stretch reflex and do not cause pain.

This diagram will give you an idea of a "good stretch":

← A STRETCH →		
An Easy Stretch	The Developmental Part of Stretching	A Drastic Stretch
(hold for 20–30 seconds)	*(hold for 30 seconds or longer)*	*(do not stretch in the drastic stretch)*

The straight-line diagram represents the stretch which is possible with your muscles and their connective tissue. You will find that your flexibility will naturally increase when you stretch, first in the easy, then in the developmental phase. By regularly stretching with comfortable and painless feelings you will be able to go beyond your present limits and come closer to your personal potential.

SECTION II—SPORT SPECIFIC ROUTINES . . .

Before and After Cycling

Approximately 10 minutes

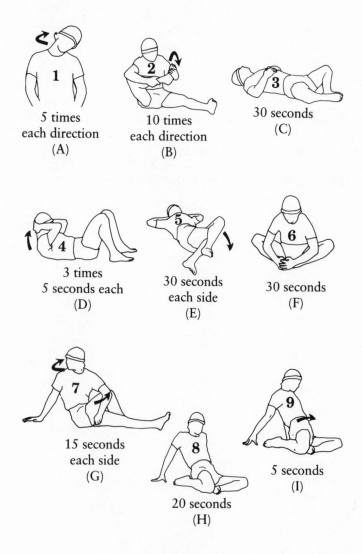

5 times
each direction
(A)

10 times
each direction
(B)

30 seconds
(C)

3 times
5 seconds each
(D)

30 seconds
each side
(E)

30 seconds
(F)

15 seconds
each side
(G)

20 seconds
(H)

5 seconds
(I)

Repeat
8, 9, 10, 11
other leg

20 seconds
(H)

30 seconds
(J)

20 seconds
(K)

30 seconds
(L)

15 seconds
each leg
(M)

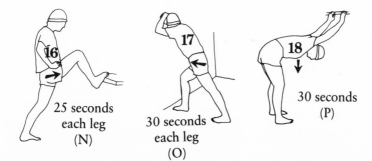

25 seconds
each leg
(N)

30 seconds
each leg
(O)

30 seconds
(P)

Before Running

Approximately 9 minutes

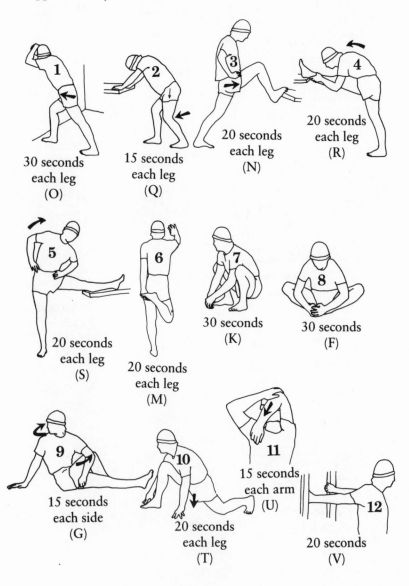

30 seconds
each leg
(O)

15 seconds
each leg
(Q)

20 seconds
each leg
(N)

20 seconds
each leg
(R)

20 seconds
each leg
(S)

20 seconds
each leg
(M)

30 seconds
(K)

30 seconds
(F)

15 seconds
each side
(G)

20 seconds
each leg
(T)

15 seconds
each arm
(U)

20 seconds
(V)

After Running

Approximately 9 Minutes

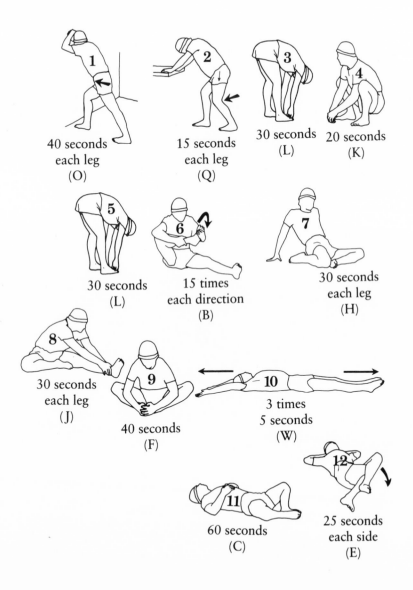

40 seconds
each leg
(O)

15 seconds
each leg
(Q)

30 seconds
(L)

20 seconds
(K)

30 seconds
(L)

15 times
each direction
(B)

30 seconds
each leg
(H)

30 seconds
each leg
(J)

40 seconds
(F)

3 times
5 seconds
(W)

60 seconds
(C)

25 seconds
each side
(E)

Before and After Swimming

Approximately 10 Minutes

10 seconds
each arm
(X)

5 times
(Y)

20 seconds
(P)

30 seconds
(Z)

10 seconds
each leg
(AA)

25 seconds
each leg
(T)

30 seconds
(K)

20 seconds
(BB)

15 seconds
each arm
(CC)

30 seconds
(F)

3 times
5 seconds each
(D)

10 seconds
each side twice
(DD)

5 seconds
each direction
(W)

SECTION III—THE EXERCISES...

Exercise A, Neck

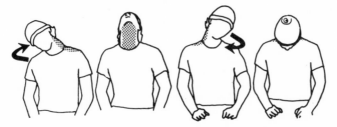

Sit in a position that is comfortable. *Very slowly* roll your head around in a full circle as you keep your back straight. While you are rolling your head around slowly you may feel that you should stop and hold a stretch at a particular place that feels tight. Do so, but don't strain. If you are holding a position, be relaxed and the area will gradually loosen up.

These stretches for your neck will help you sit or stand with better posture when you find you are slouching.

Exercise B, Ankle

Rotate your ankle clockwise and counterclockwise through a complete range of motion with slight resistance provided by your hand. Rotary motion of the ankle helps to gently stretch out tight ligaments. Repeat 10–20 times in each direction. Do this to both ankles and feel if there is any difference between ankles in terms of tightness and range of motion. Sometimes an ankle that has been sprained will feel a bit weaker and tighter. This difference may go unnoticed until you work each ankle separately and compare.

Exercise C, Groin

Relax, with knees bent and soles of your feet together. This comfortable position will stretch your groin. Hold for 30 seconds. Let the pull of gravity do the stretching.

Variation: From this lying groin stretch, gently rock your legs as one unit (see illustration) back and forth about 10–12 times. These are real easy movements of no more than 1 inch in either direction. Initiate movements from top of hips. This will gently limber up your groin and hips.

Exercise D, Neck

Interlace your fingers behind your head at about ear level. Now, use the power of your arms to slowly pull your head forward until you feel a slight stretch in the back of the neck. Hold for 5–10 seconds, then slowly return to the original starting position. Do this 3–4 times to gradually loosen up the upper spine and neck.

Exercise E, Back and Thighs

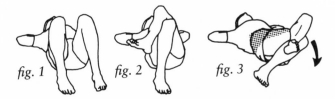

fig. 1   fig. 2   fig. 3

After gently stretching the groin, bring your knees together and rest your feet on the floor. Interlace your fingers behind your head and rest your arms on the floor (fig. 1). Now lift the left leg over the right leg (fig. 2). From here, use left leg to pull right leg toward floor (fig. 3) until you feel a good stretch along the side of the hip or in the lower back. Stretch and be relaxed. Keep the upper back, back of head, shoulders, and elbows flat on the floor. Hold for 30 seconds. *The idea is not to touch the floor with your right knee, but to stretch within your limits.* Repeat stretch for other side, crossing right over left leg and pulling down to the right.

This stretch position can be a real help if you have sciatic[1] problems of the lower back. If so, hold only stretch tensions that feel good. Never stretch to the point of pain.

Variation: Some people, especially women, will not feel a stretch. If that is the case with you, use opposite tension to create a stretch:

To do this, hold down the right leg with the left leg, as you try to pull the right leg back to an upright position (but, because you are holding the right leg down with the left leg, the right leg won't move). You will get a stretch on the side of the hip area. This technique is good for people who are tense as well as for those who are extremely limber in this area.

---

1. The sciatic nerve is the longest and largest nerve of the body. It originates in the lumbar portion of the spine (lower back) and travels down the entire length of both legs and out to the great toe.

Exercise F, Groin and Buttocks

Put the soles of your feet together and hold onto your toes. Gently pull yourself forward, bending from the hips, until you feel a good stretch in your groin. Hold for 40 seconds. Move from the hips, not head and shoulders.

Remember—no bouncing when you stretch. Find a place that is fairly comfortable that allows you to stretch and relax at the same time.

If you have any trouble bending forward, perhaps your heels are too close to your groin area.	If so, keep your feet farther out in front of you. This will allow you to get movement forward.

Variations: Hold on to your feet with one hand, with your elbow on the inside of the lower leg to hold down and stabilize the leg.

Now, with your other hand on the inside of your leg *(not on knee)*, gently push your leg downward to isolate and stretch this side of the groin. This is a very good isolation stretch for people who want to limber up a tight groin so that the knees can fall more naturally downward.

Exercise G, Spine

The spinal twist is good for the upper back, lower back, side of hips, and rib cage. It is also beneficial for internal organs and will help keep your waistline trim. It will aid in your ability to turn to the side or look behind you without having to turn your entire body.

Sit with your right leg straight. Bend your left leg, cross your left foot over and rest it to the outside of your right knee. Then bend your right elbow and rest it on the outside of your upper left thigh, just above the knee. During the stretch use the elbow to keep this leg stationary with controlled pressure to the inside.

Now, with your left hand resting behind you, slowly turn your head to look over your left shoulder, and at the same time rotate your upper body toward your left hand and arm. As you turn your upper body, think of turning your hips in the same direction (though your hips won't move because your right elbow is keeping the left leg stationary). This should give you a stretch in your lower back and side of hip. Hold for 15 seconds. Do both sides. Don't hold your breath; breathe easily.

Exercises H, I, J, Thigh

A sitting stretch for the quadriceps: First sit with your right leg bent, with your right heel just to the outside of your right hip. The left leg is bent and the sole of your left foot is next to the inside of your upper right leg. (You could also do this stretch with your left leg straight out in front of you.)

 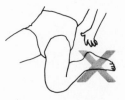

In this stretch position your foot should be extended back with the ankle flexed. If your ankle is tight and restricts the stretch, move your foot just enough to the side to lessen the tension in your ankle.

Try not to let your foot flare out to the side in this position. By keeping your foot pointed straight back you take the stress off the inside of your knee. The more your foot flares to the side, the more stress there is on your knee.

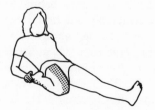

Now, slowly lean *straight back* until you feel an easy stretch. Use your hands for balance and support. Hold this easy stretch for 30 seconds.

Some people will have to lean back a lot further than others to find the right stretch tension. And some people may feel the right stretch without leaning back at all. Just be aware of how you feel and forget about how far you can go. Get into what *you* can do and don't worry about anyone else.

Do not let your knee lift off the floor or mat. If your knee comes up you are overstretching by leaning back too far. Ease up on the stretch.

Now slowly, and with complete control, increase into the developmental stretch. Hold for 25 seconds, then slowly come out of it. Switch sides and stretch the left thigh the same way.

Can you feel any difference in tension in the two stretches? Is one side more limber than the other? Are you more flexible on one side?

After stretching your quads, practice tightening the buttocks on the side of the bent leg as you turn the hip over. This will help stretch the front of your hip and give a better overall stretch to upper thigh area. After contracting the butt muscles for 5–8 seconds, let the buttocks relax. Drop your hip down and continue to stretch the quad for another 15 seconds. Practice to eventually get both sides of the buttocks to touch the floor at the same time during the quad stretch. Now do other side.

Note: Stretching the quad first, then turning the hip over as the buttocks contract will help change the stretch feeling when you return to the original quad stretch.

If, during the stretch, there is any pain in the knee joint, move the knee of the leg being stretched closer to the midline of your body and see if you can find a more comfortable position.

Moving your knee closer to the midline of your body may take the stress off of the knee, but *if there is pain which does not subside in any variation of this position, discontinue doing this particular stretch.*

fig. 1   fig. 2

To stretch the hamstrings of the same leg that was bent, straighten the right leg with the sole of your left foot slightly touching the inside of the right thigh. You are now in the straight-leg, bent-knee position (fig. 1). Slowly bend forward from the hips toward the foot of the straight leg (fig. 2) until you create the slightest feeling of stretch. Hold this for 20 seconds. After the stretch feeling has diminished, bend a bit more forward from the hips. Hold this developmental stretch for 25 seconds. Then switch sides and stretch the left leg in the same manner.

During this stretch, keep the foot of the straight leg upright with the ankle and toes relaxed. Be sure the quadriceps are soft to the touch (relaxed) during the stretch. Do not dip your head forward when initiating the stretch.

I have found that it is best to first stretch your quads, then the hamstrings of the same leg. It is easier to stretch the hamstrings after the quadriceps have been stretched.

Use a towel to help you stretch if you cannot *easily* reach your feet.

Exercise K, Groin, Lower Back, Ankles

Many of us get tired in the lower back from hours of standing and sitting. One position which helps to reduce this tension is the squat.

From a standing position, squat down with your feet flat and toes pointed out at approximately 15° angles. Your heels should be 4–12 inches apart, depending on how limber you are, or as you become familiar with stretching, depending on exactly what parts of your body you want to stretch. The squat stretches the front part of the lower legs, the knees, back, ankles, Achilles tendons, and deep groin. Keep knees to the outside of your shoulders. Knees should be directly above big toes in this squat position. Hold comfortably for 30 seconds. For many people this will be easy, for others very difficult.

Variations: At first there may be a problem with balance: usually falling backwards because of tight ankles and tight Achilles tendons. If you are unable to squat as shown, there are other ways to learn this position.

Try the squat on the downward slant of a driveway or hillside

or by leaning against a wall with your back.

You could use a fence or pole for balance by holding onto it with your hands.

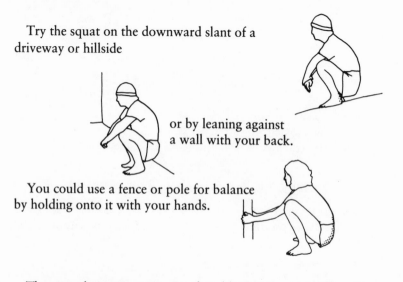

The squat becomes a very comfortable position and helps relieve any tightness in the lower back.

Be careful if you have had any knee problems. If pain is present discontinue this stretch.

To increase the stretch in the groin, place your elbows on the inside of your upper legs, gently push outward with both elbows as you bend slightly forward from your hips. Your thumbs should be on the inside of your feet with your fingers along the outside borders of the feet. Hold stretch for 20 seconds. Do not overstretch. If you have trouble balancing, elevate your heels slightly.

To stand up from the squat position, pull your chin in slightly and raise straight up *with your quadriceps doing all the work and back straight.* Do not dip your head forward as you stand up: this puts too much pressure on your lower back.

Exercise L, Lower Back, Hips, Hamstrings

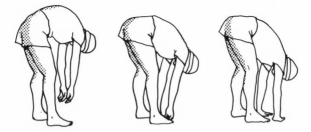

Start in a standing position with feet about shoulder-width apart and pointed straight ahead. Slowly bend forward from the hips.

Always keep knees slightly bent during the stretch (1 inch) so lower back is not stressed. Let your neck and arms relax. Go to the point where you feel a slight stretch in the back of your legs. Stretch in this easy phase for 15–25 seconds, until you are relaxed. Let yourself relax physically by mentally concentrating on the area being stretched. Do not stretch with knees locked or bounce when you stretch. Simply hold an easy stretch. Stretch by how you feel and not by how far you can go.

When you do this stretch you will feel it mostly in the hamstrings (back of thighs) and back of the knees. The back will also be stretched, but most of the stretch will be felt in the back of the legs.

Some of you will be able to touch your toes, or just above the ankles. Although we are different in flexibility, we do have one thing in common: we are all stretching our muscles.

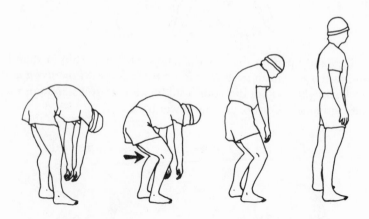

Important: Any time you bend at the waist to stretch, remember to bend your knees slightly (1 inch or so). It takes the pressure off your lower back. Use the big muscles of the upper legs to stand up, instead of the small muscles of the lower back. Never bring yourself to an upright position with knees locked.

Exercise M, Thigh, Lower Leg

To stretch the quad and knee, hold the top of your *right* foot with your *left* hand and gently pull your heel toward your buttocks. The knee bends at a natural angle when you hold your foot with the opposite hand. This is good to use in knee rehabilitation and with problem knees. Hold for 30 seconds, each leg.

Exercise N, Hamstrings

Place the ball of your foot up on a secure support of some kind (wall, fence, table). Keep the down leg pointed straight ahead. Now bend the knee of the up leg as you move your hips forward. This should stretch your groin, hamstrings, and front of hip. Hold for 30 seconds. Do both sides. If possible, for balance and control, use your hands to hold on to the support. This stretch will make it easier to lift your knees.

Variation: Instead of having the foot on the ground pointed straight ahead, turn it to the side (parallel to the support), then stretch as above. This stretches the inside of the upper legs. Hold for 25 seconds.

Exercise O, Calf

To stretch your calf, stand a little ways from a solid support and lean on it with your forearms, head resting on hands. Bend one leg and place your foot on the ground in front of you, with the other leg straight behind. Slowly move your hips forward, keeping your lower back flat. Be sure to keep the heel of the straight leg on the ground, with toes pointed straight ahead or slightly turned in as you hold the stretch. Hold an easy stretch for 30 seconds. Do not bounce. Stretch other leg.

Exercise P, Shoulders

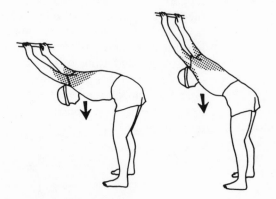

Another good upper body and back stretch is to place both hands shoulder-width apart on a fence or ledge and let your upper body drop down as you keep your knees slightly bent (1 inch). (Always bend your knees when coming out of this stretch.) Your hips should be directly above your feet.

Now, bend your knees just a big more and felt the stretch change. Place your hands at different heights and change the area of the stretch. After you become familiar with this stretch it is possible to really stretch the spine. Great to do if you have been slumping in the upper back and shoulders all day. This will take some of the kinks out of a tired upper back. Find a stretch that you can hold for at least 30 seconds.

The top of the refrigerator or a file cabinet are good to use for this stretch. Do it slowly. It can be done practically anywhere: all it takes is a little thought and some doing.

Exercise Q, Achilles Tendon

To create a stretch for the calf and Achilles tendon, lower your hips downward as you slightly bend your knee. Be sure to keep your back flat. Your back foot should be slightly toed-in or straight ahead during the stretch. Keep your heel down. This stretch is good for developing ankle flexibility. Hold stretch 25 seconds. The Achilles tendon area needs only *a slight feeling of stretch.*

Exercise R, Hamstrings

Now, while looking straight ahead, slowly bend forward at the waist until you feel a good stretch in the back of the raised leg. Hold and relax. Find the easy stretch, relax, and then increase it. This is very good for running or walking.

Variation: If you cannot easily touch your toes, rest more of your leg up on a table or platform of some kind that is at a comfortable height for you. Then you will be able to use the side of the table or ledge for balance and support as you get the right feeling of stretch in the hamstrings.

Exercise S, Hamstrings

To stretch the inside of your raised leg, turn the foot that is on the ground so it is parallel to the support. Face your upper body in the same direction as your down foot and turn your left hip slightly to the inside. Slowly bend sideways with your left shoulder going toward your left knee. This should stretch the inside of your upper leg. Hold an easy stretch for 15 seconds and a developmental stretch for 20 seconds. Be sure to keep the knee of the down leg slightly bent. Do both legs.

Exercise T, Thigh

To stretch the muscles in the front of the hip *(iliopsoas)*, move one leg forward until the knee of the forward leg is directly over the ankle. Your other knee should be resting on the floor. Now, without changing the position of the knee on the floor or the forward foot, lower the front of your hip downward to create an easy stretch. Hold for 30 seconds. You should feel this stretch in the front of the hip and possibly in the hamstrings and groin. This is excellent for lower back problems.

Do not have your knee forward of the ankle. This will hinder the proper stretching of the hip and legs. The greater distance there is between the back knee and the heel of the front foot, the easier it is to stretch the hip and legs.

Exercise U, Shoulder, Upper Arm

Here is a simple stretch for your triceps and the top of your shoulders. With arms overhead, hold the elbow of one arm with the hand of the other arm. Gently pull the elbow behind your head, creating a stretch. Do it slowly. Hold for 15 seconds. Do not use drastic force to limber up.

Exercise V, Shoulders, Chest

Another stretch is to hold on to a fence or both sides of a doorway with your hands behind you at about shoulder level. Let your arms straighten as you lean forward. Hold your chest up and chin in.

Exercise W, Total Body

point
your
toes

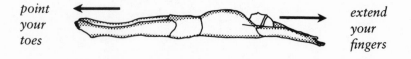

extend
your
fingers

Elongation Stretch: Extend your arms overhead and straighten out your legs. Now reach as far as is comfortable in opposite direction with your arms and legs. Stretch for 5 seconds, and then relax.

Exercise X, Shoulders

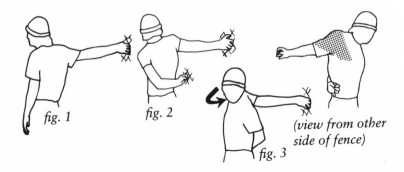

fig. 1   fig. 2   fig. 3

(view from other side of fence)

This stretch is for the front of the shoulders and arms. You need a chain-linked fence, doorway, or wall. Face the fence and hold onto it (or press against it) with your right hand at shoulder level (fig. 1). Next, bring your other arm around your back and grab the fence (or whatever you are using) as in fig. 2. Now, look over your left shoulder in the direction of your right hand. Keep your shoulder close to the fence as you slowly turn your head (fig. 3). Trying to look at your right hand behind you gives you a stretch in the front of the shoulders.

Stretch the other side. Do it slowly and under control. The feeling of a good stretch is what is important: *not how far you can stretch.*

Variation: From the previous position, stretch your arm and shoulder at various angles. Each angle will stretch the arm and shoulder differently. Hold for 10 seconds.

Exercise Y, Shoulders, Chest

Most of us have a towel in our hands at least once a day. A towel can aid in stretching the arms, shoulders, and chest.

Grab the towel near both ends so that you can move it, with straight arms, up and over your head and down behind your back. Do not strain or force it. Your hands should be far enough apart to allow for relatively free movement up and over your head and down behind your back.

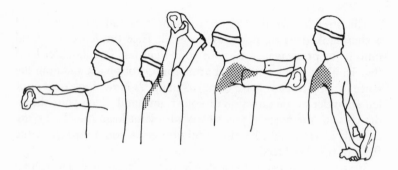

To increase the stretch, move your hands slightly closer together and, keeping the arms straight, repeat the movement. Go slowly and feel the stretch. Do not overstretch. If you are unable to go through the full movement of up, over, and behind while keeping your arms straight, then your hands are too close together. Move them farther apart.

You can hold the stretch at any place during this movement. This will isolate and add further stretch to the muscles of that particular area. For example: if your chest is tight and sore, it is possible to isolate the stretch there by holding the towel at shoulder level with arms straight behind you, as shown above. Hold for 10–20 seconds.

Exercise Z, Thighs, Lower Legs

Most women will not feel much of a stretch in this position. But for tight people, especially men, this lets you know if you have tight ankles. If there is a strain, place your hands on the outside of your legs for support as you balance yourself slightly forward. Find a position you can hold for 20–30 seconds.

If you are tight, do not overstretch. Regularity with stretching creates positive change. There will be noticeable improvement in ankle flexibility within several weeks.

Exercise AA, Thighs, Ankles, Achilles Tendon

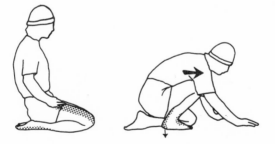

Bring the toes of one foot almost even or parallel to the knee of the other leg. Let the heel of the bent leg come off the ground ½ inch or so. Lower heel toward ground while pushing forward on your thigh (just above the knee) with your chest and shoulder. The idea is not to get the heel flat but to use the forward pressure from your shoulder on your thigh to give an easy stretch to the Achilles tendon. All that is needed to adequately stretch the Achilles tendon is a *very slight stretch*. Hold 15 seconds.

This stretch is great for tight ankles and arches. Be sure to work both sides. Here again, you will probably find that one side is a lot different than the other in flexibility and feeling. As we get older or go through periods of inactivity and then are active again, there is a lot of stress and strain on the ankles and arches. One way to reduce or eliminate the pain and soreness of new activity is to stretch before and after exercise.

Exercise BB, Forearm, Wrist

A Forearm and Wrist Stretch: Start on all fours. Support yourself on your hands and knees. Thumbs should be pointed to the outside with fingers pointed toward knees. Keep palms flat as you lean back to stretch the front part of your forearms. Hold an easy stretch for 20 seconds. Relax, then stretch again. You may find you are very tight in this area.

Exercise CC, Arms, Chest

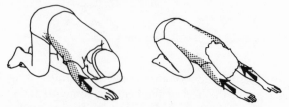

With legs bent under you, reach forward and grab the end of the carpet or mat. If you can't grab on to something, just pull back with straight arms while you press down slightly with your palms.

You can do this stretch one arm at a time or both at the same time. Pulling with just one arm provides more control and isolates the stretch on either side. You should feel this in your shoulders, arms, lats *(latissimus dorsi)* or sides, upper back, and even your lower back. When you do this for the first time you may only feel it in the shoulders and arms, but as you do it more you will learn to stretch other areas. By slightly moving your hips in either direction you can increase or decrease the stretch. Don't strain. Be relaxed. Hold for 15 seconds.

Exercise DD, Neck

With the back of your head on the floor, turn your chin toward your shoulder (as you keep your head resting on the floor). Turn chin only as far as needed to get an easy stretch in the side of your neck. Hold 5 seconds, then stretch to the other side. Repeat 2–3 times.

Index